Same old

Same old

Queer theory, literature and the politics of sameness

Ben Nichols

Manchester University Press

Copyright © Ben Nichols 2020

The right of Ben Nichols to be identified as the author of this work has been asserted by him in accordance with the Copyright, Designs and Patents Act 1988.

Published by Manchester University Press
Oxford Road, Manchester M13 9PL
www.manchesteruniversitypress.co.uk

British Library Cataloguing-in-Publication Data is available

ISBN 978 1 5261 3283 3 hardback
ISBN 978 1 5261 6381 3 paperback

First published by Manchester University Press in hardback 2020

This edition published 2022

The publisher has no responsibility for the persistence or accuracy of URLs for any external or third-party internet websites referred to in this book, and does not guarantee that any content on such websites is, or will remain, accurate or appropriate.

Typeset by New Best-set Typesetters Ltd

Contents

Acknowledgements	*page* vi
Introduction: Same old	1
1. Useless	39
2. Reproductive	75
3. Normative	114
4. Reductive	151
Coda: Same again	187
References	198
Index	214

Acknowledgements

Acknowledgement is due to the Arts and Humanities Research Council who provided the funding for the initial stages of this work.

Jane Elliott and Mark Turner were exemplary mentors during this period without whom this project would not have been possible.

Heather Love and Hugh Stevens came into contact with the project at the culmination of its first stage and provided completely invaluable feedback and advice. Their support since this time has been beyond what I could have hoped for and I am very grateful to them both for this.

James Whitfield and Patrick Preston both read drafts at a late stage in the project's development and offered very helpful feedback.

Jason Edwards has been not only a long-term source of intellectual and professional guidance but a great friend too. His reading of the entire manuscript at the final stage of its development offered the project exactly what it needed.

I would like to extend my gratitude to David Shenton for his extremely kind permission to use an image from his graphic novel *Stanley and the Mask of Mystery* on the front cover of the book. I can't think of a better image to have used. I would also like to thank two anonymous peer reviewers for their very helpful suggestions on improving the manuscript. Moreover, sincere thanks are due to Matthew Frost at Manchester University Press who has been incredibly patient.

Finally, I thank Les Andy (who is also sometimes very patient) from whom I am still trying to learn what's important in life and who has, really, made everything possible.

The image on the front cover of this book is © David Shenton. Used here by permission.

Acknowledgements

The digital copy of the image on the front cover was provided by the British Library and is reproduced with their permission © British Library Board (YK.1993.b.975, p. 49).

An earlier version of Chapter 4 was printed as 'Reductive: John Rechy, queer theory and the idea of limitation', *GLQ*, 22.3 (2016), 409–36. © 2016, Duke University Press. Republished by permission. www.dukeupress.edu.

Introduction
Same old

In April 2014 an account on Tumblr caused a small stir in the online press. *Buzzfeed*, *Slate* and the *Huffington Post* all ran stories about *Boyfriend Twin*, a blog dedicated to collecting pictures of (predominantly) gay male couples who look exactly alike: that is, like identical twins. 'Because what's sexier than dating yourself?' asks the blog's irreverent tagline.[1] The account garnered a range of responses, from a mixture of curiosity and unease at the uncanniness of the twins ('We're not entirely sure how we feel about this,' said the *Huff Post* (Nichols 2014; see also Broderick 2014)), to mild disappointment about the fundamental conservatism apparently expressed in their attraction to each other (Bloomer 2014), an idea that draws on a wider tendency to imagine attachments to familiarity and similarity as politically reactionary. A contributor quoted in the *Slate* article briefly addresses one reservation about the phenomenon – that it 'confirms the whole dumb Freudian model of homosexuality as a kind of narcissism' (Bloomer 2014) – but *Boyfriend Twin* also playfully highlights something undeniable in culture that grounds this reservation: that within the terms we have for understanding sexual attraction, and for understanding what are often assumed to be the most consequential dividing lines between us, gay people are defined as being attracted to that which is 'the same' as us. The still dominant terms we have for understanding sexual definition – heterosexual and homosexual – split sexual definition on the basis of the perceived sameness or difference of the gender of one's sexual object. Of the myriad ways of defining sexual desire and orientation that could have endured from nineteenth-century sexology, it is sameness and difference along the axes of sex and gender that continue to shape dominant understandings of sexual identity most powerfully. Within this paradigm, the distinctiveness of gay people has in part been defined by our orientation towards sameness.

Since its emergence as arguably the most prestigious framework for scholarly understanding of non-heterosexual desire and culture in Anglophone academia, queer theory has consistently troubled queer people's association with sameness. In influential works, scholars as diverse as Eve Kosofsky Sedgwick, Michael Warner and Sara Ahmed have all compellingly suggested that our culture's definition of queers in this way is misguided and problematic. Sedgwick, for example, homes in on the historical moment in the late nineteenth century often credited with the crystallisation of modern sexual identity. In a reading of Oscar Wilde's play *The Importance of Being Earnest* (1895), she suggests that critics play into the 'homogenizing heterosexist scientism of homo/hetero' (Sedgwick 1993: 67) when they read gay desire in the play in relation to sameness, ignoring, for example, Wilde's apparent investment in eroticised differences in age. Wilde's play resists the '"homosexual" homo-genization' (ibid.: 58) taking place with particular vigour at the time of his writing and continued by scholars today. In an influential essay on the prominent psychoanalytic definition of gay desire, Warner has similarly argued that imagining only gay attraction as a love of the same is a displacement of the narcissism in all desire. Defining gay desire as a 'sexuality of sameness' (Warner 1990: 203) serves an ideological purpose for dominant culture to convince itself that not all sexuality – including normative heterosexuality – is reliant on a kind of narcissism or ego-erotics. He argues that the self-evident fact that gay people are obviously interested in those who are different from them – that their interest is in more than 'relations of mere sameness' (ibid.: 191) – throws into relief the ideological function of defining gay people as oriented towards the same. Sara Ahmed (2006: 96), in her book *Queer Phenomenology* (2006), argues that the 'association between homosexuality and sameness is crucial to the pathologizing of homosexuality as a perversion that leads the body astray'. Therefore, this idea 'needs to be contested' (ibid.). As we can see, queer scholarship has tended to understand queers' association with sameness as the tool of a dominant order seeking to marginalise and misrepresent queer lives.

This scepticism about understanding homosexuality as an attraction to a 'sameness' in gender also overlaps with an orientation against a much wider range of related ideas. As with much criticism tied however nominally to a desire for political transformation in the name of marginalised people, queer theoretical writing tends to rely on positions in which it poses values like heterogeneity, variety, multiplicity and change in opposition to a prevailing order that is imagined as seeking sameness in the forms of homogeneity, fixity, mainstreaming and conformity. The wider rhetorical and political commitments of queer theoretical work are shared with other kinds of cultural criticism with similar roots in post-structuralist theory and in scholarship whose focus is the politics of specifically social differences: race, class, gender and dis/ability, to name only a few. But these commitments in turn also borrow from an even wider cultural dispensation, beyond leftist thought, in which whatever is related to sameness is maligned, devalued, denigrated. Queer theory's frequent orientation, then, lines up with the power of many ideas that broadly embody or express the definitional sameness of homosexuality to magnetise censure and hostility: for example, boredom, repetition, plagiarism, copying, banality, the status quo, ordinariness, habit, predictability, quietism, stasis, formalism, stagnation, statism, regulation, convention, automation, consumerism, mass production, complicity and standardisation.

But what is it about these ideas that tends to seem so problematic? Even as it has maligned sameness, queer theory has also provided persuasive terms for understanding the roots of its own aversion. It was the contention of foundational work by scholars such as Sedgwick, Warner, Judith Butler and Lee Edelman that the marginalisation of non-heterosexual people was not only a matter of the material treatment of a given body of people but was underpinned by some of the most deep-seated philosophical and cultural assumptions. In the famous opening to *Epistemology of the Closet* (1990), for example, Sedgwick (1990: 1) writes that 'an understanding of virtually any aspect of modern Western culture must be, not merely incomplete, but damaged in its central substance to the degree that it does not incorporate a critical analysis of modern homo/heterosexual definition.' That is, the centrality of homo/hetero definition as a means for understanding sexuality and personal identity in the modern West means that it is 'full of implication, however confusing, for even the ostensibly least sexual aspects of personal existence' (ibid.: 2). Sedgwick gives a long list of examples of discursive nodes, or binary hierarchies, that might be inflected by this split: 'secrecy/disclosure, knowledge/ignorance, private/public, masculine/feminine, majority/minority, innocence/initiation, natural/artificial, new/old, discipline/terrorism, canonic/noncanonic, wholeness/decadence, urbane/provincial, domestic/foreign, health/illness' (ibid.: 11). This universalising move, which was shared in alternative form by other theorists, was crucial to the self-understanding of the new field of queer theory and has indelibly marked subsequent queer theorising: rather than focusing solely on the culture and experiences of those defined as lesbian and gay, queer theoretical work was able to find the inscriptions of sexual power structures in the apparently least sexual of places.[2] However, whilst one of the nodes that Sedgwick mentions is, of course, the split 'same/different' (ibid.), it seemed to Sedgwick (and it has seemed to many others) that an anti-homophobic inquiry should proceed in the name of the different and difference. For example, one of the many axioms that make up Sedgwick's introduction to *Epistemology* is '[p]eople are different from each other', but the correlative fact is seemingly ignored: if everyone is different from each other then, if this is true, they at least have their difference from everyone else to make them all the same (ibid.: 22). As we will see in various ways over the following pages, one move that Sedgwick's sense of the universal significance of sexual definition has authorised has been to imagine that anything related in any way at all to difference, deviance or transgression can be embraced as what necessarily pertains to non-hetero sexualities. But reading this another way, the centrality of sexual definition to many forms of knowledge can also be read in the disregard that our culture and our theoretical frameworks have shown towards sameness, tending most often to take it for granted that difference is the necessary sign of political and ethical effectiveness.

The link forged by Sedgwick (and others) between queerness and forms of 'difference' responds to how a dominant culture has marginalised queers through precisely this link: by rendering us abject outsiders. In this respect, Sedgwick's move can be understood within the framework of Foucauldian 'reverse' discourse. Foucault (1998: 101) famously writes that, at a crucial point in the history of sexuality, homosexuals began to adopt the medical terms that had been used to discredit them: 'homosexuality began to speak in its own behalf, to demand that its legitimacy or "naturality" be acknowledged, often in the same vocabulary, using the same categories by which it was medically disqualified'. There was, therefore, a certain strategy of defiance and deflation in adopting these terms that had pathologised queers as abnormal, deflating the power of those terms to disqualify by embracing them. As

Heather Love (2007: 2) reminds us, the embrace of the word 'queer' in late 1980s activism was a similar strategy: taking a slur and repurposing it for political ends. The strategy of queer activism and theory was to embrace the abject difference that queers had been imagined to embody. However, there has been much less scope to explore how the discourse on the link between queers and sameness might also be 'reversed': instead, this association is one, as we saw above, that it has seemed more appropriate to aversively resist. Queer scholars have arguably been selective about which terms that have been used to denigrate homosexuality they might defiantly embrace.

A more recent trend in queer scholarship, however, has begun to look to a wider range of ideas with which queers have historically been associated. Scholars in this evolving anti-redemptive strain in queer theory such as Edelman (2004), Love (2007), Elizabeth Freeman (2010), Jack Halberstam (2011) and Kadji Amin (2017) have looked to ideas that have been deemed unduly negative, backward or otherwise out of step with the political project of queer studies in order to question aspects of the field's foundational self-understanding. Not all of these scholars have proposed a defiant embrace of the ideas they discuss, but all share an interest in exploring what the affirmative or redemptive project of queer theory may have precluded. Scholars such as Love and Amin have examined how historical queers have often made use of, or understood themselves through, terms that contemporary *queer politics and theory* have denigrated. Arguably this is a slight variation on 'reverse' discourse: queers are not here defiantly speaking back to a dominant order using its own terms but rather, through in some ways embodying the dominant or apparently problematic, are framed as having something to teach a queer theory that may have presumptively excluded a given set of ideas.

Same old develops this queer theoretical work of exploring how queers have operationalised and embodied terms and ideas that are in tension with the values of contemporary queer theory. Over the next four chapters, I dwell in particular on more moments in queer culture, like *Boyfriend Twin*, which play on or invest in sameness in a way that is at odds with contemporary scholarly assumptions. I argue that aspects of past and present queer cultures can and do make us think again about the frameworks that queer theory has provided. Each of the chapters takes an idea that queer scholarship has defined itself in opposition to, understanding this opposition as closely related to queer theory's defining aversion to sameness, and explores how that idea has been central to aspects of queer culture in the long twentieth century. The historical period I focus on begins in the late nineteenth century around the time of the Wilde trials in 1895 and moves forward through the emergence of lesbian and gay liberation movements to the present day. This is a significant period in queer history that is understood by historians to have been responsible for the 'homo/hetero' sexual definition that now seems so crucial to our understandings of human subjectivity and that also saw the emergence of a visible, publicly available and established queer culture (Weeks 1989). Focusing on this period, the specific cultural lens I use in this book is literature or literary writing, but each chapter also opens out on to empirical and social aspects of queer culture. For example, I use feminist speculative fiction from across the twentieth century to interrogate queer theory's framing of 'reproduction' as a dreary commitment to 'more of the same' and to revisit the value of same-sex communities. A range of 'lesbian middle-brow' novels from the earlier twentieth century, I argue, both formally and thematically equate lesbianism with ordinariness and encourage reflection on the queer opposition to normativity, foregrounding the important reasons for some queer investments in ordinariness. Another chapter looks at fiction on sexual seriality and sexual typing from the later part of the twentieth century, as well as the practice of listing, documenting or recording sexual partners, to explore its investments in the kind of 'reductionism' that queer theoretical writing often assumes to be bad. And in the chapter that follows this introduction, I start with *fin-de-siècle* queer aestheticism to interrogate queer scholarship's investment in usefulness or 'making a difference' and as a way of registering other forms of scepticism towards utility that have been a part of queer history, such as in the liberationist writing of Guy Hocquenghem. To the list at the end of the third paragraph of this Introduction, then, we could add the ideas that structure each of the following chapters: uselessness, reproduction, normativity and reductionism.

In what follows of this book, I will be describing a paradoxical and counterintuitive situation in which many of those phenomena that have seemed most anathema to queer scholars are associated with the sameness that in modern Western sexual definition has also marked homosexuality. In its very structure, I will suggest, queer theory maintains a paradoxical gay-aversiveness. Such gay aversiveness was famously the subject of Leo Bersani's *Homos* (1995), a powerful critique of queer theory from the mid-1990s, which he opened with the provocative conclusion that 'No one wants to be called a homosexual' (Bersani 1995: 1). For Bersani, queer theory's disdain for lesbian and gay sexual identities echoed the denigrated status of these identities within the broader culture and, moreover, made little sense for a field that could, or should, have been interested in the specificity of gay forms of being. In this book, I chart how this disdain for homosexuality carries through into the aversion towards a much broader set of ideas that embody or express sameness.[3] Not only does no one want to be called a homosexual, but no one wants anything to do with the sameness that has defined homosexuals either.

Literary or imaginative writing is, in various ways, a helpful route in to a discussion of the place of sameness within queer theory and culture. For one thing, it is not, on the whole, regarded as argumentative or expository writing and so is not marked by the need to persuade that defines, say, politically engaged scholarship. This need to persuade can make engaged scholarship more strongly attached to ideas related to difference which more often tend to generate agreement and approval. (What political project, after all, could hope to win support by the promise to keep things the same?) The frameworks available for studying fictional writing also encourage us to think most emphatically about both form and content and so to take account of the wide array of ways of addressing sameness that we can see in queer culture. Equally, some of the most influential queer theoretical formulations were devised via literary readings and there is a distinct tradition of queer literary scholarship, which is not the case for all aspects of queer culture. It therefore seems appropriate to ground a critique of queer theory in a sense on its own terms – via the kinds of literary readings that were so integral to its early formation. Moreover, this book's investment in such readings is also a structural investment in sameness as there are already queer accounts in one way or another of most of the works I address in the following chapters. They are all taken from a significant period in the history of queer culture, as I have indicated above. In emerging from this context, the literary works I address perhaps cannot help but speak to wider concerns of queer life and to the extratextual worlds that made them, as well as to arguments in queer theory and scholarship. Equally, we should not underestimate the agency of literary works within social life. For example, scholars have often argued that Radclyffe Hall's *The Well of Loneliness* (1928) played a crucial role in formulating and disseminating a version of modern lesbian identity, as I discuss in Chapter 3. On the level of content, too, these literary works show us that standing against the forms of sameness that contemporary theory opposes has no necessary or transhistorical relation to queer lives and histories. Stephen Gordon in *The Well*, for example, longs to be normal in a way that makes little sense in the context of contemporary queer frameworks with their opposition to all forms of normativity. The readings of imaginative literature, then, are a starting point for raising questions of broader significance and consequence across queer culture: for example, about lesbian ordinariness, about sexual typing and about the need to establish and reproduce cultures as well as disrupt them.

But what is the practical importance, in the end, of this attention to sameness? For one thing, the readings in the chapters that follow bring into focus the modest social value of the ideas they explore. In the chapter on queer aestheticism, we see that Henry James's novels show that if one does not 'make a difference' then one is at least not making things worse. The utopian worlds of feminist speculative fiction show that 'reproduction' – literalised as a process of creating 'more of the same' – need not seem as problematic as it often does in queer scholarship when what is being reproduced are non-homophobic utopian worlds. The protagonists of lesbian middle-brow writing encourage us to view queer subjects' desire to be normal through more sympathetic eyes, showing how conformity and normality can provide a welcome respite from the otherwise exhausting burden of censure and disapprobation. Finally, writing in the genre of the 'stud file', or the catalogue of sexual partners, shows that reducing people to sexual types or numbers can be the occasion for erotic pleasure. In a more theoretical register, reducing people in this way can also help to foreground some of the ethical potential of being 'reduced' or abandoning the commitments to human individuality and complexity that can lead to aggression and violence. But beyond the direct values of these forms of sameness, attending to them in the way that I do here also has what, following Love (2007: 12), I would call a 'diagnostic usefulness'. In her now classic book *Feeling Backward* (2007), attention to 'negative' affect in queer history helps to diagnose the enduring experiences of marginalisation and victimhood in the present. My approach in *Same old*, however, can help us diagnose the displacement sometimes at work when undesirable social forces are associated with sameness. For example, in Chapter 2, I note how many scholars have suggested that Charlotte

Perkins Gilman's reproductive maternalism goes hand in hand with a questionable racial politics prevalent within late nineteenth and early twentieth-century feminism. In these scholars' accounts, racism always generates an imagination of pure and unsullied reproduction and any valorisation of reproduction will be similarly imbricated in a chauvinistic attachment to a certain racial formation. Whilst it seems clear that strong forms of racism frequently rely on fantasy images of non-hybrid racial continuation, it seems less clear to me that any concept of reproduction will be tied to a particular racial formation. I argue that scholars, such as the critics of Gilman who suggest that it is reproduction per se that is problematically racist, are relying on the rhetorical force and authority that accrues from associating any given idea, political process or interpretative move with sameness. 'Reproduction' as a commitment to keeping things the same names the problem in shorthand, but is not able on its own to explain adequately the workings of racism. It is not clear that sameness and its cognate ideas are necessarily discriminatory. By the same token, it is not clear that difference and its cognate ideas will necessarily be anti-homophobic, anti-sexist or anti-racist, but to celebrate these cognate ideas does draw on a general tendency of concepts related to difference to generate approval and agreement. Not only does such a celebration frequently rely on tacit assumptions about sameness, but it also obscures the workings of those social forces that are often cited as queer theory's antagonists and which in the forms of discrimination, marginalisation and intolerance seem more often to work through insidious forms of differentiation.

However, I do not intend to argue, as some have done, for abandoning difference altogether, where 'difference' means specifically social difference. As we will see, a number of scholars and commentators on the political left have, at various points in recent times, suggested that a politics focused on social differences – often known as 'identity politics' – has got in the way of a more general and effective emancipatory politics. By contrast, I do not see the politics of social difference becoming any less significant in our times. Instead, my interest is in why consequential social identities – sexuality, race, class, gender, dis/ability – seem more important or interesting when presented in the abstract as *differences* rather than in terms of the specific, material identities that they are. Why does *queerness* – mobile, dynamic, flexible – seem more compelling to scholars and activists than the seemingly intractable categories that continue to shape people's lives: *gayness, lesbianism, bisexuality*? This may seem like the kind of cultural materialist position which was prevalent in the 1990s and argued in favour of concrete social identities against the apparent postmodern excesses of queer theory (Morton 1996; Sinfield 1998). But it is also about the formal or rhetorical associations that accrue to ideas: how 'identity' does not just point to social realities but at the same time connotes fixity and coherence. Why have queer scholars reversed the discourse on queer difference but not on queer sameness? There are stark rhetorical battle lines drawn across scholarship and activism that see good forms of difference opposed to apparently bad or reactionary forms of sameness. But taken together, the chapters in this book offer a challenge to this situation by showing that queer culture is frequently many of the things that queer theory disapproves of: useless, reproductive, normative, and reductive. In light of the works I address, I argue, we can interrogate the ease with which what seems unbearable or undesirable about almost any phenomenon can be displaced on to some form of sameness: the unpleasantness of a commute on to the fact that it is done every single day, the emptiness of a job on to the repetitiveness of the tasks it involves, the intolerableness of a heterosexist and racist world on to the forms of conformism that they are frequently taken to require. To supplement the approaches sometimes named as the 'politics of difference', then, I offer the 'politics of sameness', which is intended to be an optic through which to interrogate how forms of sameness come to seem inherently problematic. Being against sameness, I argue, does not help us understand fully how social problems work. To make this point, over the following chapters I offer a series of careful readings of concepts that embody a maligned sameness to interrogate the critical idealism that would presumptively position them as firm antagonists for any kind of engaged scholarship.

Repetition without a difference

'Clones go home.' These are the words that the artist Keith Haring famously stencilled on to the pavements of New York's East Village in the 1980s (Kolossa 2004: 15). The 'clones' that the slogan targets were the seemingly identical gay men – in uniforms of plaid shirts, jeans and moustaches (some of them, no doubt, boyfriend twins) – who were perceived to be dampening the bohemian air of the neighbourhood with their sense of conformist masculinity imported from the more upmarket West Village. Haring's sentiment has been echoed by other community voices who have similarly found something to deride in clones' unthinking attachment to sameness, their apparently herd-like mentality and lack of independent thought (Holleran 1982). The image on the front cover of this book, for example, taken from David Shenton's graphic novel *Stanley and the Mask of Mystery* (1983), gently mocks the clone's misplaced sense of individuality in the context of his fundamental conformity. In specifically queer theoretical discourse, where clones, or related ideas around identical repetition in queer culture, have been addressed, it has not been to celebrate a simple investment in being like others or the enjoyment of sameness, but rather to recuperate this figure to prestigious theoretical models about the dissolution of self, meaning and language. For example, Tim Dean has suggested that clone figures can be seen to emblematise the model of ontological breakdown, or de-differentiation, that has been elaborated by Leo Bersani over the last twenty years or so (which I discuss in more detail below), in which Bersani has identified decentred and dispersed forms of human subjectivity operating in aspects of queer life, as well as in high art. Dean (2002: 30) also uses heuristics such as Derridean *différance* or the Lacanian Real, or what he calls 'otherness', to represent this 'zone of undifferentiation', or an 'ontological sameness' (ibid.: 31) which resists identity in so far as, in this account, identities make things discrete from other things. The clones' desire to look similar to other people is freighted with a theoretical weight which turns that desire into another expression of prestigious accounts of the dissolution of the self. The simple attachment to type and taxonomy that we continue to see throughout contemporary queer culture – bear, butch, femme, daddy, twink – becomes interesting only as it can be transformed into an emblem for self-difference. The clone, I suggest, is a model for how sameness has been treated in queer scholarship: either straightforwardly maligned, or else, where celebrated, celebrated for something other than the simple fact of sameness.

The scholarly gesture in which a form of 'sameness' actually works against *sameness* – understood as integration, coherence and substance – has been foundational for queer theoretical writing. For example, we have seen this repeatedly in critiques of what has arguably been the most enduring antagonist of queer scholarship: *identity*, where this means self-sameness, or stable and enduring being. Judith Butler's account of the performativity of gender is perhaps the most famous version of this, where she argues that the forced repetitions necessary to consolidate gender identity also allow for repetitions with a difference that create opportunities for living gender otherwise. The opportunity of repetition is when it is not actually exact repetition. But this is an opportunity built into repetition from the start as, according to Butler's theoretical model, exact repetition is simply not possible. Drawing on post-structuralist tenets, Butler argues that self-present identities constitute 'ontological locales' that are 'fundamentally uninhabitable' (ibid.: 186). The idea of any self-presence is fundamentally undercut by the means of its enunciation: the repetition required to perform gendered identity actually works against the 'economy of the same' and its 'reductive efforts of univocal signification' (ibid.: 132). As I discuss in more detail in Chapter 4, Butler has returned to this model repeatedly in her writing to show that the need to repeat which is fundamental to meaning-making will also, always, inevitably, lead to instability and difference. The model has proved singularly adaptable to the various contexts of her work: gender identity, re-signifying hate speech and even reconceptualising universality. It has also been very influential for other scholars and we can see the spirit of it when Dean (2002: 31) claims, in the essay mentioned above, that the clone figures a 'sameness irreducible to identity', or a kind of sameness (like Butler's repetition) that undercuts belief in fixity and coherence.

Another key influence for Dean, as mentioned briefly, is the work of Bersani. Even though he is the theorist to have offered the most sustained treatment specifically of sameness in queer studies, as with others Bersani nevertheless marshals this against 'identity'. For example, *Homos* is framed as a critique of what he perceived to be an excessive anti-identitarianism in early 1990s queer theory which precluded thought about the specificities and affordances of sexual identity. But attending to the specificity of gay identity in his work reveals, for him, how homosexual identity actually contains within it the possibility of figuring the breakdown of any specificity or identity whatsoever. The 'category of homosexuality' (Bersani 1995: 5), or what he prefers to call 'homo-ness' (ibid. 7), provides him with a model for figuring a non-antagonistic way of relating in so far as it involves understanding oneself as in some sense 'the same' as what one is relating to and therefore does not aggressively uphold differences. 'Sameness' is therefore a heuristic for understanding this less strictly differentiated and more mobile version of subjectivity. Homosexuality is valuable as a model for Bersani only in so far as it is an 'anti-identitarian identity' (ibid.: 101), in so far as it can be formulated as containing the mobility that always undoes fixed identities. If Bersani is sometimes associated with the formulation of a model of gay desire as self-shattering, it is also the case that what homo-ness facilitates is a process of 'self-extension' (ibid.: 7). That is, homo-ness designates a universal correspondence of being within which human subjects are no longer definitively differentiated but exist as relay points in a constant mobility of minutely differing forms. In homo-ness subjects are inescapably continuous with the world around them. The self is not destroyed, but is dissipated in a 'vast network of *near sameness*, a network characterized by relations of inaccurate replication' (ibid.: 146, original italics). Sameness is valuable in so far as it is not really fully itself: it remains 'inaccurate', 'near' rather than fully centred.

If Bersani's terms for understanding sameness have been influential, I would argue that it is because, as for Butler, they map on to prestigious theoretical models that have on the whole tended to have forms of *difference* as their foundations. For example, even though he has distanced himself from 'deconstructive readings' (Bersani 2010: 172), it would seem to me that a key precursor to Bersani's work is deconstruction. (Dean implicitly makes a similar point in the essay cited above when he also offers Derridean *différance* as a heuristic for understanding the clone.) In a well-known formulation, Derrida (2002: 26) writes that there are 'only, everywhere, differences'. In the Derridean account of signification, there is no final point of authentic meaning, only signs pointing to other signs, always introducing some detour or deferral in meaning. For Bersani (2010: 147), similarly, it is crucial that 'differences are inviolable'. The point is that for both thinkers there's something necessary or inevitable about how sameness is never possible: either the fact of our situatedness within signification or the necessary spatial expansiveness of subjectivity means that difference is just inevitable. Within this metaphysical tradition, difference is the proper condition of the world: faith in identity, substance, stability etc. is misplaced, if not pernicious. The transit of this idea through various kinds of scholarship in the 1980s and 1990s would be difficult to track comprehensively, given how widespread the consensus is, but we could certainly see it taken up influentially by literary scholars (Barbara Johnson (1980; 1987)), queer theorists (Lee Edelman (1994)) and political theorists (Iris Marion Young (1990)). In terms that have become well-used, Johnson (1980: x, original italics) writes of this post-structuralist difference as necessitating 'differences *within*' that split any self-defined unity from itself in contrast to 'differences *between*' that separate self-contained entities from each other. This difference within is something like a transcendental necessity. The way in which signification works, and our necessary situatedness within signification, means that self-identity is impossible: we are all subjects of the signifier, subject to the impossibility of our identities and separated from what we think of as ourselves. An upshot of this post-structuralist consensus has been to see any belief in a kind of integrated wholeness as a politically problematic fiction. For example, in *Homographesis* (1994), arguably the most sustained piece of queer post-structuralist criticism ever produced, Edelman (xix) dismisses such belief as a commitment to the 'logic of the same': he offers his own analysis to 'deconstruct the repressive ideology of similitude or identity itself' (ibid.: 22–3). The repressiveness of identity and similitude, however, seems to be left implicit in its association with the 'logic of the same'.

Beyond Bersani, other thinkers who have very valuably highlighted the links between sameness, queerness and homosexuality also often draw on a related theoretical lineage. Madhavi Menon has recently offered an account not of queer sameness but of queer universalism or what she calls 'indifference'. The kind of 'difference' to which Menon (2015: 3) is opposed is social difference, understood along familiar lines: 'identitarian difference' that leads to 'identity politics' which misrepresents the social complexities of existence and can be problematically divisive. By contrast, the universalism or indifference that she endorses is an inevitable force that disrupts the formulation of stable differences: 'a universal structure that is the failure of identity' (ibid.: 22). What makes this universalism 'queer' is its resistance to stability and also its relation to 'desire' understood in psychoanalytic terms as a fundamentally corrosive and disruptive force, rather than any relation to historical (identitarian) queers (ibid.: 16). We can see in this account the spirit of post-structuralism, of Butler and Bersani, but Menon's most explicit debt is to another theorist: Alain Badiou and his critique of ethical systems based on the recognition of differences, such as those that predominate in contemporary multiculturalism. As Badiou (2001: 25, original italics) writes in his short polemic *Ethics*, 'Infinite alterity is quite simply *what there is*'. Therefore 'differences hold no interest for thought' and 'amount to nothing more than the infinite and self-evident multiplicity of human-kind' (ibid.: 26). The more properly ethical task consists in '*recognizing the Same*' (ibid.: 25, original italics). This means actively working towards generic truths that emerge as 'events' or radical breaks in any given social situation: differences are simply what is the case and The Same erupts as a radical difference (singular) that interrupts this status quo. Badiou argues for an ethics that thinks in terms of generic truths that are entirely indifferent to everyday differences: 'Only a truth is, as such, *indifferent to differences*' (ibid.: 27, original italics). Within Badiou's ethics and politics of radical newness the only things that are acceptable are constant revolution and innovation: the only ethical position is to encourage transformation constantly and tirelessly. There is no room for stability or the continuity of what is established: 'The Same' is only in the service of radical difference in the form of radical change. To argue against difference, Badiou turns it into a form of sameness: the simple and banal fact of what is the case, the uninteresting status quo.

As we have seen, then, work that explores 'sameness' is also often pitched against 'identity' and 'identity politics'. While they approach the question from a specific angle and have specific theoretical and political axes to grind, the writers above join a diverse range of scholars who have, in various ways over the last twenty years, taken the politics focused on social difference to task for stressing too extensively how people differ from each and for not spending enough effort on articulating forms of common experience or common social good. Other scholars from at least the mid-1990s have sought to move away from particularity, specificity and difference as a means of rejuvenating calls for a general emancipatory politics on the left. We could trace this position more broadly across the social sciences (Wendy Brown (1995)) and the humanities (Amanda Anderson (2006)), as well as specifically within queer theory (James Penney (2014)). While these writers by no means represent a united trend, they all indicate an undercurrent of thinking along the same lines: their positions signal a movement away from an emphasis on social differentiation towards a theory on the left that more emphatically makes claims about collective forms of life and communal political goals. Penney, for example, also draws on the work of Badiou to critique queer theory for being too caught up in sexuality to consider broader projects for social change. A Badiouian Event, by contrast, addresses itself to people on the level of 'generic humanity' (Penney 2014: 187). His work therefore offers the possibility of 'general social emancipation' (ibid.: 47) in contrast to queer theory's apparently self-interested factionalism. We see commentary on the left returning to this idea again and again. A recent version can be found in Mark Lilla's *The Once and Future Liberal* (2017) which blames 'identity politics' for the splintering of the left that, he claims, led to the election of Donald Trump. The embrace of sameness or universalism by queer critics arguably goes hand in hand with this larger tradition of rejecting 'identity politics'.

By contrast with some of these preceding positions, the kinds of sameness that I am concerned with in this book are not those that portend a grand ontological disintegration or that seek to move away specifically from social differences. Such differences may certainly be the causes of violent disagreement, but they also offer the possibility of pleasure and empowerment and, moreover, show no sign of becoming any less operative or significant. If anything they are becoming more and more relevant in a way that perhaps brings into question the utopianism of the strong anti-identitarianism in queer theory from the early 1990s. Indeed, an interest in sameness does not have to mean abandoning social difference – embracing sameness can also mean embracing social 'identity' as that which has been widely maligned for the apparent limitation it imposes on broader movements for social transformation. Rather than the philosophical accounts of sameness that draw on Lacan and Badiou, I am interested in how a much wider range of everyday ideas suffer a simple fate of being denigrated: the desire to be 'like' others, a commitment to keeping things as they are, a simple lack of interest in innovation. Often these ideas do appear in queer theory in slightly more grandiose forms: normativity, reproduction, reductiveness. These are not necessarily 'everyday' ideas in these forms, but alongside 'identity' they are certainly more systematically disavowed or rejected in the everyday or ordinary business as usual of queer theory. Sameness, in Badiou as much as Bersani, has meant the dissolution of the self and familiar boundaries, the dramatic traversal of limits and containers. It has not really been a reconceptualisation of what is important to these thinkers – which remains mobility, innovation, etc. – but rather a renaming of what is best in the service of those ideas. *Sameness which means sameness* remains a problem in this work: conformity, limitation, the status quo, identity, integration. It is these persistent antagonists of queer theory and critical theory more broadly that are my concern in what follows.

Certainly, there is a scattered history of recognising the importance of these ideas for specifically queer scholarship that runs from the late 1980s to the present day. I have already mentioned the recent work of Menon to articulate what she calls a queer universalism or 'indifference'. Similarly to Dean, Mikko Tuhkanen (2002a) has also drawn on the work of Bersani to contribute to the conversation on queer sameness, but has largely tended to follow him in imagining the idea of sameness as primarily valuable in so far as it indexes a grand (at least in terms of its theoretical articulation) ontological disintegration. Jonathan Flatley has focused not on sameness but on 'likeness' in the life and work of Andy Warhol. Flatley (2017: 7) argues that Warhol's tendency to 'like' a lot of things, as well as his interest in forms of repetition and serial collecting, were ways of imagining 'new, queer forms of affection and relationality' based more on the apprehension of similarity than of differences. We can see echoes of Bersani in Flatley's account and, as with Bersani, Flatley is keen to distinguish what he is offering from a belief or faith in identity: 'It is important to emphasize that this being *alike*, this "lived similarity", is both experientially and conceptually distinct from being equal or identical' (ibid.: 5, original italics).[4]

Yet there are other scholars who have offered more thoroughgoing interrogations of the theoretical co-ordinates that underlie these contributions. For example, there is a fascinating moment in Diana Fuss's *Essentially Speaking* (1989), which is not the book usually regarded as Fuss's primary contribution to queer theory (that is, her edited collection *Inside/Out* (1991)), where she suggests that the prevalent post-structuralist scepticism towards essence presumes in favour of difference, in a way that is particularly pertinent for lesbian and gay studies. Within post-structuralist feminist theory, the 'signification of "homo" has been linked to the politics of the phallocratic "Same," whereas the meaning of "hetero" has been associated just as insistently with the more respectable politics of "Difference"' (Fuss 1989: 111). Within this theory, then, 'heterosexuality operates as the apotheosis of "heterogeneity" and functions to displace what is perceived to be the more conservative, reactionary effects of the practice of "homogeneity"' (ibid.). Fuss asks an important question: 'Is there, in fact, an anti-homosexual bias in current theories of sexual difference, and if so, how has a de-privileging of the "homo" in favor of the "hetero" operated to keep these theories of sexual difference in place?' (ibid.). Around the same time, in another volume that has arguably fallen out of the canon of queer theoretical texts, the collection edited by Cadden and Boone, *Engendering Men: The Question of Male Feminist Criticism*, Wayne Koestenbaum (1990: 182) traces the birth of 'gay reading' back to Oscar Wilde's interest in mechanical reproduction and copies: 'gay criticism needs to develop a theory of typing or copying that wipes the tarnish off clones'. 'To consider replication degrading is, literally, homophobic: *afraid of the same*' (ibid.: 182–3, original italics). Slightly more recently, Brad Epps (2001) has critiqued the 'fetish of fluidity' in queer theory, arguing that its own penchant for the mobile has itself become paradoxically fixed as its proper commitment and moves too quickly to the rejection of identities that still operate in the world. But despite this suggestive, scattered history, considerations of sameness have never been sustainedly established as the basis from which queer thought should proceed. On the contrary, what has been perceived as the proper motivator for queer theory is *difference*, understood not only as social difference but also as a much wider field of ideas sometimes only tenuously, if at all, related to the differences entrenched in the structures of social life. It has been, and remains, difficult to shake the assumption that *difference* is the necessary anchor for any socially progressive, politically engaged kind of theory and activism.

The homo in homonationalism

A range of influential scholars have argued the opposite of many of the positions in the previous section: namely, that queer theory is not attentive enough to various forms of social difference which should be brought more firmly within the queer theoretical purview. However, these scholars also share a conviction that this should not mean something involving 'identity' or 'identity politics': there is agreement, across apparent theoretical divides, that these should be avoided. For example, in an important special issue of *Social Text*, the editors David Eng, Jack Halberstam and José Esteban Muñoz (2005: 1) set the scene for a critique of queer theory on the basis that it is too focused on sexuality and not attentive enough to other kinds of difference, calling for a 'renewed queer studies' that commits with greater clarity and vigour to intersectionality. 'Surely, queer studies promises more than a history of gay men, a sociology of gay male sex clubs, an anthropology of gay male tourism, a survey of gay male aesthetics' (ibid.: 12). The intersectional approach that they endorse opposes the 'homogeneity' and

Introduction: Same old

'universalizing tendencies' (ibid.: 13) of 'reactionary (identity) politics' (ibid.: 4). Eng (2010: 41) has continued this critique in his monograph *The Feeling of Kinship* in which he argues for a 'renewed intersectional approach' in queer studies. For Eng, this renewal is an important means of combating 'queer liberalism', or the neoliberal political formation in which certain lesbian and gay subjects are afforded civil rights on the proviso that they conform to normative kinship arrangements by buying into a kind of 'identity politics' (ibid.: xi). Intersectionality is intended to bring back to view the social differences that queer liberalism apparently attempts to flatten and, in particular, bring to light the processes of racialisation that attend liberal rights claims. The move to assimilate to a liberal model is a forgetting of 'social difference' (ibid.: 10) and intersectionality is meant to bring this back into the frame. Jasbir Puar has taken these arguments a step further by arguing that we need to complement intersectional analyses with a rubric of assemblage. For Puar (2007: 212), intersectionality remains insufficiently dynamic because it conceptualises component parts of identity as 'separable analytics' that can be 'disassembled', whereas assemblage theory 'is more attuned to interwoven forces that merge and dissipate time, space, and body against linearity, coherency, and permanency'. Intersectionality encases difference 'within a structural container that simply wishes the messiness of identity into a formulaic grid, producing analogies in its wake' (ibid.). Puar's argument is made in the context of her account of 'homonationalism', or what she calls a 'structure of modernity' (Puar 2013: 337), in which lesbian and gay minority difference is actually used by nation states to bolster nationalist projects, or, in other words, becomes a form of 'identity politics' (Puar 2007: 211). Intersectionality has become another form of 'diversity management' (Puar 2012a: 53) rather than a genuine way of attending to difference. For her, assemblage promises a better solution.

These interventions have also been amongst the latest in a wider range of longstanding reservations about how difference can be co-opted, commodified or otherwise distorted by institutions and governments as well as interpretative practices: that is, how difference can be solidified into 'identity'. For example, the analysis of homonationalism is only a recent development in work that has noted how difference can be institutionalised in the form of corporate commitments to diversity, which really only attend to those differences that have been sanitised, depoliticised, ratified and pre-defined as acceptable. Versions of this account can be found in arguments from the 1990s against the tokenistic inclusion of ethnic minorities (Spivak and Gunew 1993), or against the commodification or appropriation of minority racial identities (hooks 1992: 21–39), or against an 'empty pluralism' that treats frictions arising from social difference only as a matter of personal prejudice rather than structural inequality (Mohanty 2003: 193). More recent versions can be found in accounts of the 'non-performativity' of diversity cultures which only pay lip service to difference (Ahmed 2012: 116), or the institutionalisation of new social movement difference in the post-1968 university and the way in which 'power' can work 'through difference in order to manage its insurgent possibilities' (Ferguson 2012: 4). These scholars all provide warnings against how difference can be downplayed even as it seems to be being honoured or protected: they provide warnings against not taking difference seriously enough. Writing specifically about feminist theory, Janet Jakobsen (1998: 26) suggests that the 'politics of "difference"', with difference in quotation marks, is problematic, not because of anything to do with difference, which is still celebrated, but because it plays into the 'economy of the same' in US politics, which rewards social movements who are able to articulate themselves as a unity. The resulting 'reductive pluralism' is no good because it turns difference into 'homogeneity' (ibid.: 10). In 'reductive pluralism,' 'empty pluralism' and 'diversity management', then, difference is a problem because it becomes like sameness.

The rhetorical alignment of many of these thinkers has a varied genealogy. On the one hand, there are the post-structuralist foundations from the previous sections, though Puar's interest in assemblage arguably owes more to Gilles Deleuze than to Derrida. However, queer of colour (and other) analyses have insisted that queer theoretical work that is interested in intersectionality draws, often tacitly, on feminist work from the preceding decades (Muñoz 1999: 6–11, 21–2; Ferguson 2004). Certainly, we can see that a shift in the rhetoric of women of colour feminism has been particularly influential in this regard. In 1977, the Combahee River Collective (1983: 210) can offer their approach to 'struggling against racial, sexual, heterosexual, and class oppression' by understanding these oppressions as 'interlocking' as a form of 'identity politics' (ibid.: 211), in so far as it derives from their identities as black women. However, later writers such as Cherríe Moraga, Gloria Anzaldúa and Audre Lorde all embraced *difference*, rather than identity, as that which mainstream feminist thought had not adequately recognised.

Mainstream feminism came to be associated with 'homogeneity' and an adequate account of social life with difference (Lorde 1984: 116; see also Moraga and Anzaldúa 1983). Indeed, we can see this influence in Butler's work that I cited above; it is not only metaphysical difference but intersecting social differences that undermine the notion of a univocal identity (Butler 1999: 7). Queer theoretical work, then, begins to appear at a time when it seems newly possible or appropriate to combine post-structuralist and sociological forms of difference. In the words of William B. Turner's (2000: 134) genealogy of queer theory, 'in an important sense, "queer" served as the conceptual connection between the politics of difference that some feminists, lesbians, and gay men had cultivated and the philosophical language of difference that Foucault, among others, initiated'. In this account, queer theory emerges to provide something like an exemplary relation to difference understood in philosophical *and* sociological terms: it channels both the energies of politicised writers defending social difference from the apparent risk of homogenisation or reduction to stereotype and a post-structuralist scepticism towards the project of establishing fixed unities. However, this also means that difference began to lose its specificity – rather than a means of making sure people were paying attention to social identity, or paying attention to the ramifications of social categories within social life, it transformed into a wider field of ideas often taken to be implicitly good. For example, in a well-cited essay, Cornel West (1990: 29) credits 'Black diaspora women' over the preceding decade with the move towards the 'new cultural politics of difference' that he celebrates for how it seeks to 'trash the monolithic and homogeneous in the name of diversity, multiplicity and heterogeneity' (ibid.: 19). But it is not clear what logical relation 'diversity, multiplicity and heterogeneity' actually have to consequential social categories, even as these have been the ideas that a wide range of socially engaged scholarship has privileged.

Returning to Puar and Eng, we might ask in a similar vein what logical relation the 'homo' and the 'queer' have to the social forces that they critique. All the thinkers in the first paragraph in this section take a common approach in so far as they associate the nationalism and liberalism they anatomise not only with undesirable forms of sameness (universalism, grids, homogeneity) but also with gay people, whether that's the gay men in the nightclubs in the *Social Text* issue or the lesbian and gay liberal subjects living under homonationalism. For example, for

Eng and Puar, the historical shift that they name as 'queer liberalism' and 'homonationalism' respectively, and what is presented as most problematic about this shift, does not have any fundamentally necessary relation to gay people. Puar (2013: 337) calls homonationalism a 'structure of modernity': it names a shift to a new historical phase in which the forms of minority difference that might previously have offered radical political potential are actually celebrated and utilised by modern nation states for their state-building and neo-imperialist ends. Any other form of maligned (or apparently formerly maligned) minority difference might be the basis for a similar argument. Yet there seems to be something uniquely rhetorically compelling about the 'homo' prefix. Similarly, for Eng, the problem with 'queer liberalism' is that it is a form of liberalism, where liberalism means a political position that is deliberately blind to social differences because it is attached to abstract freedom and equality. The problem in queer liberalism actually has no specific intrinsic relation to queers: it is a generic force for flattening social difference. Yet queers again seem like the easiest or most appropriate target, perhaps because of the sameness that this form of liberalism seems to be bringing about: it locates queerness in the 'private sphere of intimacy, family, and bourgeois respectability as *sameness*' (Eng 2010: 43, original italics). In Puar's and Eng's analyses gay people seem somehow better suited to carrying the burden of the unacceptable forms of sameness associated with liberalism and nationalism. These scholars suggest most strongly the relation that I am arguing undergirds much aversion to sameness. They materialise the link between gay people and sameness that this book is about.

Could it be, then, that the longstanding, extraordinarily durable and oft-repeated injunction against *identity* is one way that queer theory has maintained a paradoxical gay-aversiveness at its core? It is ideas like 'identity' that frequently form the foils for queer theoretical argumentation, as well as ideas like homogeneity, coherency and grids that we have seen scholars such as Puar and Eng malign, which I explore in this book. As discussed above, my approach does not accord with the more prominent models available for understanding 'sameness' in queer scholarship and culture, which imagine it as a force of grand ontological disintegration with profound ethical implications. A project with closer ambitions to mine is another that I mentioned above: Koestenbaum's (1990: 182) argument, really from before the moment of queer theory, that 'gay criticism needs to develop a theory of typing or copying that wipes the tarnish off clones'. Rather than an account that recuperates the clone to established and highly prestigious theoretical models (the kind of account we saw Dean provide at the beginning of the previous section), Koestenbaum calls for gay criticism to come up with adequate tools for accounting for the clone's interest in types and copies. By the same token, over the chapters that follow, I explore the manifest ways in which queers have performed investments in the kinds of sameness that queer scholarship has tended to distance itself from structurally.

Rather than with Bersani's particular account of sameness, then, my approach has more in common with a separate set of ramifications of his work. That is, Bersani's interest in 'sameness' stems from a broader project: his scepticism towards what he famously called the prevailing 'culture of redemption' in which art in particular, but also life more broadly, can be seen as valuable only if it is redemptive, exalts humanity, protects human dignity and has an agency in the world that can be seen as a vector of the Good (Bersani 1990). Such investment in human sovereignty can lead to violent defensiveness, such that abandoning proud identities and recognising the 'sameness' of humanity with itself and the world can create less aggressive being. For Bersani, abandoning the redemptive imperative is a way to embrace this 'sameness'. Whilst they have not necessarily taken up his interest in sameness per se, various scholars such as Edelman, Love, Freeman, Halberstam and Amin have continued to explore the implications for queer theory of refusing to embrace the culture of redemption in the way that he does. Whether arguing for a completely unmotivated embrace of negativity as a means of refusing the imperative of redemption (Edelman 2004), or for paying attention to affects, experiences and objects of study which may read as irredeemably backward or out-of-date (Love 2007; Freeman 2010; Halberstam 2011), these scholars have revealed what redemptive approaches have obscured. Love (2007: 2) suggests that queer theory in particular lends itself to such anti-redemptive positions because the very slur that names the field ('queer') has always 'evoked a long history of insult and abuse'. Amin has also recently contributed to scholarship in this vein by examining the attachments of Jean Genet to phenomena that queer thought has tended to see as problematic, such as racial fetishisation and pederastic desire. By fully accounting for the 'disturbing attachments' of Genet, and thereby de-idealising him in the canon of queer thought, Amin (2017: 4) suggests that a fuller account of social life is made possible, making space for 'disturbing attachments' to 'race, history, and geopolitics'. My ambition in the following pages is to do something similar: I identify a critical idealism structured around the rejection of sameness in queer theory and show how the specificity and particularity of queer culture is at odds with this in consequential ways.

Whilst the temptation to abandon all redemption, such as that provided by justification in terms of political usefulness, is strong, I nevertheless want to try to articulate something similar to Amin's project or Love's (2007: 12) sense of the 'diagnostic usefulness' of queer abjection. On the one hand, as I argue in Chapter 1, the imperative to justify an approach in terms of its usefulness, or the 'difference' it makes, is part of the rhetorical dispensation that I am seeking to interrogate. The epistemological project of this book would suggest that the implicit power of appeals to making a difference is linked to the similarly taken-for-granted hierarchy of difference over sameness in sexual definition. On the other hand, this epistemological inquiry is nevertheless attended by an ethical or practical one: to what extent does a default privileging of difference and denigration of sameness obscure the functioning of the social forces against which much queer theoretical writing would seek to organise itself? My suggestion is that engaging with sameness might be a way to focus greater attention on how social domination functions. A casual association of the forces of social domination with sameness may provide a neat rhetorical shorthand, it may appeal to what often seems a default sense that sameness is damaging and unhelpful, but it does not necessarily adequately explain the functioning of that domination. However, whilst Love looks specifically at negative queer affect from the past as a way of acknowledging that those ways of feeling bad are not necessarily things we have got over, this book is not about affect. I do not survey ways of feeling bad in queer representation as a means to show how such bad feelings continue to structure queer lives and alert us to the enduring, intimate effects of homophobia, which Love registers so eloquently. I do, however, share with Love a refusal to jettison what seems out of place. In my case, what has come to seem out of place are the forms of sameness that are surveyed in the chapters that follow. The chapters help to diagnose those situations in which a constant aversion to sameness might obscure scenarios in which, say, homophobia or sexism or racism do not function through forms of sameness at all. The diagnostic purpose of the book, then, would be to invite us to think more carefully about where and in what ways, exactly, sameness might be a problem or the cause of a problem. Surely it cannot just be *because it is sameness*, or, if this is the case, then surely we must think about where the idea that sameness in itself is a problem comes from.

In this regard, *Same old* is also influenced by systematic attempts to understand the habits and shapes of entire fields of study, such as in the recent work of Robyn Wiegman. In *Object Lessons* (2012), Wiegman (1) charts how participants in what she calls 'identity knowledges' formulate their objects of study so as to reassure themselves that the work they undertake with these objects in mind will serve their social justice goals. Wiegman seeks to study the political desires that motivate identity knowledges, to examine the sense that we can ever make our objects of study adequate to the political importance that we invest them with. Acknowledging that there are many ways in which scholars have answered the question of what will provide the most politically defensible forms of scholarship, Wiegman seeks to examine the 'answer's ardent pursuit' (ibid.: 5), or the very act of seeking an object that will finally provide the politically pure analysis sought. Wiegman seeks to 'interrupt' the idea that 'if only we find the right discourse, object of study, or analytic tool, our critical practice will be adequate to the political commitments that inspire it' (ibid.: 2–3). She moves away from the 'golden rule' that 'objects and analytics of study can be made to deliver everything we want from them' (ibid.: 28). She remains convinced of the idea that 'objects can resist what we try to make of them' (ibid.: 30). I'm doing something like that in this book: showing how queer subjects frustrate the radicality we might prefer to invest in them, in so far as radicality is commonly indexed primarily to investments in difference. That is, it is my suggestion that making forms of difference the necessary shibboleths of queer-positive political engagement is not necessarily a way of ensuring a queer-positive politics. People marginalised because of sexual nonconformity have no necessary relation to difference: their lives are not more accurately reflected by forms of difference. For example, Wiegman briefly discusses the example of the AIDS crisis to show how the critical idealism of queer theory's staunch anti-normativity does not enable understanding of how queer investments in marriage might be a way of healing some historical injuries that arose as a result of the crisis, during which, say, intimate partners were denied access to their dying or dead loved ones (ibid.: 339–40). Amin has also recently powerfully drawn on Wiegman's work to make his argument that it is only when the ideals of queer theory are deflated that space is made for thinking through the actual particularities of social life.

In this book, then, I am continuing in the vein of Wiegman and Amin to ask fundamental questions about what the role of queer scholars and scholarship is and should be. On the one hand, should it be to learn the protocols and imperatives of a specific academic field which has been influenced by a range of prestigious French theoretical texts, and bears the hallmarks of many of the assumptions that thread through contemporary engaged scholarship, so as to secure legitimacy and belonging within that field? On the other hand, should it be to be interested in all the manifold ways of living, of giving expression and form to, non-heterosexual existence, even as this may conflict with the imperatives of that field as it is currently imagined? At the beginning of this section, I quoted Eng, Halberstam and Muñoz (2005: 12) in their argument that 'queer studies promises more than a history of gay men, a sociology of gay male sex clubs, an anthropology of gay male tourism, a survey of gay male aesthetics'. To my mind, though, there are unfortunately no established protocols within history, sociology or anthropology for any kind of analysis like this. That which queer studies is supposedly moving beyond would surely need to have secured some level of legitimacy for the point here to be anything other than a rhetorical one. In the chapters that follow, what I offer strays perhaps too close to the 'survey of gay male aesthetics' that they mention. Many of the works that I address are linked to the kinds of lesbian and gay identities that scholars such as Eng et al. have often called for us to move beyond. By contrast, I do not imagine that these identities are inherently politically pernicious. In this book, I dwell on these identities and their expression in a range of literary works, on the myriad ways of giving form to queerness that these works allow access to, and indeed would argue that even now there is no scholarly framework for taking a 'survey of gay male aesthetics' seriously. But I also argue that doing this can help to revise some of the most prevalent and durable theoretical frameworks that queer scholarship operates within.

It gets blander

Few aspects of lesbian and gay aesthetics have combined an undeniable centrality to queer lives with a manifest tendency towards sameness quite so clearly as coming out stories. Across the genres in which they have appeared, these stories have often been deemed repetitive, formulaic and boring, relying on stock characters like the troubled teenager and stock plots like the final, harmonious integration of a lesbian, gay or bisexual identity. In this latter respect they are also liable to attract the ire of the many scholars addressed in the previous paragraphs whose intellectual projects have centred on the debunking of stable identity and a preference for avant-garde forms. Still, though, as a genre, they will not seem to go away, transforming their tedious repetitiveness into a dogged persistence, continuing to manifest aesthetic as well as political shortcomings. However, it is much less common to recognise that the boring repetitiveness of these stories may be connected to the material conditions of minority cultural production. When a culture has few formal institutions for its transmission, dissemination and development, its proponents are likely to have to go over what others have done before and see others going over what they may think of as already achieved. It may be necessary to repeat the same positions again and again when there are no grounds from which to feel that one's culture is securely established. A boring repetitiveness may be tied in to the experience of social marginality. I want to suggest here that we should recognise how queer culture shares with other minority cultures this necessary tendency towards sameness. Might minority cultures, out of necessity, be boring?

The assumption that guides literary commentary on coming out stories is that they should certainly *not* be boring. For example, in one of her many essays on aspects of lesbian and gay literature, the author Dorothy Allison (1995: 199) laments the 'monotonous regularity' with which coming out novels were published in the wake of Rita Mae Brown's bestselling *Rubyfruit Jungle* from 1973. Similarly, in an oft-cited article, Sarah Schulman critiques lesbian writers for writing coming out novels in which the characters' lesbian sexuality is the primary focus of the work. She complains that much lesbian fiction is 'preachy and didactic, filled with stiff, one-dimensional characters' (Schulman 1995: 166). Moreover, the narrative structures and writing styles are 'uptight and repetitious' (ibid.). She calls on writers to 'stop re-proving the same formulaic arguments' in order to better represent the 'complexities' of lesbian and gay lives (ibid.: 168). Writing in a more scholarly-theoretical vein, Judith Roof (1996: 111) discusses a character from the TV series *Roseanne* who comes out as lesbian in the 1992–93 season of the show, and registers her disappointment at this declaration of identity as an aesthetic judgement: the character Nancy becomes 'boring' whereas she had previously been dynamic and irreverent. In any case, we see that many of the aesthetic judgements that have been made about coming out stories cluster around a set of ideas: boredom, monotony, repetitiveness.

But it isn't just in terms of their apparent aesthetic failings that coming out stories have been critiqued. The coming out story's political shortcoming has been imagined as its promotion of a stable, coherent sexual identity. While coming out stories take many generic forms – autobiographical testimonials, novels and young adult fiction – they all share a focus on recognising, accepting and publicising a sexual identity and preference. In her book-length study of the genre, Esther Saxey (2008: 15–33) traces its roots back to the consciousness-raising groups of second-wave feminism and related novels of emerging feminist consciousness by authors such as Marge Piercy, Marilyn French and Margaret Atwood. Just as feminists sought to share experiences of making female identity in a patriarchal world in order to empower others, so queer people have sought to share their coming out stories for similar reasons. But this focus on identity is one of the key characteristics for which it has been critiqued over the years. For example, Roof's critique that I cited above is primarily made on philosophical grounds. She suggests that the narrative structure of these stories, in which teenage tribulations frequently lead to a final resolution in adult sexuality, privileges a standard developmental model that is overladen with heterosexual meanings. The stories mimic the Freudian account of heterosexuality as what proper and healthy adults will eventually grow into. Their emphasis on a final and coherent realisation of identity, even as this is a non-heterosexual identity, is a way of reinscribing what Roof (1996: xxxv) calls this 'heteronarrative'. Embodying the particular style of queer literary and cultural studies scholarship that emerged in the 1990s, Roof imagines any commitment to a coherent identity as problematically caught up in a presumptively heterosexual logic. Reading the stories collected in an anthology from the early 1990s called *What a Lesbian Looks Like* (1992) put together by the National Lesbian and Gay Survey in the UK, Roof (1996: 104) laments that they all have the 'same narrative structure'. She bemoans this tendency of lesbian and gay writing to replicate the defining structures of heterosexual narrative: she asks wearily, 'Why is the story always the same?' (ibid.: xxvi). As I have indicated, though, queer stories, more than any, may have good reason for repeatedly being the same.

Certainly, the stories do, frequently, seem to repeat themselves. For example, the editors of *The Coming Out Stories*, a canonical anthology published in 1980 by the lesbian-feminist Persephone Press, recognise in their introduction that contributions to the volume are defined by similarities and patterns (Stanley and Wolfe 1980: xvii). One contributor, Deidre McCalla, is able to recognise the repetitiveness that tends to mark coming out stories by wearily distinguishing her own story from them: 'There were no long, painful years of suffering in silence, nor any early adolescent fears of being sexually different. I never went to a summer camp and to the best of my recollection, never had a crush on any of my gym teachers' (ibid.: 12). She identifies many of the key milestones in the coming out stories in this anthology, but other life experiences she might have picked up on that appear with striking regularity include being from a small or non-metropolitan town (ibid.: 7, 23, 79), finding new freedoms while studying for an advanced degree (ibid.: 31, 60, 100) or ending their stories on the final, triumphant recognition of lesbian identity and community (ibid.: 43, 78, 124). It is this latter aspect, of course, that is also particularly important. In their introduction the editors suggest that the lives of out lesbians have been omitted from the historical record and that their anthology is a small step towards correcting this omission so that women going through similar experiences in the future will not have to find their own ways completely in the dark, or, in other words, so that they have a blueprint for their own identities to copy or emulate.

Perhaps this built-in repetitiveness is why coming out stories themselves continue to be repeated. That is, if the ambitions of the editors of *The Coming Out Stories* are to give gay people some legs to stand on during the development of their non-heterosexual consciousness, then it's clear that their efforts are themselves part of a repetitive, or iterative, process that is still, and may always be, ongoing. We see evidence of this in the continuing popularity of coming out stories in high-profile campaigns such as the 'It Gets Better' project started in 2010 in the US by the popular relationship columnist Dan Savage. Originally begun as a video uploaded to YouTube addressed to gay teenagers, the project has grown into something much larger with tens of thousands of videos now uploaded to its dedicated website and hundreds of thousands of followers on Twitter. Amongst the project's outputs is an anthology of short testimonials: *It Gets Better: Coming Out, Overcoming Bullying, and Creating a Life Worth Living* (2011). Whilst this is different from the earlier coming out stories in many ways (it's published by a major mainstream publisher, and features essays from heterosexual celebrities and politicians as well as from everyday LGBTQ people), there are also many similarities. For example, in an overwhelming majority of the first-person accounts, the narrator will describe feelings of difference and alienation from a small-town religious or else otherwise highly traditional background. This is followed by bullying at high school, accompanied by suicidal thoughts, or even a suicide attempt. Things get much better after high school or in college: many end up surrounded by supportive friends and with a long-term partner. The It Gets Better project has garnered new criticisms, beyond the more common reservations about the coming out story's investment in identity: queer scholars have also critiqued it for the normalised image of queer life that it seems to promote and for privileging the exceptionalism of queer youth suicide over more structural and entrenched forms of everyday inequality (Puar 2012b). Sidestepping these critiques somewhat, my interest is in the repetition that this volume also embodies. Sometimes it's almost as if the contributors to the volume recognise that their stories are likely to seem uninteresting and frequently the actual process of coming out is quickly skirted over or else is revealed to be banal. One contributor, Darren Hayes, former lead singer of the band Savage Garden, explicitly recognises the potential of coming out stories to bore their audiences: self-effacingly he writes, 'You don't need to know my long, boring coming-out story', even as he has been enlisted to provide exactly this (Savage and Miller 2012: 151).

But just as the stories in these volumes are marked by kinds of repetition, many of the contributors recognise that coming out is, by definition, a repetitive process. 'There are more scenes, more ways to come out. The process is a long one, going on daily' (Martha Pillow in Stanley and Wolfe 1980: 10). 'There are more entries – many more comings out since then' (Ellen Roe Anthony in ibid.: 69). 'I think coming out is a life-long process' (Caryl B. Bentley in ibid.: 79). One story makes the point by repeating the phrase 'I had come out' in relation to different scenarios (ibid.: 53–5). Within a presumptively heterosexual world, a non-heterosexual person has to come out again and again, in every new context defined by those presumptions. Moreover, the editors of *The Coming Out Stories* make it clear that coming out involves gradual self-realisation as women develop a lesbian consciousness out of the scraps that dominant culture provides for them. With no models for what a lesbian life might look like, they recognise that the women in the anthology have had to piece together gradually what they can from the materials available. In the introduction to *Testimonies* (1988), another early collection of coming out stories, Tina Portillo writes that the stories in the volume will be 'the kind of history-book-making testimonials that we all need' (Holmes 1988: 8). Without solid institutions for passing on and developing queer history and culture, queer people are left having to reinvent the wheel, and Portillo's hope is that *Testimonies* is a step towards a situation where queers don't have to constantly do this. Karen Barber, the author of the Introduction to the second edition of *Testimonies*, agrees: 'Each story told becomes a part of our community's history, reminding us how times have changed, or as the case may be, how much things have stayed the same' (Barber and Holmes 1994: 7). The editors of *The Coming Out Stories* also suggest that the stories serve to right the historical wrong in which lesbian history has been concealed: 'Our anthology represents that ongoing process of rediscovery of ourselves, our continuing reclamation of our lives and our strengths' (Stanley and Wolfe 1980: xv). It is the lack of this history and the lack of institutions for transmitting it that result in the repetitiveness of queer experience, which coming out stories emblematise and embody.

The stories dramatise this need for most robust information flows in how their narrators frequently dwell on teachers, reading and libraries. Some of the contributors are themselves school instructors who induct students into the ways of lesbian life (e.g. Roselle Pineda in Holmes and Tust 2002: 104), but overwhelmingly the narrators across all the volumes I have addressed so far (and more) are at some point students with formative romantic interest in their teachers: gym teachers, English teachers or generalists (Stanley and Wolfe 1980: 71, 100, 156, 209, 221, 233; Holmes 1988: 35, 54, 60, 94, 105, 142; Barber and Holmes 1994: 102, 52; Holmes and Tust 2002: 25, 36). Teachers, of course, are people who promise access to information and knowledge; they are guides and mentors at formative points in life. Books can also play this role and many of the narrators of these stories are keen readers. One of them has an 'insatiable desire for reading' (Stanley and Wolfe 1980: 25). Another scrabbles for information: 'I read what I could find on the subject of homosexuality to try to understand where it came from, what it meant' (ibid.: 165). For another, the only way she survived was 'through books' (ibid.: 233). Another 'voraciously read[s] novels, biographies and autobiographies about famous women's lives and the difficulties and choices we faced' (Holmes 1988: 88). Another tells us: 'I was very into books as a child and read pretty much everything I could get my hands on' (Holmes and Tust 2002: 94). The institutions that frequently facilitate access to all these books are libraries. The contributors to all volumes find lifelines in libraries that furnish them with access to materials that help them understand their incipient sexual identities. As children, contributors spend their weekends in their local libraries where they gain 'priceless' knowledge that they carry 'secretly' and 'proudly' (Stanley and Wolfe 1980: 196, see also 236), later studying 'abnormal psychology textbooks' (ibid.: 79), and using university library catalogues for 'tracking down psychiatric books which described in gruesome detail the case histories of "female homosexuals" and left nothing to the imagination' (ibid.: 156). Others use the university library to meet future love interests (ibid.: 96), form relationships with trainee librarians (ibid.: 239) or become librarians themselves (Sarah Holmes, editor or co-editor of all volumes of *Testimonies*, is described as a 'corporate librarian' (Holmes and Tust 2002: back cover)). The stories paint pictures of people thirsty for knowledge: lusting after teachers in particular, finding a lifeline in a library (and often working in one) and reading whatever they can get their hands on. The narrators are desperate to find ways to learn other than through (painful) experience and, as we have seen in the explicit terms in which the collections are framed, to enable others to bypass this experience too. Combined with their framing as tools to fill in gaps in the historical record, the stories begin to suggest the importance of a specifically sexual politics of information management.

The absence of robust and reliable sources of information has social and political consequences. Without the structures in place to learn about the advances of those who have gone before, without ways of passing on collective memory, LGBTQ culture is often given no choice but to start from scratch, going over what may have already been done elsewhere. In her more recent writing, Schulman has taken up this issue in her commentary on the state of LGBT literature. Rather than criticising authors' writing, though, she has instead lamented the lack of support structures for LGBT literary culture. This leaves LGBT authors to fight for attention from the kinds of mainstream support structures within which their work is often made to seem like a minority irrelevance, or which tend to assume that LGBT content precludes writing from the category of serious literature. Combined with the absence of structures for passing on established culture and collective memory in gay communities, this leads to the repetition of scenarios from the past. An example she gives is an apparent 'glitch' on Amazon in April 2009 which removed all titles listed as 'lesbian and gay' from its bestsellers lists as part of a policy of de-ranking 'adult' material. Schulman's contention is that the reaction to this from the LGBT community would have been stronger if there were more robust structures for schooling people in how exactly this kind of thing has happened before and has been the way in which the mainstream has belittled LGBT cultural production: simply as pornographic 'adult content' (Schulman 2012: 133–53). As we have seen, the coming out story is often imagined as a way of providing some of the collective memory that Schulman is talking about, laying some of the groundwork for those emerging into LGBT culture. However, we could also suggest that these stories embody in some way the problem that they overcome: the seemingly redundant repetition of what has already gone before. Yet, as the literary scholar Jane Elliott (2006: 1701) reminds us in her discussion of the tendency of feminist theory to conflate the new and different with the politically valuable, 'things may stay true longer than they stay interesting'. If coming out stories are not interesting, then we might recognise that this has as much to do with the necessity of repetition that comes from being in a minority position as it does with the failure of cultural imagination. Can we accept that there might be good reasons that being boring should be a part of gay culture?

Coming out stories then help us think more broadly about sameness and queer culture. On one hand, if the repetition that these stories embody so well is a product of our social marginality, then we might suggest that this is something that the true liberation of queers would free us from. But at the same time perhaps there's scope for us to see that this boredom is not just something that we are doomed to, but something we might recognise as structurally necessary, or even embrace. One way to understand this is to return to the idea of 'reverse' discourse: we are put in a position where our marginality makes us need to repeat.

We could fight against this, invite queers to reinvent themselves and create something new, but we could also take the position of repetition that a dominant culture has ascribed to us and find enjoyment or power in this. Coming out stories, as I have said, embody the problem that they are also supposed to overcome: they are highly repetitive, but they are supposed to alleviate repetition, or form an information network that means that future queers don't have to go over the same ground again. However, at the same time, the stories offer models to follow, actually facilitating repetition, or, in theory, making it easier to repeat. Critiques of coming out stories for being repetitive perhaps ignore something fundamental about queer and other minority experience: that it is intimately bound up with boring repetition. Marginal lives are likely also to be repetitive ones. Coming out stories help us see that there may, in specific ways, be an intimate connection between sameness and queer culture.

The following chapters continue to explore this conjunction: queer culture's enduring investment in the forms of sameness that queer theoretical frameworks have been less good at honouring or recognising. The first chapter examines the place of uselessness in the history of queer representation by looking back to the moment of *fin-de-siècle* aestheticism. I examine how the aestheticist reservations about the utilitarianism and vulgarity of late nineteenth-century society were also reservations about the value or necessity of difference (legible most clearly in the idiomatic rendering of usefulness as 'making a difference'). Whilst many queer aesthetes who resisted the imperatives of utility could be appropriate here, I focus in particular on two protagonists from the novels of Henry James: Rowland Mallet in *Roderick Hudson* (1875) and Gabriel Nash in *The Tragic Muse* (1890). Rowland and Gabriel are repeatedly associated neither with a revolutionary socialism (advocated by Oscar Wilde), nor with a sensuous appreciation of art (advocated by Walter Pater) but rather with 'theory' or 'theories'. Like James himself, they are aesthetic characters deemed impractical and overly analytical: thoroughly useless, their inclinations are to leave things mostly the same. I imagine their particular brand of theoretical uselessness as an interesting counterpoint to recent scholarship in queer studies that we have already encountered and that has sought to refigure what can be considered meaningfully political by turning its attention to the idea of failure or to apparently 'useless' affective states. Where this embrace of queer failure or uselessness is imagined to have some form of political potency, or in other words is imagined to be useful, Rowland and Gabriel receive no such redemption. Situated in a history in which queer theory itself has been subject to charges of uselessness from scholars apparently better attuned to the materialities of lived experience, Rowland and Gabriel serve to flag up a longer history of intimate connection between queers and uselessness.

Chapter 2 examines lesbian feminist speculative fiction from across the twentieth century in order to reconsider queer theory's widespread rejection of reproduction, particularly in the wake of Edelman's (2004: 2) influential critique of 'reproductive futurism'. The ease with which Edelman rejects reproduction is imagined to have something to do with its rhetorical association (in his rhetoric and beyond) with copying, or creating more of the same. Edelman rejects not just biological reproduction, however, but all forms of reproduction, including the perpetuation of all social and political forms, which he imagines to be necessarily tied up with a dominant heteronormativity. The theoretical foundations of his argument (derived from deconstruction and psychoanalysis) make it impossible for him to see any kind of sameness as anything other than the embodiment of a pernicious and conservative order. However, in novels ranging from Charlotte Perkins Gilman's *Herland* (1915) to Nicola Griffith's *Ammonite* (1993), and many in between, I argue that the worlds presented are structured around forms of reproduction – biological and social copying (and sometimes literalised in the form of cloning) – that are none the less in no way heterosexual and certainly not heteronormative. Moreover, these novels dramatise the importance of structures for reproduction – for keeping things the same – especially where the conditions being reproduced are the result of minoritarian struggle.

Chapter 3 begins by noting that, of all the things that could be credited with a structuring role in the formation of modern lesbian identity, scholars often return to something as ordinary and dowdy as a middle-brow novel: Hall's *Well of Loneliness*. I read Hall's work, alongside that of other 'lesbian middlebrow' writers from the early twentieth century against queer theory's longstanding rejection of normativity. From its earliest articulations, queer scholarship has taken it for granted that its enemies are, in Warner's (1993: xxvi) oft-cited phrase, 'regimes of the normal', but the sharpness of this critique has morphed into a more general position in which any kind of normativity or conformism is intrinsically suspect. By contrast, in *The Well*, the famous lesbian protagonist Stephen Gordon longs to be normal precisely because of its association with sameness and the opportunity it provides to be 'like' everyone else. In Hall's earlier novel *The Unlit Lamp* (1924), the protagonist Joan Ogden's unwillingness to change the life of familial conformity that she finds in many ways stifling and intolerable leads her to abandon hope of making a life with her female lover: she chooses the path that embodies a regime of the normal. In Mary Renault's *The Friendly Young Ladies* (1944), written, according to Renault, in response to Hall, the lesbian couple of the novel's title repeatedly see themselves as emphatically 'ordinary'. These middle-brow novels are the occasion to reflect on what keeps anti-normativity at the heart of queer theoretical strategy: the opportunity it provides of opposing a stultifying, conformist, assimilationist sameness.

In agreement with some of his critics, the fourth chapter suggests that John Rechy's fictional writings are reductive. Whilst Rechy protests against his frequent categorisation as a 'gay writer' in terms of the problematic limitation and reduction it apparently constitutes, his fictional (and semi-fictional) writings such as *City of Night* (1963), *Numbers* (1967) and *The Sexual Outlaw* (1977), amongst others, repeatedly embody and represent the forms of reduction he decries. They are 'reduced' to descriptions of a gay casual sex world that is itself described as performing various kinds of 'reduction'. In this, it is part of a broader tradition of writing in the vein of the 'stud file', or the account of sexual seriality that we can see across twentieth-century queer writing in the work of Samuel Steward, Renaud Camus, Jane Delynn or Samuel Delany. However, both post-structuralist commitments to non-identity and 'politics of difference' approaches have opposed reductionism because of the limitation and sameness that it would seem to impose. It is in this chapter that I provide the most sustained reading of the work of Bersani, who articulates the potential value of reduction in the context of his broader argument endorsing 'homo-ness'. However, Bersani ultimately echoes the consensus against reduction, endorsing an enabling reductionism in opposition to a static, limiting and homogenising version. Rechy's writing, I argue, facilitates both the endorsement and the interrogation of Bersani's terms: in the end, we see that Rechy does not reject the forms of reductionism that Bersani does in order to give a familiar and comprehensible rhetorical shape to his work. This chapter suggests that Rechy's writing in particular encourages us to

Introduction: Same old

recognise the reductiveness of queer culture, which queer theory may prefer to disavow.

Taken together, the following chapters challenge the assumption that we must at all costs avoid the useless, reproductive, normative and reductive. There is no logical reasoning that accompanies the assertion that these ideas necessarily lead to undesired or unwanted ends. Instead, the assumption that often attends these ideas is that sameness itself *is* the unwanted and undesired end. Whilst I am not necessarily looking for something better, for an approach that will fully redeem what I might be seen to be suggesting is the failure of extant queer theory, I do provide an account of what underwrites some common rhetorical formations in queer theoretical writing. This point is borne out by the inconsistencies in the chapters that follow. For example, whilst Chapter 1 suggests that the apparent necessity of usefulness is related to how the useful can be seen to make a difference, hence rendering the useless a realm of abject, unpalatable sameness, subsequent chapters also relate the *useful* to forms of sameness. For example, in Chapter 3, in *The Well of Loneliness*, Stephen Gordon's desire to be useful is imagined to be part of her desire to be normal, ordinary and unremarkable. In Chapter 2, usefulness and efficiency for Gilman signify homogenised, hyper-utilitarian factory-like processes which reduce human individuality. Contradictions like this mean that this book does not offer any clear form of sameness to embrace: I do not suggest that, say, if only we embrace either uselessness or usefulness we will arrive at a perfected politics. The point is not to say that one approach or the other is the right one, that, say, uselessness is always associated with sameness and so therefore embracing it will offer a politics or way of life that can offer some salvation from any current shortcomings. Instead, the point is to show how forms of sameness can be adapted to fit rhetorical context. When arguing in favour of the useless, utilitarian logics are cold, excessively rational, machine-like, inhuman and homogenising. When arguing in favour of the useful, that which is not instrumentalisable is seen as an ineffectual, murky swamp of indistinction. Both situations can provide the opportunity of opposing some form of sameness. This is the point, then: that forms of sameness frequently give shape to what we oppose, and, moreover, they seem to many, including queer theoretical scholars, somehow better suited or more appropriate for doing so. I would evoke Bersani (1995: 1) again: 'No one wants to be called a homosexual.' Even decrying those phenomena that it has often seemed most important for queer work to oppose, then, may be ways of aligning against the sameness that also defines homosexuality.

Notes

1 See www.boyfriendtwin.tumblr.com.
2 For related arguments see: Butler 1999; Edelman 1994; Warner 1993.
3 I discuss Bersani at more length below and in Chapter 4. More recently, David Halperin (2012: 50) has made the case for the value of a 'traditional gay male culture' that has a durability in the world that, he argues, queer theory has taught us to feel is suspiciously essentialist and problematically backward. I discuss Halperin at more length in the Coda.
4 Although her account is not emphatically queer in the way that Flatley's is, Kaja Silverman has offered an account of 'analogy' that also echoes Bersani. Silverman (2009) argues that, until the sixteenth century, analogy and resemblance played a much larger role in prevalent conceptions of the world than they have since this point. She seeks to uncover attachments to a similar kind of resemblance in a range of modern artists and suggests that they imagined this resemblance to offer 'another kind of human relationality' (ibid.: 4).

1

Useless

The queer associations of *fin-de-siècle* British aestheticism have been well documented by scholars who have dwelled on the nonconforming sexual lives of figures such as Walter Pater, Oscar Wilde and Vernon Lee.[1] Such is the effect and influence of these figures that the very crux of aestheticism – embracing art for art's sake against an apparently inhumane, instrumentalised and utilitarian world – has come to evoke the air of social and sexual transgression. Wilde (1994: 6) of course famously embraced art as 'quite useless' but nevertheless central to a revolutionary project of individual self-realisation. Pater adopted an insubstantial 'position of retreat' as a means of diverting the public gaze from his homosexuality, finding pleasure in 'hesitancy, reticence, and indecision' in a world that demanded decisive participation (O'Connell 2015: 972, 981). Lee positioned herself against the 'productivist ethos' of a materialist and consumerist society (Denisoff 2006). This anti-utilitarian energy has also threaded through the subsequent history of queer commentary and representation. David Halperin (2012: 238, original italics) identifies the persistent tendency to value '*pleasure* over *utility*' in twentieth-century gay male culture, arguing that this expresses the desire for a better life that can redeem the deprivations of reality within a drearily heteronormative world. Guy Hocquenghem (1993: 108, 148) linked the instrumentality of a capitalist world with the heterosexual reproduction that orients it, defiantly embracing homosexuality as 'non-utilitarian' and 'useless' within this reproductive order. More explicitly than with the earlier aesthetes, in Hocquenghem's account the uselessness of art aligns with queers' uselessness in failing to produce children, shibboleths of valuable endeavour in a world whose emphasis on productivity finds an intimate analogue in reproductive heterosexuality. Owing an intellectual debt to Hocquenghem, more recent queer theorists such as Lee Edelman (2004), Heather Love (2007), Elizabeth Freeman (2010) and Jack Halberstam (2011) have been energised by embracing what has seemed useless to queer theory in order to question aspects of the field's self-understanding.

In this chapter, I explore the place of uselessness in the history of queer representation by returning to the moment of aestheticism and in particular to two characters in two novels by Henry James: Rowland Mallet in *Roderick Hudson* (1875) and Gabriel Nash in *The Tragic Muse* (1890). These novels are from the history of aestheticism but are also about aesthetes and aestheticism in various ways. As I will go on to argue, they offer a new way of thinking about the centrality of uselessness to queer history. Mallet is an independently wealthy man with a 'lively suspicion' (James 1980: 4) that he is a 'useless creature' (ibid.: 7) and the novel might be seen to suggest that it is this ambivalent sense of himself and his desire for some form of redemption that motivates his patronage of the fledgling sculptor who gives the novel its title. This patronage, in turn, gives the novel its plot: Rowland takes Roderick to Europe, to give him the opportunity to hone his artistic skill. Futility is restored, however, as all comes to nothing: identifying with his patron in all the wrong ways, Roderick himself becomes a dissipated 'useless lout' (ibid.: 352) before, in the end, taking his own life. Gabriel Nash in *The Tragic Muse* is only the most futile of a host of useless people who populate the novel. In spectral form there is George Dallow who in life cared only for his collection of precious things and eschewed the imperative to play a responsibly political public role. There is Nick Dormer, who, having attained such a role, surrenders it to commit himself to the full-time painting of portraits. But Nash, having influenced Nick in his abandonment of a political career, and always inclined to flippant over-analysis, is the only one thought by Nick's mother to be of 'no human use' (James 1995: 470), good for nothing but talking, quipping and theorising: the '[in]human use[s]' of the verbose aesthete.

In what follows, I want to put these novels, and Rowland and Gabriel in particular, in conversation with how uselessness has been taken up most recently by queers in queer theoretical work that has turned its attention to the terrain of uselessness in the forms of failure, backwardness and negativity. As discussed above and in the Introduction, scholars like Lee Edelman, Heather Love, Elizabeth Freeman and Jack

Halberstam have for varying reasons looked to apparently unhelpful, dated or outmoded forms of social engagement. Whilst for Edelman this has been to abandon all political intervention as irrevocably complicit in the valorisation of the future, for Love, Freeman and Halberstam the embrace of forms of apparent negativity has helped to problematise what can count as meaningfully political, and to keep politics open to the unexpected effects of what might in many ways seem hopelessly apolitical. This scholarship continues in the vein established by early queer theoretical formulations that sought to hold on to the unknowability of queerness in the face of demands to specify exactly what political use it might have (Berlant and Warner 1995). However, a tension I note in this chapter is that this work often turns its attention explicitly to that which has been deemed 'useless', while, at the same time, arguing for how what has been dismissed as useless can, even if only in modest ways, be use*ful*. As Jack Halberstam (2011: 4, 21) writes, turning to the useless, or, in the terms of his project, 'us[ing] the experience of failure', can still be a way of 'making a difference'. In this chapter, I want to suggest that this strategy of legitimising uselessness or failure derives its effectiveness from an implicitly accepted preference for difference over sameness. Moreover, I argue that the James characters that I focus on here can help us reflect on this situation: they neither encourage an embrace of the radical negativity that Edelman endorses nor demonstrate how the uselessness of Rowland and Gabriel can be redeemed through its relation to unexpected political effects, or, in other words, through its fundamental usefulness. Far from suggesting that making a difference is necessary, then, I argue that Rowland and Gabriel show the value, in some contexts, of leaving things the same. Indeed, it is only when, for example, Rowland tries to pander to the pressure to 'make a difference' which he feels bearing on him from multiple directions that he takes on the mentorship of Roderick which ultimately leads to Roderick's death. Had he not tried to 'make a difference', the novel could be seen to suggest, then at least he would not have made things worse in this way.

It is important to acknowledge, though, that the work cited in the previous paragraph has been offered, sometimes implicitly, in response to those who have castigated queer theoretical writing for its apparently apolitical indifference to strong programmes of political intervention. Like Gabriel, queer theoretical writing has had to defend itself from the suggestion that it is of 'no human use', or unable to provide clear programmes for political change, and (unlike Gabriel) it has done this, as in much of the work cited above, by foregrounding how it turns in a more oblique than direct way to political usefulness. Queer theory has been, and continues to be, critiqued by sexuality studies scholars in the social sciences or with strong commitments to historical materialist methods for not being properly political, not meaningfully able to 'make a difference' on its own, and insufficiently in tune with the supposed realities of people's lives. Frequently, as I will explore, a feature of these critiques is not to dismiss queer inquiry altogether, but rather to reformulate it and to replace the 'theory' in queer theory with 'studies'. 'Queer studies' has come to signify a more materially engaged and politically effective form of queer scholarship that has moved beyond the limitations of 'theory'. As above, I want to think about the response to this scholarly move that James's characters encourage. Both Rowland and Gabriel come to be associated in their respective novels precisely with 'theory' (James 1980: 242) or 'theories' (James 1995: 56). As in contemporary scholarship, theory in the novels represents non-applied thought and abstraction, which stands in tension with a prevailing imperative to 'do' or commit to practical achievements, but the novels do not suggest that this necessarily needs to be instrumentalised in some way. Indeed, as I suggested above, it is when Rowland tries to 'make a difference' that things go down the pan.

One of the reasons that I suggest these novels can encourage reflection on queer scholarship is their established significance within it. Both novels have garnered significant attention from critics across their reception histories who have picked up on queer themes in various ways. Amongst *Roderick Hudson*'s earliest reviewers, Grace Norton recognised an 'anomalous relation' (Hayes 1996: 14) between Roderick and Rowland that has, in subsequent criticism, been recognised as more clearly homosexual or homoerotic.[2] Various contemporary reviews of *The Tragic Muse* recognised in Gabriel Nash a similarity to the generic representation of the aesthete, and more particularly to Wilde (ibid.: 221, 236, 238). More recent critics have been able to suggest that, owing to associations of the artistic with the queer in the late nineteenth century, the novel's aesthetes like Nash and Nick are homosexual.[3] Building on this work, I want to flag up further how Rowland's and Gabriel's queer identities are formed around a specific kind of theoretical uselessness. Yet, at the same time, whilst uselessness may be tied in important ways to queer identities, I also want to think of it in less social and more formal or structural terms. I suggest that what often makes the useless so unappealing is not just its direct social association with queers, but how it is mixed up with a rhetorical dispensation that takes it for granted that only those ideas that can be properly associated with difference are helpful, correct and necessary. The novels are of interest in the context of this book for how they refuse to endorse the imperative to 'make a difference'. Indeed, while in contemporary idiom 'making a difference' means 'making a positive difference' – with the value added subsumed into the idea of difference itself – the novels, as I indicated above, show how making a difference can mean making things worse. The novels, I argue, simply do not share an assumption that difference is necessarily for the best.

In important ways, then, this is why I focus on these James novels, rather than on any of the other familiar figures associated perhaps more readily with British aestheticism. That is, whilst it may seem appropriate when addressing uselessness in queer literary history to engage figures like Oscar Wilde or Walter Pater as emphatic proponents of 'art for art's sake in opposition to the utilitarian doctrine of moral or practical usefulness' (Mendelssohn 2007: 5), I will argue that the James novels I consider here help us to see some of the ways in which even Wilde and Pater achieve certain kinds of usefulness. Wilde (1994: 6) may claim in the Preface to *The Picture of Dorian Gray* (1891) that 'all art is quite useless', but he makes clear elsewhere that this uselessness could nevertheless have a thoroughly practical or useful aspect in transforming a dehumanising, capitalist world into an egalitarian, socialist one (Wilde 1973). In this sense, Wilde's position could be seen as a progenitor of the contemporary queer theoretical arguments that we saw above in which what is deemed useless is none the less marshalled to various, albeit sometimes modest, forms of usefulness. In his famous 'Conclusion' to *The Renaissance* (1873), Pater (1986: 153) advocates a way of living that involves surrendering to the gathering of as much sense experience as possible, to 'getting as many pulsations as possible into [our] given time'. What interrupts this process is the formation of 'theories' that distance us from the 'things we see and touch' (ibid.: 152). For Pater, it is no good to develop a 'theory or idea or system' and no use to formulate what he damningly calls 'abstract theory' (ibid.: 153). For him, theory represents a ruinous and damaging alienation from sense experience. As Daniel Cottom (2003: 147) has suggested, Paterian aestheticism's faith in sense experience has parallels with more conservative tendencies in cultural studies to call for a greater focus on the supposed material realities of people's lives which can function as an 'absolute law to humanity', over and above anything that might be principally theoretical. James's characters, on the other hand, are never redeemed from their association with theory and the useless abstraction it denotes. James's own reputation and status is also key here: in a review of James's work published in the aestheticist journal *The Yellow Book*, Lena Milman (1895: 72) criticises his writing for being 'too analytical', and lacking in 'passion'. Such a statement from an important vehicle of aestheticist and decadent work, coupled with the strategies of emphatically aestheticist writers like Wilde and Pater, marks James with a particular kind of uselessness: one that is more concerned with analysis than with simple, sensual fun.

Moreover, as I will explore in the second section below, James's novels demonstrate that the kinds of strategies that can be mobilised to justify both wildly aestheticist and prosaically practical life paths are often the same. Both novels make clear, for example, that what might be seen as both properly useful 'practical' and less legitimate 'artistic' lives emerge and justify themselves with recourse to difference; both lives are equally attempts to escape the clutches of a sameness attributed to the other life path. So, as we will see, in *Roderick Hudson*, Mr Striker, the responsible and successful lawyer from whose employment Roderick escapes to Rome, talks, in a turn of phrase seemingly convinced by the authority of procreation, of the importance of sensibly distributing the 'seed we sow' (James 1980: 47), while mocking the imitation on which he imagines Roderick's study of sculpture to rely. Roderick, on the other hand, as we will also see, figures his artistic creation as creating offspring, marvels at the transcendent power of creation, whilst deprecating the 'repulsive routine' – the unbearable sameness – of his work for Mr Striker (ibid.: 20). Both sides, in justifying themselves, have to disavow the sameness that the other would impute to them. In *The Tragic Muse*, Nick Dormer escapes from a political life, and its attendant imperative to 'do', into an artistic career, only to redeploy this imperative as better honoured by the making of art. He deprecates his life as a professional politician because of the unproductive 'humbug' it forces him to speak (James 1995: 242): art better suits his felt need to 'do something' (ibid.: 118). Far from being abandoned, the imperative to do is in fact better served by an association with art or art-making.

Being theoretical, though, only gets Gabriel dismissed as a 'twaddler and a bore' (ibid.: 63). Being theoretical in these novels does not help Rowland or Gabriel gain legitimacy and, I would suggest, for these characters, constitutes a disregard for difference in two ways: it is a way of rejecting the idea that there is a difference between the life paths of art and practicality, as well as a way of rejecting the idea that we see in both of these paths that an association with forms of difference is a necessary form of self-legitimation. Not capitulating to the rhetorical demands of this negotiation between life paths, Rowland and Gabriel remain associated not with art or practical achievement but with theory. In doing this, though, they do not offer themselves as useful in any way. They do not achieve anything. Instead, they represent a stubborn intransitivity in the face of the otherwise inevitable validity of difference-making. In his defence of the uselessness of higher education, Daniel Cottom (2003: 203) argues that we should treat the educational system as a 'standing cultural commitment against the tyranny of stupidity in any form: the market, technocracy, the state, even the people'. The uselessness of education is not necessarily put to any clear use, but simply constitutes an opposition to undesirable social forces like 'the market'. In a similar way, I suggest, Rowland and Gabriel constitute a blockage or hindrance to the idea that any sort of difference must necessarily be made. I think we can see their uselessness as a 'standing commitment' against the tendency that we can see in some queer scholarship to make the useless into the useful. They represent a standing commitment against the easy validation that the idea of making a difference provides.

What difference does it make?

A concern often voiced around early queer theoretical formulations was that they were too closely linked to post-structuralist theory to facilitate meaningful political intervention. For example, in his contribution to the oft-cited anthology *Fear of a Queer Planet* (1993), Steven Seidman (111) suggests that post-structuralist gay and lesbian theory might be too involved in textual analysis and criticism to provide 'any positive program for change'. He imagines instead a more 'pragmatic approach' (ibid.: 137) that combines post-structuralism's commitment to non-identity with the 'politics of difference' that critiques the social exclusions of movements based on single-axis and unitary identities (ibid.: 117). Post-structuralism's strong anti-identitarianism is critiqued as a way of 'denying differences by either submerging them in an undifferentiated oppositional mass or by blocking the development of individual and social differences through the disciplining compulsory imperative to remain undifferentiated' (ibid.: 133). Seidman argues against what seemed at that time to be the hallmark of queer theory by suggesting that we need identity in some instances to stay attuned to local struggles and he locates pragmatic and practical programmes for social change in the mediation between a strong identity politics and a post-structuralist refusal of self-present identity. To be effective, he suggests, queer theory needs to combine the two approaches.

Despite the fact that, as I suggested in the Introduction, a formative queer move was to mediate in precisely the way that Seidman advocates, his impression of queer theoretical writing as unhelpful and aloof from the material conditions of oppression has often been taken up in sociological writing. In Seidman's edited volume *Queer Theory/Sociology* (1996), for example, we see various thinkers provide versions of his argument. Steven Epstein (1996: 145) argues that an 'encounter' between queer theory and sociology would be productive because sociology could tutor queer theory out of its bad habits: the way in which its focus on texts leaves out 'crucial questions about social structure, political organization, and historical context' (ibid.: 157) and involves a 'reduction of complex cultural codes' (ibid.). Whilst sociology can teach queer theory to pay more attention to these specific contexts, queer theory is apparently only useful in so far as it can empirically prove its insights about the pervasive influence of the epistemology of the closet on the basis of what sociology deems to be adequate proof, within the accepted protocols of sociological method: by showing 'concretely' the 'precise ways in which sexual meanings, categories, and identities are woven into the fabric of society' (ibid.). Other contributors to the volume make very similar arguments (Gamson 1996; Stein and Plummer 1996). The rhetorical satisfaction that comes from imputing insufficient usefulness to one's opponents overrides an acknowledgement that the strategy for usefulness spelled out is already one proposed by those opponents.

By no means confined to the 1990s, in the twenty years since the publication of *Queer Theory/Sociology* many scholars writing from sociological perspectives have recapitulated these positions. For example, we can read again the accusation that queer theory operates only 'at the level of cultural texts' (Edwards 1998: 472) and as a form of merely 'cultural critique' (ibid.: 481). The shift away from the social sciences, which are 'directly founded upon a strong [...] political engagement with the social world' towards 'literary and psychoanalytic studies' in dominant lesbian and gay theorising '*does* make a difference' (ibid.: 474, original italics), which is that it shifts towards a whole raft of approaches that *do not* make a difference, or cannot be seen to in a sociological paradigm. In still more recent work, we read that queer theory is unable to account adequately for the 'empirical world and the sociohistorical forces that shape sexual practice and identity' (Green 2002: 522). Instead, it uselessly 'focuses on social dissolution and a self evacuated into discourse' (Green 2007: 33–4). More recently still, Heather Love's (2015) work on postwar sociology argues that queer theory has been impoverished by not having recognised its foundation in the close attention to the social world that this work has encouraged.

However, it is by no means only on the basis of disciplinary division that queer theory is imagined to be useless. Donald Morton, an English studies professor, has repeatedly critiqued queer theory essentially on the basis that it is not 'Marx's historical materialism' (Morton 1996: 2). According to Morton, queer theory is a project to 'assert the *primariness of sexuality/libidinality, the autonomy of desire, and the freedom of the sexual subject from all constraints*' (ibid., original italics). Queer theory is therefore hopelessly complicit with an exploitative, late capitalist status quo, in so far as, like capitalism, it encourages diversification in what is unnecessary, needless and useless: desire. Queer theory is complicit with capitalism's 'expansion, reproduction, and commodification of desires (for profit)' (ibid.: 29). It therefore stands in contrast with socialism's concern 'with fulfilling needs' (ibid.). 'Overcoming capitalism would involve returning to the more fundamental level of addressing human *need*, represented by use value, and a consequent cancellation of all those *(needless) desires* produced by capitalist commodity fetishism at the level of exchange-become-surplus-value' (ibid.: 4, original italics). Moreover, in so far as queer theory is the spawn of postmodernism, it tends to stray towards 'ahistorical idealism' (ibid.: 3), towards a sense that truths, phenomena and identities are fundamentally ungraspable. Queer theory's anti-realism therefore threatens to abandon attention to the material bases of oppression: 'From the materialist perspective identities are not textual mirages but intersections of historically produced subject positions in which various marginalized subjects are exploitatively and oppressively situated' (ibid.: 14).[4]

A similar position has been recapitulated in more recent queer scholarship, albeit a position less emphatically offered in terms of historical materialism. David L. Eng, Jack Halberstam and José Esteban Muñoz (2005: 2–3), for example, in their 'Introduction' to the 'What's Queer About Queer Studies Now?' special issue of *Social Text*, frame their contributors' essays as a reassessment of the 'political utility of queer', a re-evaluation of the 'utility of queer as an engaged mode of critical enquiry'. Utility and engagement come in the form of the potential of queer work to focus greater attention on sites of intersection with 'other modes of difference' – 'including race, gender, class, nationality, and religion, in addition to sexuality' (ibid.: 1) – or on what Morton calls 'historically produced subject positions'. For Eng et al., the political utility of queer stands in tension with ideas like that of a 'mass-mediated consumer lifestyle' (ibid.), the conceptualisation of the public sphere in terms of its 'homogeneity' (ibid.: 13), and the 'universalizing tendencies' of the institutionalisation of gay shame (ibid.). Utility is positioned against various manifestations of an unpalatable sameness: the 'mass', 'homogeneity' and the universal. For Eng et al. it is 'queer theory' that is demonised as nothing more than a 'metanarrative about the domestic affairs of white homosexuals' (ibid.: 12), in opposition to the apparently more capacious 'queer studies' of their title that better serves an imagined 'political utility'.

This transition in vocabulary can be found across the positions outlined earlier in this section. In the 'Introduction' to *Queer Theory/ Sociology*, for example, Steven Seidman (1996: 18, 24) gestures towards a future in which queer theory and sociology can teach each other important lessons, but, interestingly, when this gesture is made, the dialogue turns into one between 'queer studies' and sociology, pointedly *not* 'queer theory'. 'Studies', it seems, is the more workable, more palatable, more collaborative version of the 'theory'. We also see this shift in vocabulary in Steven Epstein's (1996: 159) essay: again, the future of mutual transformation is one that witnesses the move to 'queer studies' rather than 'theory'. Donald Morton, too, implicitly rejects the 'theory' in 'queer theory', which, as he makes clear, is associated with those French postmodern thinkers whom 'theory' in the Anglo-American humanities designates (Barthes, Derrida, Baudrillard and Foucault are names that he mentions). What is needed instead is what he calls a 'materialist queer studies' that 'theorizes sexuality in relation to the largest possible understanding of social need' (Morton 1996: 30). 'Studies', as in Eng et al., promises a greater attention to multiple social differences, as well as more engagement with material reality and is contrasted implicitly with the narrow and useless 'theory'. As Matt Bell (2011: 106) has recently written in a brief treatment of this rhetorical shift in the way of naming queer inquiry, the 'movement toward expanded capacity' that takes place in the move from 'queer theory' to 'queer studies' also 'entails the exclusion of a certain sameness'. 'Theory' does not promise any programme for change: it does not make anything happen. *Studies*, by making a difference, by being useful, acquires some of its palatability from the implicit sense that difference is to be preferred over sameness.

An alternative strain in queer theory, however, has sought to interrogate the ease with which both scholars and activists oppose engagement with material reality to the useless, unproductive or apolitical. For example, in *Homographesis*, Lee Edelman has written about a problematic AIDS activist rhetoric that demonises apparently apolitical gay men, supposedly fixated on pleasure and consumption. For Edelman, this strategy of delegitimising certain queers effectively repeats the structuring of subjectivity in the modern West in which a dominant white heterosexual male emerges through defining itself in opposition to the narcissism and passivity of the homosexual. Dominant masculinity embraces 'active engagement with otherness', 'movement into and authority over a world located outside of, and defined as different from, the self', '[a]ctivity, change, sociality, civilization, life itself' (Edelman 1994: 104). All of this depends upon the transcendence of 'imaginary intersubjectivity', associated with the passivity of gay men in so far as they fantasmatically submit to anal penetration and consequently come to represent the 'subject's fall from master to matter' (ibid.). The AIDS activist position that Edelman delineates cannot endorse 'responses to "AIDS" that appear to turn "inward" and towards the "self" instead of outward and toward "others"': such inward-facing responses are deemed 'narcissistic' and 'apolitical' (ibid.: 106). Proper political engagement, then, is figured as the 'unselfish, socially conscious alternative to the self-centred and destructively hedonistic pleasure associated with a gay sexuality defined, as in the phobic discourse of the culture at large, by the mirror and the anus' (ibid.). Edelman seeks to resist the 'essential but, at moments, too narrowly conceptualized "politics" of "activism"' (ibid.: 110). Edelman's expanded politics would include the 'theoretical interrogation sometimes dismissed, from the "activist" perspective, as merely "academic"' (ibid.: 112). Equally, it is a kind of politics that 'would require the recognition that powerfully "political" effects can be generated even by those who would seem, from an "activist" perspective, to be a- or anti-political' (ibid.: 113): by drag queens, for example, and the unexpectedly rousing effects of the 'narcissistic splendor of their campy posturing before the law's ascetic eye' at the Stonewall Inn in 1969 (ibid.). When scholars like Eng et al. suggest that queer studies' 'utility' lies in its attention to 'other modes of difference', then, they rely, at least rhetorically, on the transcendence of the 'imaginary intersubjectivity' – the sameness – associated in Edelman's account with homosexuality.

In his more recent work, Edelman has moved towards a position that has even more powerfully embraced that which is useless. In *No Future* (2004), he argues that every intervention made in the name of a better future is already folded into the heterosexist logic of reproductive futurism. The way to refuse this logic is to refuse the justification for action on the basis of political good. As a way of reading the heterosexism that attends attributions of usefulness, he turns to an essay by Jean Baudrillard (2000: 10) on cloning in which the philosopher maligns the 'dissociation of reproduction from sex' through reproductive technologies. The up-shot: '[a]mong the clones [...], sex, as a result of this automatic means of reproduction, becomes extraneous, a useless function' (ibid.). Without the alibi of procreation, sex amongst clones, amongst those marked by their eerie sameness, like that which cannot be seen to 'make a difference' within conventional political models, is a 'useless function'. Suggesting that we reject the consoling alibis that insist on the value of usefulness, Edelman calls on queers to embrace their relation to the useless death drive with which they are associated in logic such as Baudrillard's. Queers, consequently, should forsake '*all* causes, *all* social action, *all* responsibility for a better tomorrow' (Edelman 2004: 101, original italics).

However, other recent queer theoretical texts have developed arguments along the lines of Edelman's earlier insight about the unexpected political effects of what might seem apolitical. Heather Love, as we saw in the Introduction, turns her attention to various representations of queers from the late nineteenth and early twentieth centuries, which might seem useless, outdated or 'backward' from the perspective of current LGBT politics. She writes of having resisted the 'criterion of utility as a standard of judgment' (Love 2007: 146), in order to argue that these representations have an 'oblique rather than direct' relation to what affirmative politics would deem useful (ibid.: 29): 'they teach us that we do not know what is good for politics' (ibid.: 27). Elizabeth Freeman (2010: xiii) similarly turns her attention to 'whatever has been declared useless' for queer politics. She analyses works of visual art for the way in which they employ what might seem anachronistic and argues that they confront viewers with the 'interesting threat' of the 'genuine *past*-ness of the past' (ibid.: 63, original italics) by offering images that challenge the seeming inevitability of the present. Jack Halberstam (2011: 11) has similarly turned to 'counterintuitive modes of knowing such as failure and stupidity' as modes of 'resistance' (ibid.) that can help 'confront the gross inequalities of everyday life in the United States' (ibid.: 4).

All of these writers, then, suggest that unexpected political effects can come from what might seem politically impotent. So, the 'theory' dismissed, sometimes implicitly by its replacement with the roomier 'studies', might have the kinds of unpredictable political effects that someone like Halberstam attributes to what might seem like failure (he describes his allegiance to what he calls 'low theory' (Halberstam 2011: 1)), or that Edelman wants to imagine can take place through the 'theoretical interrogation' that some might dismiss as excessively academic. The sharp distinction, then, between, on the one hand, what is imagined to be responsible engagement with a material world with the intention of social transformation and, on the other hand, a useless disengagement from clearly instrumentalisable action, loses some of its legitimacy in this queer theoretical work. This work suggests that we cannot necessarily know in advance what actual effects any particular intervention will have. What does not have a clearly transformative role in politics might none the less create very powerful effects.

But as this reference to powerful effects might suggest, frequently the embrace of forms of uselessness in these texts is justified on the basis of the good it can do, or, in other words, on the basis of how it can be useful. Heather Love's interest in the abject representations she surveys is in their 'diagnostic usefulness' (Love 2007: 12), or the way in which they might tell us something about the enduring affective fallout of social exclusion. For Elizabeth Freeman (2010: 59), what she analyses as 'temporal drag' is a 'usefully distorting pull backwards' that puts 'necessary pressure on the present tense' (ibid.: 64). Halberstam (2011: 15) similarly turns to the 'utility' of the modes of failure he examines. His belief in 'low theory' is, as we have seen, a belief in 'making a difference by thinking little thoughts and sharing them widely' (ibid.: 21). Even Lee Edelman (2004: 7), whose abandonment of usefulness may seem the most thoroughgoing of all, insists that embracing the figural status of the death drive is a way to 'intervene in', 'refuse[]' (ibid.: 11) and 'ruptur[e]' (ibid.: 17) the 'reproduction' (ibid.: 7, 11, 17) of the social world defined by reproductive futurism, to interrupt its unbearable continuation of the same old conditions. I spend more time on Edelman's relation to reproduction in the next chapter, but for now we might note the resemblance his thorough rejection of reproduction bears to Donald Morton's rejection of the 'reproduction' he associates with capitalism (Morton 1996: 29). In a number of queer theoretical accounts, the terrain of the apparently useless is embraced only in so far as it can, in Halberstam's words, 'mak[e] a difference' to the reproduction of social form. Edelman's argument in *No Future* does not necessarily escape his earlier ambitions in *Homographesis* to have his arguments 'make a critical difference' (Edelman 1994: 23).

As many of these theorists show, the allure of the useful, or of 'making a difference', is a hard one to resist. A real challenge, then, when making any kind of argument about uselessness is dealing with the institutional, political and personal demands to articulate why, in the end, it might prove useful. Of course, common sense and the dictates of academic publishing declare that there must be a reason for making an argument. What *is* the point? What difference *does* it make? As Daniel Cottom (2003: 204) has suggested, though, when dealing with the useless, it may be necessary to retain a 'definitive inefficiency' in explaining why one cares about it, even when it is an abject uselessness 'emerg[ing] from the despair that eats away at our satisfactions and that questions even our greatest and most pleasing certainties'. I suggest that the 'pleasing certaint[y]' manifest in the move to make the useless useful, the common sense that declares there must be a point or a reason, is an expression of the unquestioned value and palatability of what can be seen to be associated with making a difference. Rather than saying exactly what good will come of simply sticking with the useless, the unhelpful and the non-transformative, then, perhaps all we can do is to stress again our ambivalence about the imperative of difference that seems to underwrite the desire to say what good any particular thing will do.

I cannot prove the value of the uselessness of James's characters, but, then again, I do not want to: what they are in this chapter for, I argue, is to temper the very demand that they should have a use. Whilst from some quarters James is an author with a social conscience, with scholars like John Carlos Rowe (1998: 7) attempting to get readers to think of him as a 'critical social theorist', he also remains a figure of arguably unhelpful privilege: as Rowe also notes, it is a 'quixotic task' because of James's 'central role, along with T.S. Eliot and other literary moderns, in the history of Anglo-American New Criticism' (ibid.). Whilst this is not all he is, James is also a figure of white, male, class privilege. He is by no means an exemplary model for the kind of transformational politics that figures like Eng, Halberstam and Muñoz seek to reinvigorate with their attention to the 'political utility' of queerness. Nor am I suggesting that his characters are exemplary models for some other, thoroughly anti-political, Edelmanian position: they are not included here to be put to any use whatsoever. If they do have a point, it is resistance to having one. Any unease about the uselessness of these novels may be an object lesson in how difficult it is just not to be so convinced that difference is necessary. The uselessness of Rowland Mallet and Gabriel Nash is not a productive uselessness, or one that shatters entirely all social form, but rather a sort of banal uselessness that just does not make anything, at all, happen. However, I want to argue, as we will see especially in the figure of Rowland Mallet, that the desire to leave things the same is also a recognition that making a difference can sometimes mean making things worse.

Making the grand difference

On the one hand, both *Roderick Hudson* and *The Tragic Muse* may seem to provide aestheticist ways of accounting for the social marginality of art as a result of its opposition to a regime of practicality that takes difference as its sovereign value. That is, as I will detail at the beginning of this section, these novels provide rhetorical schemes for associating art with useless forms of sameness. However, ultimately I argue that even an affinity with art and art-making in these novels gets redeemed through its association with various forms of difference, leading ultimately to utilitarian redemption. Certainly, scholars have mapped James's novels on to forms of aestheticism, suggesting that Roderick Hudson represents the embodiment of a Paterian emphasis on sense experience

(Ellmann 1999: 25; Freedman 1990: 133). Following such readings, we might imagine that it is Roderick's art-making that presents an opposition to a moralistic insistence on practical doing and achievement. However, scholars who have addressed James's relation to aestheticism have tended to imagine it less as a straightforward recapitulation to the tenets of its proponents than as a reworking or reimagining of those tenets to his own ends: *Roderick*, for example, is often read as a denunciation of Pater's particular brand of aestheticism (Ellmann 1999: 26; Freedman 1990: 140). In partial agreement with some of these critics who suggest that James had an oblique or 'equivocal' (Ohi 2005: 747) relationship to some of the proponents of British aestheticism, I will turn towards the end of this section, and in the penultimate section below, to how the substantive resistance to these regimes of difference-making can be located in the abject theoreticalness of Rowland and Gabriel.

To begin, then, I would like to survey how it is artist characters like Roderick and Nick Dormer who might be seen to offer an opposition to the imperative of utility. In *Roderick Hudson*, Rowland learns from his cousin Cecilia not only about the roguish Roderick but about the ways in which he contrasts with his brother Stephen too, who was a 'plain-faced, sturdy, practical lad', 'the making of a useful man', 'very different from his brother' (James 1980: 23). Roderick, echoing her sentiment, tells Rowland that he has 'been very different from Stephen': 'idle, restless, egotistical, discontented' (ibid.: 32). His mother, consequently, prefers her son's apprenticeship at Mr Striker's law firm as a 'much safer training' than a career as a sculptor: she finds sculpture an 'insidious form of immorality' (ibid.: 23). Similarly, Mr Striker, Roderick's employer at the beginning of the novel, can contrast the promise of an artist's life – 'a tempting doctrine to young men with a taste for sitting by the hour with the page unturned, watching the flies buzz, or the frost melt, on the window-pane' (ibid.: 46) – with his own earthy humility: 'I'm a plain practical old boy, content to follow an honourable profession in a free country' (ibid.: 47). Roderick's fiancée Mary Garland, too, comes from a family of clergymen who are emphatically 'ministers' rather than 'theologians', who 'don't take a very firm stand upon doctrine', who 'haven't time to find reasons and phrases', but are 'practical and active' instead (ibid.: 59).

In *The Tragic Muse*, the case is much the same. Nick's mother Lady Agnes has fairly definitive views on the 'comparative dignity of the two arts of painting portraits and governing nations' (James 1995: 377). Favouring the latter, of course, she has 'no aptitude for aimlessness', which she associates with art-making, and thinks it 'vulgar' (ibid.: 61). For Julia Dallow, the woman Nick Dormer will eventually marry, with her 'personal impatience of unapplied ideas' (ibid.: 321), the 'humiliation of her youth' was having to deal with her late husband's 'flat inglorious taste for pretty things' and 'his indifference to every chance to play a public part' (ibid.: 280). She cannot countenance 'even an oblique demand for the same spirit of accommodation', the 'same concessions', in her relationship with Nick (ibid.). Wealthy family friend Mr Carteret cannot believe Nick's decision to give up his seat in the House of Commons: '[d]o you pretend there's a nobler life than a high political career?' (ibid.: 337). The faintest sense of such a pretence leads Carteret to dismiss Nick as a 'trifler' (ibid.: 333). Nick's friend Peter Sherringham keeps an 'unembarrassed eye on Downing Street', an intent attention he contrasts with the impression of 'futile aestheticism' that he worries his association with the actress Miriam Rooth might cause him to make (ibid.: 141). Miriam Rooth herself is 'horribly disappointed' that Nick does not aspire to be a 'great statesman': 'What was so useful, what was so noble?' (ibid.: 360).

Roderick and Nick, then, can seem like the ones who challenge puritanical dictates via their 'futile aestheticism'. In *Roderick Hudson*, we learn that Roderick, during the little time he spent at a 'small college,' gave a 'good deal more attention to novels and billiards than to mathematics and Greek' (James 1980: 23). After some initial creative success in Rome, he separates from Rowland, ending up in Baden-Baden where he learns 'terribly well how to do nothing' (ibid.: 99). From there, what Rowland calls Roderick's 'fatalism' (ibid.: 226) seems only to become more pronounced: he becomes a 'useless lout' (ibid.: 352) and ends up dead, a 'vague white mass' at the bottom of a Swiss gorge (ibid.: 387). In *The Tragic Muse*, Lady Agnes complains that Nick 'used to have so *much* sense of responsibility' (James 1995: 24, original italics). Grace agrees that nowadays '[h]e does so little – takes no trouble' (ibid.: 42). He is 'aware that for the most part he didn't pass for practical; he could imagine why, from his early years, people should have joked him about it' (ibid.: 457). It is perhaps an awareness that informs his response to Biddy's remark about his 'high ability' as an artist: Nick replies that he is 'no use *really*!' (ibid.: 26, original italics). Within the terms of these oppositions, then, both Roderick Hudson and Nick Dormer might be seen to be the useless ones in so far as the paths they choose are contrasted with the more 'useful' courses of Stephen Hudson, on the one hand, and a political career, on the other.

Indeed, the novels often seem to strengthen this opposition between art and practicality by also associating art-forms beyond Roderick's sculpture and Nick's painting with uselessness. The theatre in particular enters the firing line. The acting teacher Madame Carre, for example, is 'strange, almost grotesque', a 'queer vision of the darkness', no doubt because of the way in which she 'mouth[s] and mimic[s] in the drollest way' (ibid.: 85). At the novel's first encounter with Madame Carre, Peter informs Miriam that this lady will give her the '*réplique*' (ibid.: 89). The French term – 'cues' in English – highlights a relation to sameness: '*réplique*' also means 'replica'. Similarly, going to see Miriam in a London theatre, Peter thinks fondly of the '*répétitions générales*' to which he had gone in Paris (ibid.: 378). Again, the French phrase – 'dress rehearsals' in English – highlights the repetition that characterises the theatre. It is a repetition that is the occasion for some complaint, as we see in Peter Sherringham's excoriation of the 'strange passion of the good British public for sitting again and again through expected situations, watching for speeches they had heard and surprises that struck the hour', as well as their 'critical sense' which is 'ignobly docile' for 'not insisting on something different, on a fresh brew altogether' (ibid.: 309–10). This theatrical repetition, as well as many people's attachment to it, is cause for mockery and criticism.

Roderick, too, comes to be associated with the copying that also characterises the theatre. For example, he initially thinks of himself as 'above all an advocate for American art' and that the simple step Americans need to take in order to produce the 'greatest works in the world' is to 'be true to ourselves, to pitch in and not be afraid, to fling Imitation overboard and fix our eyes upon our National Individuality' (James 1980: 26). Roderick, however, throws over throwing over 'Imitation' fairly quickly, as Rowland asks him if he would like to go to Rome: 'speedily consign[ing] our National Individuality to perdition', Roderick 'respond[s] that he should like it first rate' (ibid.: 26–7). In Rome, Roderick is 'to study', says Rowland to an incredulous Mr Striker: '[h]ow do you study sculpture anyhow?' 'By looking at models and imitating them' is the answer Rowland provides. 'Do you hear, madam?' Mr Striker continues disparagingly, 'Roderick is going off to Europe to learn to imitate the antique' (ibid.: 44). But it is imitation at which we have already seen the young sculptor succeed. After he delivers an impersonation of Mr Striker, we are told that Roderick, 'like many men with a turn for the plastic arts, was an excellent mimic' (ibid.: 20). That the impersonation is of Mr Striker's pompous reading of the Declaration of Independence at an Independence Day celebration perhaps bespeaks all the more Roderick's turn away from 'National Individuality'. As with the mockery of the repetition that characterises the theatre, then, Mr Striker's strategy is to delegitimise Roderick's study of sculpture by associating it with imitation.

In both novels, though, the artist characters recognise that allowing this association between art and sameness to stand is never going to be a persuasive way to justify what they do. Roderick works to recognise what he does within the terms of what the novel would seem to understand as growing up into properly heterosexual responsibility, away from narcissistic self-directedness. Shortly before setting sail to Europe, Roderick tells Rowland that he has become engaged to Mary Garland: '[u]nless a man's unnaturally selfish he needs to work for some one else than himself, and I'm sure I shall run a smoother and swifter course for knowing that there's a person so good and clever and charming, to whom my success will make the grand difference, waiting at Northampton for news of my greatness' (ibid.: 61–2). Leaving behind 'unnatural[] selfish[ness]', the kind of self-directedness that we earlier saw Lee Edelman equate with the dominant cultural fantasy of homosexuality, Roderick moves towards a life of 'mak[ing] [a] grand difference', which involves cultivating his artistic talents and at the same time entering into the realm of idealised heterosexuality with Mary. On the perils of aesthetic self-indulgence, Mr Striker makes sure his warning to Rowland is also very suggestive, as we saw above: the 'crop we gather depends upon the seed we sow', he says, remarking, humorously, that Roderick's 'potatoes won't come up without his hoeing them' (ibid.: 47–8). If Roderick 'takes things as almighty easy' as 'one or two young fellows of genius' Mr Striker has had occasion to observe, his seed can only be sown to waste. Responsibility, then, or 'mak[ing] the grand difference' is yoked to idealised heterosexuality in the novel (marriage for Roderick, procreation for Mr Striker).

As an artist, Roderick's redemption – his 'mak[ing] the grand difference' – also seems tied up with his *making*. So, early on in the novel, he arrives at Cecilia's, suggestively enough on her birthday, 'with his treasure done up in a morsel of old blanket' (ibid.: 16). A wrapped up gift, but also a swaddled child. In a lengthy rant on the importance of freedom to the creativity of artists, Roderick makes the comparison between artistic creation and care for a child: a 'mother can't nurse her child unless she follows a certain diet; an artist can't bring his vision to maturity unless he has a certain experience' (ibid.: 166). He also however, seems to make an equivalence between artistic creation and heterosexual (pro)creation. Talking of artists, he tells Rowland: 'I only say that if you want them to produce you must let them conceive' (ibid.). It is a kind of conception that we have already seen Roderick enjoy in Rome: '[h]e enjoyed immeasurably, after the chronic obstruction of home, the sublime act of creation' (ibid.: 76). Standing in front of 'Michael Angelo's Moses' Roderick is 'seized with a kind of exasperation, a reaction against all this mere passive enjoyment of grandeur' (ibid.: 64). Instead he is inspired into action, by the idea that if he might not 'do as much', he might at least 'do as well' (ibid.). Roderick is not the only artist-parent, though. When none of the other artists in Rome excites him, the novel tells us that there is no one 'whose genius g[i]ve[s] him the least desire to delve in the parent soil' (ibid.: 200), which is to say that there is no one whose work makes him excited about the artist who gave birth to it. His own parent soil is perhaps fecund enough. In the throes of his transformative creativity in Rome – '[h]aven't I different eyes, a different skin, different legs and arms?' (ibid.: 64) – he sets to work on 'an "Adam"' (ibid.: 76). Of course, an 'Adam' needs its heterosexual complement: '[t]he Eve was finished in three months' (ibid.: 77). It is a third of the usual gestating time, but time enough for Roderick to have made the makers of humankind. Roderick tells Rowland that he wants to be the 'original, *ab*original American artist!' (ibid.: 26, original italics): with his Adam and Eve he wants to be the progenitor of humanity.

The imperative to 'do' in *The Tragic Muse* is similarly linked to idealised heterosexuality. So, for many in the novel, Nick's properly responsible political career, his embrace of a useful 'doing', goes hand-in-hand with his marrying Julia Dallow, and his surrender of his seat in the House of Commons marks the surrender of the promise of heterosexual union. Mr Carteret, for example, tells Nick that his political career and consequent marriage to Julia 'will be of the highest utility' (James 1995: 334) and then threatens to withhold his inheritance if he does not take up a seat. Julia herself is dedicated to the 'simple idea that one ought to do something or other for one's country' (ibid.: 78). 'Pray isn't a gentleman to do anything, to be anything [...] [i]f he doesn't aspire to serve the State', she asks Nick, demonstrating that the only thing she can recognise as 'do[ing] anything' is conventional party politics (ibid.: 79). If, for Julia, the 'only decent thing' (ibid.: 77) is 'to do something or other for one's country,' or, as we saw in *Roderick Hudson*, to eschew selfish self-directedness, then it is perhaps no surprise that Roderick's sense of what would 'make the grand difference' to his artistic practice is also echoed in *The Tragic Muse*. 'Oh you're to marry?' Gabriel Nash asks slightly incredulously. '"That's what has come on since we met in Paris," Nick explained, "and it makes just the difference"' (ibid.: 255). Just like in *Roderick*, marriage can make a difference that invigorates and inspires creative action.

When Nick eventually rejects the House of Commons, however, it by no means seems to imply a rejection of the imperative to be productive. Indeed, Nick is convinced of the value of doing, but does not feel that politics makes 'just the difference'. His early account of what being MP for Harsh would entail – 'going down into a small stodgy country town and talking a lot of rot' (ibid.: 75) – demonstrates his hostility towards the political life that continues throughout the novel. The 'talking' in 'talking a lot of rot' comes in for a lot of criticism. So, he tells Julia that a 'man would blush to say to himself in the darkness of the night the things he stands up on a platform in the garish light of day to stuff into the ears of a multitude whose intelligence he pretends he rates high' (ibid.: 76). To Julia's retort that if he does not 'speak well' it is his 'own fault' because he 'know[s] how to perfectly', Nick replies that this is precisely his problem: 'I always do [...] and that's what I'm ashamed of. I speak beautifully. I've got the cursed humbugging trick of it. I can turn it on, a fine flood of it, at the shortest notice' (ibid.). He is able to muster a 'due volubility on platforms', although he feels that this is 'not really action at all, but only a pusillanimous imitation of it' (ibid.: 170). Nick, then, ultimately embraces the life philosophy of Mr Carteret, who trivialises his ambitions to paint and whom Nick might therefore be thought more likely to oppose: 'Life, for him, was a purely practical function, not a question of more or less showy phrasing' (ibid.: 189). Nick consequently avoids using 'winged words any more than he was forced to' (ibid.: 347) and, at one point admires Julia precisely for her apparently non-verbal substance: 'She had better ways of showing she was clever than merely saying clever things' (ibid.: 171).

Against the 'hollow idiotic words' (ibid.: 76) of politics Nick seems to position a more legitimate 'doing'. 'Art was *doing* – it came back to that – which politics in most cases weren't' (ibid.: 393, original italics).

Intent on 'doing', he is equally intent on doing it (whatever it is) for others: 'If I do something good my country may like it' (ibid.: 337), he says to Mr Carteret, attempting to persuade his benefactor with the difference his art might make for the country. He tells Gabriel too: the 'independent effort to do something, to leave something which shall give joy to man long after the howling has died away […] – such a vision solicits me in the watches of the night with an almost irresistible force' (ibid.: 255). Earlier in the novel, visiting the cathedral of Notre Dame in Paris, Nick is struck with inspiration: 'The great point's to do something, instead of muddling and questioning and, by Jove, it makes me want to!' (ibid.: 118). After all, Nick 'ha[s] not thrown up the House of Commons to amuse himself', but to 'work, to sit quietly down and bend over his task' (ibid.: 346). It is perhaps only slightly ironic, then, that Nick is not even a very good painter. His sister Grace says that Nick will not even 'do things people would like', that she has never seen 'such a horrid lot of things – not at all clever or pretty' as in his studio (ibid.: 371). Nick's portrait of Miriam notwithstanding, Peter concurs: his impression of Nick's works is one of 'unpromising productions' (ibid.: 399). As long as he can tell himself that he is 'doing', then, not necessarily 'doing well', Nick feels able to justify himself.

The gesture of legitimation for artists and their fans is the same as for their detractors: the difference between these positions merges into a collective intolerance of sameness. In the next section, however, I will explore the ways in which Rowland and Gabriel are never party to such forms of redemption. Instead, they represent the most sustained impediment to the assumption that any form of validation must be sought through appeals to difference. They remain useless in a way that art is rescued from being. As mentioned briefly at the beginning of this section, scholars have looked to both of the novels I engage here as evidence for James's own position on aestheticism. For example, Jonathan Freedman (1990: 140) suggests that the fate of Roderick Hudson is the statement of a position on Paterian aestheticism, showing that James thinks it reckless and unworkable: the novel is a 'resolute indictment of aestheticism'. However, he suggests that, in the character of Rowland, James begins to explore the possibility of a helpful mediation between sturdy practicality and frivolous aestheticism. Ultimately, though, this fails because of Rowland's 'neurasthetic personality' and 'hyperactive indolence' (ibid.: 138). For Freedman, Gabriel Nash also comes close to playing a 'redemptive role' in so far as he challenges 'common Victorian criteria of utility and responsibility' (ibid.: 184–5) and thereby enables the novel's artists like Nick to shed puritanical moralism and pursue their artistic careers. However, Freedman finally suggests that James's sympathies lie less with Gabriel and more with those who are able to dedicate themselves to a craft that 'bears actual fruit' (ibid.: 185). The fecundity of art and artists stands in tension with Gabriel's 'self-willed irrelevance' (ibid.: 187). This irrelevance is then valuable only to the extent that it throws into sharper relief the achievements (the 'fruit' they have borne) of the novel's artists. Whilst both Rowland and Gabriel have parts to play, they ultimately remain useless: Freedman finds more successful, more useful, versions of their roles in characters from James's later fiction, and particularly in Lambert Strether from the 1903 novel *The Ambassadors* (ibid.: 141, 192). Both Rowland and Gabriel remain useless, unable to provide the fully workable mediation between opposing life paths that is offered in James's later fiction. For Freedman, then, artists still come out on top and as I will explore more in the next section, those associated with theory get left behind.

Displeasing theories

Rather than argue against this critical sense of Rowland's and Gabriel's uselessness by suggesting ways in which they could be seen as doing any kind of good, in this section I explore them as figures of sustained intransigence in the face of any imperative, or even modest desire, to be useful. Neither gets associated with the forms of redemption that are rhetorically available to those pursuing that which seems to be straightforwardly practical, or to those pursuing the creation of art. Instead, they both come to be associated with theory, which represents an arena of abstraction, detachment and uninstrumentalised thought that does not receive any redemption in either novel. In so far as this is the case, I suggest that Rowland and Gabriel can shed light on some of the moves that I examined earlier that have taken place in recent queer scholarship. Whilst, as we saw above, sometimes it seems necessary to justify, say, the embrace of queer failure because it is ultimately more useful, the theory or theoreticalness that attaches to Rowland and Gabriel never gets such a justification. For both of these characters theory can just be theory and I think we can therefore see them as obstructing, or simply remaining unconvinced by, the idea that making any difference is necessary.

Both Rowland and Gabriel seem to operate outside of the oppositional terms within which the other characters are placed. Both in some sense 'foreign' (James 1980: 40; James 1995: 361), their lot is not to take either of the polarised courses that are set up around them.[5] In *Roderick Hudson*, for example, Rowland is ambivalent about the novel's way of structuring life along the lines of an opposition between indolence and practicality. He knows, of course, no doubt because he is 'frequently reminded', that a 'young man is the better for a fixed occupation', yet can 'perceive no advantage' in looking for one for himself (James 1980: 13). At the same time, he 'wholly lack[s] the prime requisite of an expert *flâneur* – the simple, sensuous, confident relish of pleasure': indeed, he feels himself to be 'neither fish nor flesh nor good red herring', 'neither an irresponsibly contemplative nature nor a sturdily practical one' (ibid.: 13). Recognising the polarity between the responsibly political and indulgently artistic, Rowland nevertheless thinks of himself as neither of these, but as an 'awkward mixture of moral and aesthetic curiosity' that would make him an 'ineffective reformer and an indifferent artist' (ibid.: 14). He still cannot help but feel that there are only two ways out of this 'awkward mixture', that 'moral and aesthetic curiosity' is not enough, that the 'glow of happiness must be found either in action of some thoroughly keen kind on behalf of an idea, or in producing a masterpiece in one of the arts' (ibid.: 14). But in equating these two ways out, the paths that the novel would also hold as definitively separate, Rowland perhaps shows that they are not as different as the others might think: both would provide some resolution to the malaise of Rowland's 'awkward mixture'.

Rowland seems very palpably aware of the position of uselessness he is to some extent forced to inhabit by his irresoluteness about the definitive paths of art or public life. Indeed, he is often the one to draw attention to his inertia: 'He had a lively suspicion of his uselessness' (ibid.: 4). The vaguely formulated and cursorily mentioned project he has of going over to Europe to bring back paintings to donate to a nascent American art museum is a plan that 'expresse[s] too imperfectly' his 'own personal conception of usefulness' (ibid.: 6). Consequently, he does not share his plans with Cecilia and dismisses them 'with the declaration that he was of course an idle and useless creature and that he should probably be even more so in Europe than at home' (ibid.: 7). The benefit of Europe, though, is that there he 'shall *seem* to be doing something,' the kind of dissimulation which, he recognises, is 'just the humour a useless man should keep out of' (ibid.: 7, original italics). '[I]f I don't do something on the grand scale,' he tells Cecilia, 'it is that my genius is altogether imitative' (ibid.: 5). Because he does not have a genius that is interested in being altogether original or somehow transcendently 'new' or 'different', he thinks he is 'useless'. His uselessness is indexed to sameness, to the 'imitati[on]' that Mr Striker also evokes to belittle Roderick's art-making.

Throughout the novel the people around Rowland seem only to confirm and exacerbate what he feels. So, it is Cecilia who tells him that his 'circumstances [...] suggest the idea of some sort of social usefulness', that he is a 'man to do something on a large scale' (ibid.: 5). 'Isn't a man like you doing a certain harm when he isn't doing some positive good?' (ibid.), she also asks. The way that Cecilia singles Rowland out with her suggestively typifying phrase ('man like you') is reflected elsewhere. Mary, for example, tells him that he is 'unlike other men' (ibid.: 58) because he has 'no duties, no profession, no home' and lives for his 'pleasure' (ibid.): he is the 'first unoccupied man' she has ever seen (ibid.: 56). Rowland's uselessness begins to indicate his queerness ('unlike other men'). Mrs Hudson's ambivalence emerges clearly in an earlier proclamation to Mary Garland that Roderick will be able to show her the 'practice' of art-making, but Rowland is relegated to showing her the 'theory' (ibid.: 242).

Critics have been similarly damning. Greg Zacharias, for example, criticises both Roderick and Rowland as 'selfish' (Zacharias 1990: 116), as unable to demonstrate the 'high moral responsibility require[d]' to 'assume[] responsibility for another' (ibid.: 124). Zacharias is unkind about Roderick, but the real focus of his ire is Rowland. Rowland has 'selfish motives' (ibid.: 116); the young sculptor fails because of the example Rowland sets: 'egotism, indolence, self-absorption' (ibid.: 120); Rowland is a 'harmful guide' (ibid.: 120); his patronage is a 'tyranny' (ibid.: 123); 'self-interest, not interest in the welfare of another, explains Mallet's reason for exercising power' (ibid.: 124); Rowland has a 'conceited fantasy' exposed by James as the product of a 'retarded moral development' (ibid.: 124). For Wendy Graham (1999: 103) it is only 'passive, intellectual diversion' that motivates Rowland's patronage of Roderick. Rowland is a bureaucratic 'arts administrator' (ibid.: 121) and a 'cultural Philistine' (ibid.: 141) who 'reduces Roderick to an automaton' (ibid.: 122). Elizabeth Duquette (2002: 165) suggests that Rowland's 'egotistical fantasy of art collection' is in contrast to the 'unselfish self-reliance' of Sam Singleton (ibid.: 158). Kim Bartel (2005: 176) suggests that Rowland treats Roderick 'less as a human being than as a particularly engaging work of art'. Michèle Mendelssohn (2003: 517) thinks that Rowland's investments in art are only a way out of his 'laissez-faire life of inertia'. All borrow something from the foundational sanction on same-sex sexuality that we saw earlier outlined by Lee Edelman: as unnaturally, irresponsibly, fixated on the self and not sufficiently or genuinely oriented toward otherness. It is telling, in any case, that Rowland's attempt to 'care for something or somebody' demonstrates, for Zacharias and others, his inability to do this. His 'usefulness' remains very much 'reflected', to borrow the terms the novel uses (James 1980: 37): his attempt to become useful only evidences his uselessness the more.

Whereas Rowland can sometimes demonstrate an uneasiness with his uselessness, Gabriel Nash is less apologetic. From the off, in the words of Nick Dormer, Gabriel 'think[s] rather poorly of doing' (James 1995: 251). Predictably, his usefulness is often brought quite explicitly into question. Adding to her sense of Nash's having 'no human use', for example, Lady Agnes is indignant and incredulous, taking a 'cold freedom', on Nick's saying that he wants to 'keep hold' of Gabriel Nash, to ask: 'Poor Mr. Nash, why is he so useful?' (ibid.: 50). Nash is provocatively indifferent to Biddy's conviction that one must '[c]hoose to stop' or 'reform' the 'wrongs in the world', its 'abuses and sufferings' (ibid.: 33): 'There are all kinds of machinery for that – very complicated and ingenious. Your formulas, my dear Dormer, your formulas!' (ibid.: 33), he replies. Similarly, to Biddy's suggestion that he is an 'aesthete' (ibid.: 34), Nash replies: 'Ah there's one of the formulas! […] I've *no* profession, my dear young lady. I've no *état civil*. These things are a part of the complicated ingenious machinery' (ibid., original italics). This machinery for differentiating is what underwrites Nick's party political allegiance. 'You must distinguish,' says Nick: 'Ah trust him to distinguish!', Nash mockingly admonishes (ibid.). 'He sees his "side," his dreadful "side," dear young lady. Poor man, fancy your having a "side" – you, you – and spending your days and your nights looking at it! I'd as soon pass my life looking at an advertisement on a hoarding' (ibid.: 35). Biddy cannot quite fully embrace Nash's rejection of this machinery for political differentiation. She remains convinced of doing something, or 'reform[ing]': 'what in the world *is* better?' she asks (ibid.: 35, original italics).

Nash's sense of what can count as 'doing' does not fit the kinds of opposition that a character like Biddy offers between political reform and wasteful indolence. There is a telling moment in his early conversation with Nick and Biddy:

> 'Upon my word,' said Nick, 'I don't know any one who was fonder of a generalization than you. You turned them off as the man at the street-corner distributes handbills.'
> 'They were my wild oats. I've sown them all.'
> 'We shall see that!'
> 'Oh there's nothing of them now: a tame scanty homely growth. My only good generalizations are my actions.'
> 'We shall see *them* then.'
> 'Ah pardon me. You can't see them with the naked eye. Moreover mine are principally negative. People's actions, I know, are for the most part the things they do – but mine are all the things I *don't* do. There are so many of those, so many, but they don't produce any effect.' (ibid.: 32–3, original italics)

In a way that recalls Mr Striker's advice to Rowland Mallet that he make Roderick aware of the importance of the 'seed we sow', Gabriel none the less seems to endorse the irresponsible distribution of his 'wild oats' in the form of useless 'generalizations' that lead to nothing more productive than 'tame scanty homely growth'. His only 'good' generalisations are actions that turn out to be 'principally negative' and not to 'produce any effect'. The 'duty' ascribed to doing (ibid.: 252), the 'incureable superstition of "doing"' (ibid.: 475), or the particular rhetorical construct that privileges 'doing' as such, Nash might be seen to suggest, involves an arbitrary splitting between what is doing and what is not, and an attendant value-judgement in favour of the former. James remarks to similar effect in his New York Edition Preface to *The Golden Bowl*:

> as the whole conduct of life consists of things done, which do other things in their turn, just so our behaviour and its fruits are essentially one and continuous and persistent and unquenchable, so the act has its way of abiding and showing and testifying, and so, among innumerable acts, are no arbitrary, no senseless separations. (James 1962: 347)

It is as we 'less gropingly [...] plead such differences' that 'we recognise betimes that to "put" things is very exactly and responsibly and interminably to do them' (ibid). This recognition, of course, is not necessarily germane to the 'religion of doing' (ibid.), which prefers to imagine that it can oppose itself to wasteful and illegitimate forms of (non-)effort. But it means that not doing something could potentially be seen as doing something: that is, for one thing, at least, not making things worse.

Nash's indifference about this distinction registers throughout the novel as a kind of immorality. For Biddy, early on, some of the things Gabriel says strike her as the 'highest expression of irresponsibility she had ever seen' (James 1995: 31). Indeed he explicitly rejects some of the rationales for action that other characters across both novels embrace. Talking about his 'style', he says that 'from the moment it's for the convenience of others the signs have to be grosser, the shades begin to go' (ibid.: 35). This is the reason he has to give up writing: 'Literature, you see, is for the convenience of others. It requires the most abject concessions. It plays such mischief with one's style that really I've had to give it up' (ibid.). Eschewing the logic of, say, Nick Dormer, whose career in art is redeemed by the possibility it provides of doing something good for his country, Gabriel rejects all formal creative endeavours for the benefit of others. In contrast with Julia's 'personal impatience of unapplied ideas' (ibid.: 321), Nash would seem to have a personal *passion* for them, gleefully distributing them, as we have seen, as his 'wild oats'. It is this that perhaps contributes to Lady Agnes's ill-feeling in Paris:

> She was disconcerted and distressed; a multitude of incongruous things, all the morning, had been forced upon her attention – displeasing pictures and still more displeasing theories about them, vague portents of perversity on Nick's part and a strange eagerness on Peter's, learned apparently in Paris, to discuss, with a person who had a tone she never had been exposed to, topics irrelevant and uninteresting, almost disgusting, the practical effect of which was to make light of her presence. (ibid.: 56)

Worse than the art itself, then, are the 'still more displeasing theories', the endless, 'irrelevant' and uninstrumentalised talk that goes on around it. Whilst she worries about Nick and Peter's turn towards such theories, it is clear that she locates their source in Gabriel, the 'person who had a tone she never had been exposed to'.

Indeed, there is perhaps no one in the whole Jamesian corpus who is more irredeemably theoretical than Gabriel Nash. The first time we meet him in the novel, he is 'imparting […] his ideas' (ibid.: 28). He is a 'paradoxical young man' (ibid.: 49), with a 'universal urbanity' (ibid.:

52). It is important, however, that he is not ashamed or afraid of paradox: he 'never cast[s] an embarrassed glance' at the 'smooth gloss of his inconsistency' (ibid.: 320) and inconsistencies cluster around him. In the words of Nick's imagination, Gabriel's 'originality had always been that he appeared to have none' (ibid.: 469). Gabriel is a person who falls easily into suggestively useless 'explanations which needed in turn to be explained' (ibid.: 113). To Peter's invocation of the 'complicated Nash', Nick responds that Nash is 'not at all complicated; he's only too simple to give an account of' (ibid.: 63). Originality in sameness, explanations that do not explain, a simplicity that cannot be articulated: if Nash's paradoxes yoke what might otherwise be thought of as incommensurable, it is perhaps no surprise that he questions the value of the difference that might otherwise keep such ideas separate. He is sarcastic in the face of what he perceives to be others' demands for difference, as when he responds ironically to Peter's claim to have seen him at the theatre 'very often before':

> Ah repetition – recurrence: we haven't yet, in the study of how to live, abolished that clumsiness, have we? [...] It's a poverty in the supernumeraries of our stage that we don't pass once for all, but come round and cross again like a procession or an army at the theatre. It's a sordid economy that ought to have been managed better. The right thing would be just *one* appearance, and the procession, regardless of expense, for ever and for ever different. (ibid.: 45, original italics)

All of this paradoxical verboseness, then, is what for Nash constitutes the 'esoteric doctrine' to which he is 'disappointed' to find Nick not 'more accessible' (ibid.: 120). Others find it inaccessible too. Miriam, for example, calls Nash 'an idiot' for not advocating the 'simplifications of practice' (ibid.: 466), apparently not aware of the fact that he is only too simple to explain. In any case, it is telling that Miriam's avowal of 'practice' must rest on a disavowal or rejection of Nash's 'displeasing theories' which in their paradoxicalness seem to offer no positive positions or strategies.

The vehicle of these theories, of course, is talk. We have already seen Nick reject a political life for the 'more or less showy phrasing' on which it relies and its consequent lack of substance, but Nash has no such qualms, embracing the 'winged words' that Nick ascribes to him. The 'words proceeding from his mouth', as Biddy observes, have a 'conspicuous and aggressive perfection' (ibid.: 28). 'I talk – I talk; I say the things other people don't, the things they can't, the things they won't,' Gabriel says 'with his inimitable candour' (ibid.: 252). In Nick's studio, with Peter, theorising about Nick's portrait of Miriam, 'Gabriel Nash had, as usual, plenty to say, and he talked of Nick's picture so long that Peter wondered if he did it on purpose to vex him' (ibid.: 313): 'Another vessel of superior knowledge – he talked, that is, as if he knew better than any one' (ibid.: 320). Talking, though, is of course in contrast to doing, as with the deceased George Dallow who liked to 'talk' only about his precious 'things', 'scarce ever about anything else' (ibid.: 157), who, in Julia's exasperated phrase, 'was always talking' (ibid.: 182). Here are Nick's impressions of Nash in his studio, 'true as ever to his genius while he lolled on a divan and emitted a series of reflexions that were even more ingenious than opportune':

> He had grown used to Gabriel and must now have been possessed of all he had to say. That was one's penalty with persons whose main gift was for talk, however inspiring; talk engendered a sense of sameness much sooner than action. The things a man did were necessarily more different from each other than the things he said, even if he went in for surprising you. (ibid.: 348)

Nash, not, as we have seen, an 'aesthete', not so much a subscriber to the adage of *l'art pour l'art* as of 'blah *pour* blah' (or, even more facetiously, 'blah blah blah'), might be seen to make a way of life out of the talking that Nick certainly cannot think of as action. Nash's sense that we saw earlier of the universality of doing is implicitly dismissed as the kind of talk that 'engender[s] a sense of sameness'. Instead, a difference is introduced to divide up the universal doing: a difference that loads Nash with sameness so he can be dismissed, in Peter Sherringham's words, as a 'twaddler and a bore' (ibid.: 63) and so that what he says can be dismissed, in Biddy's words, as the 'twaddle of the underworld' (ibid.: 33). Contrary to the position we have seen James outline – to "put" things is very exactly and responsibly and interminably to do them' – in this passage Nick cannot equate talking with doing.

Moreover, James's work has itself often been subject to the kinds of critiques levelled at Nash. One contemporary reviewer complains of *The Tragic Muse* that the 'talk [...] is so vague, so ineffective that we can only hope [it] is not intended to show us what life should be' (Hayes 1996: 225). Another writes of the 'close attention needful at times, to disentangle the thread of this elusive variety of talk', 'always a little exasperating to the average member of society' (ibid.: 229). Another bemoans James's presentation of a 'thin solution of talk', a 'flow of talk [that] is perpetual' but does not succeed in 'giving a single revealing hint' (ibid.: 237): 'external, automatic talk *pour passer le temps*' (ibid., original italics). Another complains that the novel 'stagnates through three closely printed volumes of prolix conversations' (ibid.: 238). Another tells us that the novel consists of 'merely half a dozen men and women engaged in protracted conversations that lead to nothing in particular' (Gard 1968: 209).

This talk, though, seems indicatively linked to an egregious academicism. It is 'analytic, introspective and philosophical to a degree' (Hayes 1996: 221). 'It is all very well for smart undergraduates and governesses' (Gard 1968: 202). There are 'pages of monotonous analysis', such that a 'chapter lost here and there makes little difference' (ibid.: 209). But perhaps worst of all are the 'sham cleverness of [James's] conversations and illusive profundity of his analyses', which 'are more exasperating than ever' (ibid.: 200). And it is James who enters the firing line: when his characters talk – and 'they all talk on, and on; and on, and on' – 'they are as fluent, as refined, as circuitous, and as cryptic, if not quite as long-winded, as Mr. James himself' (ibid.: 233). The reviewers reinforce the sense that we saw expressed above in Lena Milman's review of James for *The Yellow Book*: that he is 'too analytical'.

The characters in *Roderick Hudson* find themselves in a similar predicament. One reviewer complains that 'there is a sameness that is monotonous in the talk of these people': 'they all talk pretty much in the same way, the way of Mr. Henry James Jr.' (Hayes 1996: 7). 'The very conversation is for the most part a reflection of Mr. James's own mental processes, and even Christina Light, the spoiled child of fashion, talks like a trained metaphysician' (ibid.: 9). Another complains that the 'conversations are often too prolonged, and the author endows all his personages with his own turn for analyzing, in consequence of which they all occasionally talk alike, blurring for the moment their individuality': this 'perpetual analysis is fatiguing'; it 'taxes the attention like metaphysics' (Gard 1968: 41). The novel is 'full of the subtle but somewhat morbid analysis that is so prominent a characteristic of Mr. James's genius' (ibid.: 78). Moreover, the 'story would have been more effective if it had been told in simpler language' (ibid.: 13).

Whilst many of these reviewers already locate the problems with the talk in James's novels in its abstraction, we can also see that they pre-empt some of the central critiques that have been aimed at theoretical writing in the humanities. James's reviewers criticise the 'sham cleverness' and 'illusive profundity' of the talk in *The Tragic Muse*. Contemporary critics, as Jonathan Culler and Kevin Lamb (2003: 3) explain, criticise theorists who 'deliberately write obscurely in order to sound profound when in fact they have nothing to say'. James's critics suggest that 'simpler language' would benefit his stories. Contemporary critics excoriate the 'merely apparent difficulty' (ibid.: 5) of theoretical writing. James's critics bemoan the 'automatic talk' in his novels. For contemporary critics, as Daniel Cottom (2003: 150, original italics) explains, intellectuals are 'worse than useless': they 'can *talk* and *write* of crisis' but no more. Not much has necessarily changed, then, in the ease with which it is possible to critique writing as 'too analytical'. James's novels and contemporary theory both come under fire for similar reasons.

According to a number of accounts both novels suffer from being full of too much talk and not enough action. This talk is monotonous and too academic or analytical. It has the effect of flattening differences and causing individual characters to blur into one.[6] Whilst these critiques are leveraged against the novels as a whole, I suggest that the novels themselves direct these kinds of critiques towards Rowland and Gabriel. For example, Gabriel's talk and 'displeasing theories' generate an uninspiring 'sense of sameness'. Aloof from the simple practicality of Mary Garland, Rowland is the one, according to Roderick's mother, to teach Mary the 'theory' of art, while Roderick can get on and show her the 'practice'. Only Rowland and Gabriel come to be associated with theory, or have the novels account for their separation from the more intelligible paths of art or practicality via their association with theory. Rather than as something to overcome, though, I do not think we need to imagine non-productive theoreticalness as a problem and I do not see that the novels necessarily invite us to make such an interpretation. We do not have to move beyond it, as Jonathan Freedman seeks to, towards the final realisation of a more useful theoreticalness in James's later novels. Rowland and Gabriel are a concerted reminder of the privileging of difference required to underwrite the assumption that usefulness is necessary. Pushing this further, we could suggest that the novels also show how it is precisely trying to 'make a difference' that makes things go wrong. It is only the sense of obligation to be useful that makes Rowland take on the patronage of Roderick which eventually results in Roderick's death. Had he left things the same, things might have, paradoxically, turned out differently.

Useless queers

Roderick Hudson ends more or less where it started: with Rowland and his cousin Cecilia together in the town of Northampton, Mass. Rowland returns 'more frequently than of old' (James 1980: 389) to the hometown of his now deceased protégé and that protégé's former fiancée to talk to Cecilia about Roderick, is ensconced in a pattern of repetition, is only the 'most patient' of mortals (ibid.: 389). By ending where it began, the novel would suggest that no significant difference has been made, no significant change has been brought about. At the same time, Rowland seems to have learned that making such a difference is not always for the best. By the end, he seems content with his pattern of return, not needing to make a difference in the way that he did at the beginning of the novel: he has learned properly how doing nothing can sometimes be the best course of action. Similarly, in *The Tragic Muse*, Gabriel Nash, perhaps more recognisably theoretical than Rowland, is so theoretical by the end of the novel that he seems to have stopped existing. Having disappeared from people's lives, the portrait that Nick has painted of him also begins an 'odd tendency to fade gradually from the canvas' (James 1995: 476). This suggests not only an affinity between Nash and his image – his copy – but also Nash's full embrace of anti-utilitarian insubstantiality: choosing a much more banal and less revolutionary way to go than Roderick Hudson's suicide, he has simply 'melted back into the elements' (ibid.: 480).

In the end, then, what are these characters good for? For one thing, Rowland and Gabriel offer a window on to thinking about the place of uselessness in the history of queer representation. We can understand both of them in relation to *fin-de-siècle* aestheticism, but they do not share the revolutionary embrace of art or the reckless submission to sensual pleasure that are associated with the key players such as Wilde or Pater. Instead, they are more thoroughly useless men, more prone simply to 'moral and aesthetic curiosity' (James 1980: 14) than making a real difference. James, too, has a more oblique than direct relation to the principle of art for art's sake. As we have seen, his approach is 'analytical', intellectual, theoretical. It is not the arch or sensual uselessness conventionally associated with aestheticism. A bit like James, both Rowland and Gabriel come to be associated with theory, which represents an arena of abstraction, detachment and uninstrumentalised thought that receives no redemption: its vehicle is the kind of talk that, above, we saw engenders a 'sense of sameness'. This relation to theory foreshadows some of the positions, rhetoric and argumentative moves that we see also in later twentieth-century queer scholarship. On the one hand, uselessness enters the purview of contemporary work via sociological or historical materialist scholarship which questions the usefulness of principally theoretical work which is imagined to be unhelpfully aloof from the real conditions of life. On the other hand, queer scholarship that has embraced the useless has done so in a way that seeks to redeem it by proving its value or usefulness. I want to suggest that Rowland and Gabriel can shed light on the implicit disciplining of queers that takes place in the rhetorical moves that we saw in the first section above in which queer *studies* comes to replace queer *theory* as a means of correcting for political short-sightedness and the erasure of difference. Rowland and Gabriel do not lead us to see that there is anything necessary, or even convincing, about this movement away from theory. At the same time, I think both characters can help to reflect on the other trend in queer scholarship that I also attended to above, which has often explicitly questioned the criteria of political utility that obtain in certain contexts. This scholarship has taught us in valuable ways to be more open-minded to the potential effects of what can seem apolitical, unhelpful and useless: the importance of what can seem impotent. However, rather than teaching us that we do not necessarily know what is best for political programmes, I think Rowland and Gabriel finally eschew any attachment at all to redeeming errands like political strategy, even strategies with highly limited and modest ambitions. For both of these characters theory can just be theory and I think we can therefore see them as obstructing, or simply remaining unconvinced by, the idea that making any difference is necessary.

It may therefore be difficult to explain exactly why we should care about their uselessness: it may, perhaps appropriately enough, be difficult to explain exactly what use their uselessness might have. In response to a similar conundrum, Daniel Cottom (2003: 203) suggests that the only thing to be done is to 'simply repeat' his sense that uselessness can represent a 'standing cultural commitment' (ibid.) against various forms of stupidity. Rather than argue for any particular good that will come of caring about Rowland and Gabriel then, I choose to embrace them because, on the one hand, they provide a window on to how a particular kind of uselessness has been intimately linked to queer lives. On the other hand, they have a firm place in this chapter in particular because my reluctance to endorse any imperative of utility, my attempt to resist the almost unimpeachable rhetoric of 'making a difference', would seem to leave no other choice.

Notes

1 The scholarship here is potentially vast. For a small selection, see the following: on Wilde: Cohen 1993; Sinfield 1994; Bristow 1995; Mendelsohn 2007. On Wilde and Pater: Dellamora 1990; Ohi 2015. On Pater: Love 2007; O'Connell 2015. On Lee: Gardner 1987; Vicinus 2004.
2 For a wide range of queer readings of the novel see: Martin 1978; Murtaugh 1996; Lane 1996; Stevens 1998; Graham 1999; Sofer 1999. For more specifically historicist readings that caution against reading modern homosexuality in the novel, preferring to see premodern forms of male same-sex intimacy see: Woods 1999; Haralson 2003; Nissen 2009.
3 As with *Roderick Hudson*, there have been a wide range of queer readings of *The Tragic Muse*, which have often read the novel as helping to bring about the queer associations of aestheticism: Wilson 1993; Haralson 2003; Salamenksy 1999, 2011. Other broadly queer readings of the novel include Lane 1996 and Rowe 1998.
4 A significantly similar approach has been offered more recently by Rosemary Hennessy, who argues for a 'return to historical materialism' (Hennessy 2000: 28–9) in opposition to the 'commodification of identities' offered by postmodern queer theory (ibid.: 34), which mimics 'capital's insidious and relentless expansion' (ibid.: 112), rather than focusing on exploitative 'social relations of labor' (ibid.: 49). More recently still, James Penney (2014: 2) has offered a particular blend of historical materialism and psychoanalysis as a way of formulating a 'genuinely universal emancipatory struggle' that can correct for queer theory's apparently narrow factionalism. Kevin Floyd (2009) has described a less antagonistic relationship between queer theory and Marxism by suggesting affinities between queer scholarship's frequent commitment to intersectional analysis and Marxism's interest in totality thinking.
5 In his biography of James, Leon Edel suggests that James was subject to a lifelong tension between practicality and art, due to his family's historical links in puritan cultures and his own ambitions to write. Edel maps this in part on to the differences between James and his older brother William (Edel

1987: 79). However, I argue that, far from providing evidence of a commitment to any such opposition on James's part, Rowland and Gabriel suggest that one does not have to exist within it.

6 Whilst I am interested here in adumbrating the ways that talk is imagined to have a formal relation to sameness, some James scholars have also associated this talk with queer social identities. See, for example Salamensky 1999, 2011; Matheson 1999.

2
Reproductive

Contemporary queer scholarship often has a vexed relationship to the idea of human reproduction. But this situation has a long history that can be traced back to at least the late nineteenth century through the various positions on the topic that have been adopted in feminist thought and writing. During the period since this time women's capacity for making more humans has been seen both as a vector of liberation and of domination; both evidence of the strength of female embodiment and a physical hindrance holding back feminist progress; both the path to women's freedom and a state tool of racialised disempowerment. Late first-wave feminists such as Charlotte Perkins Gilman or Ellen Key, for example, argued that valorising reproduction as a kind of professional, organised and managed work would not only result in the emancipation of women but would also enable broader social progress (Gilman 1998; Key 1909). Many years after this, in the 1970s and 1980s, writers such as Adrienne Rich and Mary O'Brien again articulated the importance of women's reproductive abilities to their identities and liberation as women, seeking to refuse how reproduction had been patriarchally organised, choosing instead to embrace women's reproductive capabilities as a means of celebrating female bodies (Rich 1976; O'Brien 1981). At the same time, other influential second-wave accounts heralded the opportunity that new reproductive technologies offered of completely freeing women from their association with procreation (Firestone 1972). We can see the spirit of such accounts today in scholarship that explores how reproductive technologies have begun to undo cultural assumptions linking reproduction and heterosexuality (Franklin 2007; Mamo 2007). Still others would suggest that linking women with reproductive capability has served to perpetuate an essentialised femaleness often also formulated on the basis of presumptions and exclusions to do with race, class and sexuality. Today, various facets of biological reproduction are frequently imagined as the vectors of a biopolitical control that systemically upholds racialised inequalities (Weinbaum 2004; 2019).

It is this more antagonistic relation to reproduction that has been inherited by queer theoretical scholarship. Often in queer theory, a central sanction on queers is imagined to come from our apparent failure to reproduce biologically, where biological reproduction gives heterosexuality its licence or alibi. This has been grounds for scholars and activists to refuse the idea that only reproduction gives meaning to sexual and social life. Lee Edelman's (2004: 2) critique of 'reproductive futurism' is a fervent instance of this that has had a significant impact on the subsequent shape of queer theoretical argumentation.[1] For Edelman, the figure of the Child, always fantasmatically conceived within heterosexual coupling, anchors all political visions of the future. We cannot refuse the idea of making a better future, he argues, because the refusal of the Child is unthinkable: its manipulative innocence means we can do nothing but defend it. In Edelman's account, queers figure precisely this refusal, however, in so far as they are associated with non-reproductive pleasures. They are made to embody the 'death drive of the dominant order' (Edelman 2004: 17), providing that order with a way of localising and domesticating its own relation to the drive. Edelman calls on queers to embrace their figuration as opponents to every social structure, to all forms of reproduction in so far as reproduction evokes conservation, continuation and stability. Any deference to 'the culture of forms and their reproduction' (ibid.: 48) must be abandoned. Edelman uses a psychoanalytic and post-structuralist framework for describing this situation. Queerness is understood as the death drive, or an absence at the heart of meaning, that threatens to disrupt or even destroy a social order invested in the stability of identity and ego. Edelman therefore draws on theoretical paradigms that have associated sameness with conservative and mystifying social fictions and that have preferred ideas such as irreducible complexity over stasis, the trace over self-presence, *difference* over identity. For Edelman, 'futurism merely perpetuates [a] tenacious will to sameness' (ibid.: 59). But the very bedrock of his argument relies on the assumption that sameness in the form of Imaginary wholeness, substantialised identity and the successful reproduction of social form is simply an impossibility. Consequently, any kind of reproduction – imagined as a process of keeping something the same – can only end up associated with the pernicious social forces of the dominant heterosexuality he maligns.

But does all *reproduction* – biological, social, semiotic or metaphorical – necessarily uphold the dominant heterosexuality that Edelman's Child represents? What do worlds where 'reproduction' is not the licence of a dominant and privileged sexual formation look like? These questions have driven much lesbian feminist speculative thought and fiction from across the twentieth century, which has imagined reproduction to embody the sameness that Edelman maligns but has none the less positioned it as something quite separate from heteronormativity. Some of the works I have in mind here will be familiar to many readers and have been grouped together in various configurations by scholars before because of their shared concern with imagining utopian women-only communities: Charlotte Perkins Gilman's *Herland* (1915), Joanna Russ's *The Female Man* (1975), Suzy McKee Charnas's *Motherlines* (1978), Sally Miller Gearhart's *The Wanderground* (1979).[2] A final one may be less familiar, but none the less shares the earlier fiction's concerns: Nicola Griffith's *Ammonite* (1993). All of these novels present emphatically non-heterosexual – and arguably all lesbian – worlds that are none the less organised around forms of biological and social reproduction that, crucially, are about replication, repetition and continuation, or else about keeping things the same, sometimes even in the form of human cloning. In this chapter, I explore these fictions and argue that they help us to see the conflation and confusion that happen in Edelman's account where all forms of reproduction are imagined to be associated with a politically problematic heteronormativity. This conflation is possible only within a theoretical paradigm that valorises difference as the truth of the world. An investment in keeping things the same has no necessary relation to a problematic or dominant order. My investment in the continuation of my own life does not underwrite normative heterosexuality. That is, unless you accept the theoretical underpinning of Edelman's account, which associates any investment in integration, coherence and continuation with what is politically dominant or oppressive. The novels I will go on to discuss, I argue, dramatise this quite neatly: their investments in reproduction as sameness serve to uphold lesbian, rather than heteronormative, worlds.

While she may in some ways seem out of place alongside the other authors I've mentioned so far, Gilman is central to this argument. For example, throughout her career (in essays, novels, short fiction and poems), she elaborated a worldview in which heterosexual marriage was faulted for being too invested in maintaining an oppressive social relation between women and men and not sufficiently geared towards the simple reproduction of more humans. She spells this out in her early treatise *Women and Economics* (1898), where she argues that women's economic dependence on men, or the 'sexuo-economic relation' (Gilman 1998: 19), was responsible for the notion that women were 'natural mothers', and indentured them to proprietary family units, child-rearing and housework. What Gilman proposes instead is a communal approach to 'child-culture' in which only trained professionals are responsible for raising children (ibid.: 135), as a means of freeing women from the assumption that this is their natural calling. Rather than upholding the value of the heterosexual nuclear family, Gilman's system is a way of making model citizens in an impersonal, homogenising manufacturing process. We see a particularly condensed version of Gilman's system in her well-known utopian novel *Herland* (1915). Charting unknown territory, three male explorers in the novel discover a nation constituted solely of women who after thousands of years of separation have discovered the ability to reproduce through parthenogenesis, or asexual reproduction, in which they effectively create copies of themselves. Once born, the children in Herland undergo a careful process of socialisation in which Herlandian society and values are also reproduced in them. The effect of this regularisation in reproduction ramifies across the whole of Herland: reproductive, agricultural and social processes all come to enjoy the uniform efficiency of machines, instantiating a world based on equality, social cohesion and harmony. Child-bearing and child-rearing are valorised in Herland because of their role in the perfectibility of the whole society, but valorising the Child or children in Herland cannot uphold heteronormativity because there is no heterosexuality there.

I will return to the question of how to view Gilman alongside the other more emphatically lesbian worlds presented in the other novels that I address in this chapter, but these later works certainly share *Herland*'s understanding of the importance of forms of biological and social reproduction for establishing worlds without men. For example, one of the parallel worlds presented in *The Female Man* (1975) is the future world of Whileaway where lesbian women use technology to reproduce only girls and where all children are subject to a training that creates consistency in the population. *Motherlines* (1978) imagines a fantasy world where the Riding Women, living far from the male-dominated Holdfast, have also discovered a way to reproduce without men that has resulted in their world being organised into a series of family lines made up of identical sisters. *The Wanderground* (1979) presents a world where the Hill Women, separated from the male-controlled City, reproduce through ritual 'implantment[s]' (Gearhart 1984: 44) and structure their lives around the passing on of knowledge through the 'remember rooms' (ibid.: 138). *Ammonite* (1993) presents an alien planet, discovered in the deep past by humans, where a mysterious virus kills off all men, but allows women to create new life together and ties them into a vast collective memory that stretches all the way back to these first human colonists. Many of these novels have been presented together in various configurations by scholars because of the concerns with exploring female-only worlds that they share. The novels are mostly treated as arguments about how the world could or should change but I am interested in what they say about sameness as much as change: their interest in reproduction as something that maintains as well as creates biological and social life. The investments of these more utopian novels in forms of sameness – maintenance and continuity as much as change – is perhaps why they seem to be of less interest nowadays to both scholars and popular commentators than more dystopian visions. Scholars who have charted the development of feminist speculative fiction have noted the turn away from utopianism through writing in the late 1980s (Fitting 1990), such as in Margaret Atwood's *The Handmaid's Tale* (1985). More recently, dystopia seems to continue to grip the imaginations of both feminist writers and the more general public, with the popular televisation of *The Handmaid's Tale* (2017–), the publication of the novel's sequel *The Testaments* (2019) and the emergence of many contemporary feminist dystopian novels (Gilbert 2018; Ditum 2018), all of which present worlds which demand quite emphatically to be changed. The novels I explore below, by contrast, are more about keeping things the same: they not only rely on maintaining populations through biological reproduction but also emphasise structures for passing down social information, or maintaining forms of belief and ways of life.

More recent queer theoretical work has sought to bring such forms of reproduction that are not biological into the conversation. Valerie Rohy (2012: 102), for example, has argued that, within the homophobic terms of the religious right, homosexuality is presented as a force of threatening fecundity in the way that gay people are presented as seeking to increase through influence and recruitment: homosexuality thus exhibits 'a propensity to multiply not biologically but semiotically in an unsentimental, insistent process of replication, repetition, and representation'. Far from being opposed to reproduction, in this more recent scholarship homosexuality is in fact a '*form of reproduction*' (ibid.: 108, original italics). Crucial to right-wing imaginations is the idea that homosexuals will reproduce themselves via unnatural forms of copying and imitation. Homosexuals threaten to render apparent the sameness in reproduction. Instead of disputing the idea that gay people recruit, however, Rohy argues that what we should abandon instead is the homophobic idea that such recruitment would be a bad thing. Reproduction, understood here as the imitation or copying that is crucial to passing on information and culture, is not bad if what is reproduced is desirable. Whereas for Edelman all reproduction – any investment in the continuity or coherence of established ways of life – is inevitably caught up in a reactionary misrecognition of the fundamental Real or absence that drives all meaning-making, Rohy is more in tune with the fact that good things also require reproduction.

Indeed, nothing that has any meaningful shape or durability in the world can avoid the need to reproduce itself. Such a claim has also been at the core of a recent critique of Edelman on materialist feminist grounds. Anca Parvulescu (2017: 89) has argued that Edelman works with a 'narrow concept of reproduction as procreative heteronormativity tethered to heterosexual sex' that does not take account of the wider range of activities that are needed to sustain and maintain social life. As Parvulescu notes, this kind of daily reproductive labour – social care, household labour, emotional support – has historically been disproportionately associated with women and she evokes decades of feminist scholarship that has sought to analyse the place of this kind of work in society, including the 'wages for housework' arguments from the 1970s that demanded the recognition of social reproduction as a kind of work. In a recently reissued collection of her essays, Silvia Federici (2012: 12), a key figure in Wages for Housework, also relates this need to reproduce to social movement politics: 'a movement that does not learn to reproduce itself is not sustainable'. Rohy, Parvulescu and Federici, either explicitly or implicitly, offer a counterpoint to Edelman, recognising the wide range of reproductive work that people undertake which has no necessary relation to heterosexuality, as well as the value of reproducing what we want to see more of or keep around. However, what I would add to these accounts is how strongly Edelman's argument is driven by his attachment to theoretical systems so thoroughly about *difference*. As we have seen, for Edelman, any kind of reproduction is problematically caught up in a misrecognition of the Real or absence supposedly actually at the heart of meaning. Any attachment to maintenance, continuation or endurance is intrinsically on the side of reproductive futurism. But I would argue that it is embattled and minoritised forms of life that have the clearest justification for wanting to keep things the same, particularly when they have expended a lot of energy in establishing ways of life that allow them to be safe. This is arguably why reproduction as a form of sameness is at the imaginative heart of the fiction I address in this chapter. Many of the novels in what follows show the violent worlds that the women-only communities they represent have escaped from. In the context of this it perhaps becomes more understandable that these worlds would also be attached to mechanisms for keeping themselves the same.

Some would argue, of course, that in the history of feminism it has been communities of women who have tried to separate themselves from the world in this way that have been the problem. Certainly, according to one widespread narrative of the development of feminism, it is the second-wave radical and separatist feminism which these novels reflect which was taken to task, particularly during the 1980s, for its racism and classism, or else its failure to be properly intersectional. We could suggest that Gilman's Herlanders and the women in the other novels represent the moment that is often evoked as one of sameness before 'white feminists were forced to turn their attention away from assertions of similarity and homogeneity to examinations of difference' (Kaplan 1994: 140). Certainly, there are ways of questioning this narrative for some of the later material – *Motherlines*, for example, directly addresses questions of race. But in addressing Gilman it is impossible to ignore how her emphases on sameness lead to what a number of critics over the past twenty or so years have identified as her racism or ethnocentrism. In the course of her search for a completely standardised society, Gilman advocates the compulsory socialisation – or 'Americanization' – of immigrants, the similarly compulsory education and training of what she imagines to be a wayward African American population and the schooling of young women in the importance of their reproductive choices for ensuring a healthy, homogenised future for 'the race'.

What I suggest in this chapter, however, is that, whilst Gilman's search for standardisation has racist consequences, that does not prove that there is a necessary connection between sameness and racism, even as scholars have seized on the opportunity to equate this racism with her investment in systematic forms of reproduction. In so far as critics react against Gilman's interest in sameness per se, often expressed through their use of 'reproduction' as a metaphor for the perpetuation of feminist ideas and interpretative practices, I suggest, they are borrowing from implicit judgements against sameness. Moreover, such a focus on sameness, on reproduction, may obscure the actual workings of Gilman's racism. I do not want to argue that Gilman is not racist. Rather, I want to note how a concern with racism gets registered as, or displaced on to, a concern with reproduction.

It seems clear, then, that not every act of reproduction will reproduce something bad or necessarily be implicated in a reactionary or problematic cultural logic. As a number of writers have observed, good things also require a labour of maintenance and reproduction. Clearly, not all forms of reproduction are biological and not all forms will uphold or license a dominant heteronormativity. But it is rhetorically compelling, within some theoretical projects, like Edelman's, to lump them together as embodiments of a dreary commitment to simply more of the same, as a way of accruing scholarly and argumentative authority. In the rest of this chapter, I explore key lesbian feminist speculative fictions from across the twentieth century which dramatise how a commitment to reproduction, precisely as a process of maintaining sameness, by no means necessarily upholds heteronormative worlds. Whereas Valerie Rohy uses a range of queer literary fictions that address queer aetiology and causality to develop the argument cited above (Rohy 2015), and Anca Parvulescu turns to the high literary fiction of J.M. Coetzee, my concern is with what is at once a more neglected and more obvious archive of texts that have reproduction as a form of sameness right at their centres. These fictions, I argue, offer a counterpoint to the queer theoretical dismissal of reproduction and dramatise the value of sameness for embattled and minoritised communities. The simple continuation of the lives of those who are already alive – the investment in a future that is not for children, but for us – has no logical relation to any particular sexual formation. We may want some futures, many futures, not to bring change, but to keep things the same – and surely there is nothing intrinsically politically pernicious in recognising this.

More of the same

Key to Edelman's analysis of 'reproductive futurism' is the argument that queers should not only refuse a particular heterosexual order which authorises itself through appeal to the figure of the Child but should also oppose themselves to a much wider field of political, cultural and psychic stability. Edelman suggests that queers should embrace their figural status as what undermines every social or political form, in so far as such form is always, within his argument, indentured to reproductive futurism. This therefore means abandoning every political hope for the future, turning instead to a pure negativity that scuppers 'every form of social viability' (Edelman 2004: 9). As we have seen, any deference to 'the culture of forms and their reproduction' (ibid.: 48) must be abandoned. Queerness is and should be anathema to all forms of reproduction, social and biological. But it is really only the imperatives of the particular theoretical schema that he takes as the bedrock of his thinking that necessitates this argument. In this section, I survey Edelman's argument in detail and the negotiation between ideas of sameness and difference that his theoretical co-ordinates necessitate. Ultimately, it is these co-ordinates that allow him to claim that anything that is invested in coherence, continuity, or stability – any kind of reproduction in so far as this involves producing something that is the same – affirms the conservative logic and political order grounded in presumptive heterosexuality, even as there is not necessarily any logical link between these.

In Edelman's Lacanian paradigm, the fantasy that sustains reproductive futurism is tied to structures of Symbolic meaning production. The Child comes to occupy the position of an impossible wholeness: a meaning present in itself and an identity that does not bear the 'mark of the signifier as lack' (ibid.: 39). For Edelman, this lack is a necessary part of signification, a necessary upshot of the way in which meaning is only made in the Symbolic through differential relations, where nothing means in and of itself but only in relation to other things. 'Politics', which for Edelman is always governed by the logic of reproductive futurism, 'names the struggle to effect a fantasmatic order of reality in which the subject's alienation [that is, the lack instantiated by the signifier] would vanish into the seamlessness of identity at the end point of the endless chain of signifiers lived as history' (ibid.: 8). '[H]istory' is guaranteed, however, only by maintaining the lack, maintaining the 'subject's alienation', maintaining the gap in signification necessitated by the signifier, so as to sustain the possibility of overcoming these absences in the future and therefore to keep alive the promise of any sort of future at all. Reproductive futurism relies in some sense on its own failure; success would leave nothing to look forward to in the future.

Edelman, then, reproduces the account of signification that has been central to post-structuralism and certain forms of psychoanalysis. The 'mediation of the signifier', he contends, always introduces the 'distance inherent in the chain of ceaseless deferrals and substitutions to which language as a system of differences necessarily gives birth' (ibid.: 8). This birthing of difference, for him, inhabits every linguistic act regardless of its own investment in a self-present wholeness. In a social order governed by a logic of heterosexual reproductive necessity, he argues, queerness is made to occupy the position of this gap, of what installs the constitutive 'distance' in signification, what prevents the final consolidation of meaning that futurism thinks it wants. Queerness, for Edelman, is therefore a structural position within signification, or, rather, it gives a name to the structural imperative of signification: that there is no meaning present in itself. Reproductive futurism is able to disavow its reliance on the failure of signification, on the failure of the Symbolic to provide self-present meaning, by blaming this failure on queers. By making queers embody what obstructs self-present meaning, futurism creates what it needs to keep that meaning at bay, to keep signification from succeeding, but in such a way that it can maintain plausible deniability about the fact that it has an investment in this failure. Terms derived from post-structuralism allow Edelman to give an account of the paradoxical psychic dynamic that drives reproductive futurism.

For Edelman, however, even a nominal investment in a self-present wholeness is naive deference to an impossibility. Frequently, this impossibility is mapped on to the Lacanian concept of the Imaginary, which denotes a past always superseded by virtue of every linguistic subject's necessary location in the Symbolic. Hence futurism is indentured to the 'impossible place of an Imaginary past exempt from the deferrals intrinsic to the operation of the signifying chain' (ibid.: 10), of which the Child represents the restoration (ibid.: 21, 24). Whilst the Imaginary is imagined as a realm of discrete difference in so far as it provides the fantasy of meaning present in itself, meaning that means without reference to anything else, Edelman repeatedly associates it with what is etymologically linked to sameness: 'identity'. Whilst futurism seeks to 'restore an Imaginary past' (ibid.: 21), it also seeks the 'seamlessness of identity' (ibid.: 8). Consequently, in the same way that queerness is aligned with the differential structure of the Symbolic against the Imaginary, so it embodies what refuses 'every substantialization of identity' (ibid.: 4), as what figures the 'loss of identity and coherence' (ibid.: 132), as what 'voids the promissory note' (ibid.: 149) in which identity's realisation awaits in a tomorrow that does not, in some sense *cannot*, come. What he calls 'our formation as subjects of the signifier' is a 'fact' (ibid.: 134). Differences are necessary; the sameness of Imaginary identity is only ever a fantasy.

Edelman's insistence on mapping reproductive futurism on to a structure of signification that necessitates the creation of a non-negotiable difference, I suggest, is what gives his argument a particular rhetorical effectiveness. The psychoanalytic-deconstructive paradigm in which he writes provides a familiar and comprehensible adversary in the form of Imaginary sameness. Earlier we saw Edelman claim that 'language as a system of differences' necessarily 'gives birth' to the 'deferrals and substitutions' of signification. By associating these substitutions with birth Edelman seems to imply that the differential structure of signification that he aligns with queerness is equally aligned with reproductive futurism. Through its relation to birth, the differential relations of the Symbolic seem to borrow some of what makes the image of the Child so impossible to refuse. To insist, as Edelman does, on the 'nonidentity of things' (Dinshaw et al. 2007: 181), is to cling to the structure sustaining reproductive futurism, in which things must remain non-identical to inaugurate a chain of deferrals that instantiates 'history' by projecting the achievement of identity into the future. Reproductive futurism has to maintain queerness as the gap in signification in order to keep time ticking over. What would finally put a stop to this endless deferral is what precisely must constantly be deferred (in reproductive futurism), or theorised as somehow fundamentally impossible (in theoretical accounts like Edelman's): the 'Imaginary past', or, relatedly, 'the seamlessness of identity'. Adherence to this deconstructive paradigm forecloses any possibility of sameness. Crucial rhetorical privilege is established through the neat way in which Edelman installs difference as a total significatory necessity and relegates sameness to a realm that is, in more ways than one, Imaginary.

It may be clear, though, that Edelman's description of the psychic and significatory dynamics of reproductive futurism relies on some fundamental paradoxes. For example, futurism desires significatory wholeness, but must always prevent it in order to maintain the possibility of achieving it in the future. By the same token, futurism (violently) castigates queers, but needs them to embody the bar to significatory wholeness that it requires to keep this wholeness on the horizon. The opposition between queers and futurism, then, would seem to be unsustainable in so far as each is firmly bound up with the operation of the other. In accord with the paradoxes that structure Edelman's account, both futurism and queerness are explicitly aligned with sameness. Edelman (2004: 59) writes that 'futurism merely perpetuates [a] tenacious will to sameness'; that it 'generates generational succession, temporality, and narrative sequence, not toward the end of enabling change, but, instead, of perpetuating sameness' (ibid.: 60); that its investment is in the 'rigid sameness of identity' (ibid.: 21). On the other hand, he also acknowledges that queerness is maligned for its 'repetitive investment in the Same' (ibid.: 58), is figured in terms of 'sterility and a non-productive sameness' (ibid.: 59) and conjured as a 'lethal sameness' that futurism 'condemns for its nullification of difference' (ibid.: 63). Indeed, at one point, Edelman explicitly notes the confluence between queerness and futurism's most cherished icon: the 'Child enshrines, in its form as sublimation, the very value for which queerness regularly finds itself condemned: an insistence on sameness that intends to restore an Imaginary past' (ibid.: 21).

In at least some parts of Edelman's account, it is reproductive futurism that seeks to stabilise this paradox by introducing firm distinctions between itself and queerness. Futurism generates queerness as difference in order to violently and insistently abject it:

> homosexuality, though charged with, and convicted of, a future-negating sameness construed as reflecting its pathological inability to deal with the fact of difference, gets put in the position of difference from heteronormativity that, despite its persistent propaganda through *sexual* difference, refuses homosexuality's difference from the value of difference it claims as its own. (ibid.: 60, original italics)

As we have seen, reproductive futurism needs this difference: it needs to imagine queers as an external threat. In Lacanian terms, it needs the gap or lapse in signification in order to sustain the possibility of overcoming this in the future. We see, then, that reproductive futurism's investment in sameness (continuation) is at the same time an investment in difference (queerness as what guarantees this continuation). Futurism can acknowledge its investment in sameness only in a mode of disavowal, by creating the figure that Edelman neologistically calls the *sinthom*osexual, by conjuring 'the sameness that's abjected as *sinthomo*sexuality' (ibid., original italics). Reproductive futurism needs to locate queerness and its associated sameness in a position of difference, paradoxically, to ensure business as usual. There is therefore nothing necessarily radical about queerness's difference: it is the necessary engine of futurism's conservatism.

More interestingly, Edelman is also keen to introduce a firm distinction between queers and futurism into their otherwise paradoxical association. Indeed, it is in terms of an apparently radical difference that Edelman encourages queers to understand themselves. Reproductive futurism seems to want sameness, in terms of the fantasised wholeness that the Child represents, or, alternatively, in the constancy of the movement towards that deferred end, but can acknowledge this only by projecting this investment in sameness on to the figure of the queer. But it also holds that the queer, in Edelman's account at least, cannot embrace this sameness either. Edelman calls on queers to embrace the difference as which they are conjured:

> If the queer's abjectified difference [...] secures normativity's identity, the queer's disavowal of that difference affirms normativity's singular truth. For every refusal of the figural status to which queers are distinctively called reproduces the triumph of narrative as the *allegorization* of irony [...] and thus proclaims the universality of reproductive futurism. (ibid.: 26, original italics)

For queers not to embrace their abject figuration is to 'reproduce[]' the values of reproductive futurism. Edelman does not acknowledge that embracing the abjection that reproductive futurism ascribes to queers *also* reproduces the values of reproductive futurism. Whilst the crux of his entire argument is that queers should embrace their status within futurism, Edelman is not able to embrace anything *as* 'reproduction'. At this point the paradoxes that Edelman sustains elsewhere in *No Future* are rejected for the rhetorical leverage of opposing the difference of queerness to the sameness of reproduction. Just as reproductive futurism disavows the sameness involved in its reproduction, so Edelman transposes the sameness that is associated with the queer into the 'abjectified difference' that he suggests queers should inhabit. If paradox is a figure for sameness, for the *structural* interimplication of futurism and queerness, Edelman none the less has to introduce a *rhetorical* difference, only explicitly inviting queers to identify under the banner of 'abjectified difference': they must retain the rhetorical glamour, the continuing palatability, of the exceptional.

For Edelman, then, sameness has a number of functions. He does not reject reproduction in any simple way, in that he acknowledges how queerness is implicated in futurism's processes of self-conservation, but the very structure of his argumentation frequently relies on the assumption that sameness in the form of Imaginary identifications, identity and the successful reproduction of social form is an impossibility because of the apparently inarguable fact of signification. Suggesting that futurism and queerness are structurally non-oppositional, he none the less encourages queers to embrace a position of radical difference from the deference to temporality that marks futurism. In so far as part of the problem Edelman identifies with futurism is the projective dynamic whereby it seeks to constantly create demonised figures through which to localise its own investment in the sameness of reproduction, in order to enable it to distance itself from this sameness, it is perhaps curious that Edelman would seek similarly to project a stultifying sameness on to futurism and a radically disintegrative difference on to queers. The result is that anything that 'reproduces' a set of values, or invests in the continuity of social form, is imagined as counter to the fully disintegrative energy that is supposed to attach to queers. If you aren't being properly queer, then you're participating in a mystifying fantasy of consolation in the face of the gaping maw of the Real.

Is there any way to refuse the notion that it is the reproduction in reproductive futurism that is the problem? As discussed briefly above, a number of recent scholars have addressed forms of semiotic and social reproduction that do not have the logical relation to heteronormativity that Edelman imagines all reproduction to have. Valerie Rohy, for example, is clearer than Edelman on the idea that nothing escapes the imperative of reproduction. For Rohy (2012: 108, original italics), as we have seen, the opposition between queers and reproduction does not hold because homosexuality also constitutes a *'form of reproduction'*, albeit an 'unnatural' one. That is, within anti-gay rhetoric the opposition to queers as non-reproductive takes the form of a worry that they will increase: 'The charge that gays are too sterile thus expresses an opposite horror: *they are too fertile*': queers seek to increase through 'seduction, indoctrination, contagion, or recruitment' (ibid.: 107, original italics). However, Rohy also notes a fear of homosexual reproduction in pro-gay positions that seek to justify homosexuality with recourse to biological determinism (gay genes) or to the idea that queers are 'born gay' which suggest, for example, that if gay genes exist they will not be passed on by their non-reproductive gay carriers and, crucially, that homosexuals cannot reproduce semiotically because being gay is not a choice but rather is innate. In these apparently pro-gay positions homosexuals are rendered sterile in terms of both genes and social memes. Rather than having recourse to biological determinism, Rohy argues, we should target the homophobia that manifests in the worry about an increase in homosexuals, whether on the right or the left. What, Rohy asks, is so bad about homosexual reproduction? Moreover, she questions the anti-gay division between a natural heterosexual reproduction and the unnatural process of homosexual replication through recruitment in so far as this division denies the fact that heterosexuality also has to reproduce itself semiotically and 'ideologically' (ibid.: 123). 'In this sense, the essential falsehood is not the notion that queers replicate asexually, but that heterosexuals *do not*' (ibid., original italics). As Anca Parvulescu has also argued, drawing on a broader body of materialist feminist work, forms of reproduction are necessary for everyone. For Rohy, the problem to target is not reproduction per se, but, rather, the homophobia, whether on the right or the left, that finds the idea of an increase in homosexuals distasteful or problematic. The way in which Rohy develops the traditional queer opposition to reproduction allows us to disaggregate reproduction from what gets reproduced. For Rohy, homophobia is the problem, not reproduction. Reproduction does not need to be a problem, as long as what is reproduced is not a problem.

But in addition to biological, semiotic and social reproduction, there is arguably one more significant form of reproduction that it is consequential to address: we could call this 'metaphorical' reproduction. In much politically engaged scholarship, 'reproduction' is the most prevalent metaphor for evoking the continuation of pernicious or problematic social forces. We saw this above when Edelman claims that queers' refusal to embrace the negativity as which they are figured within reproductive futurism 'reproduces the triumph of narrative as the *allegorization* of irony' (2004: 26, original italics). We could look across a wide field of scholarship for similar usages. To take just one example, Sara Ahmed's most recent book on the everyday life of being a feminist frequently locates social problems in reproductive 'familiarity and repetition' (Ahmed 2017: 9). Coming to understand 'phenomena like racism and sexism' requires an interrogation of 'how they are reproduced, how they keep being reproduced' (ibid.). She writes on how humour can be used to dismiss those deemed humourless: 'But I think humor is such a crucial technique for reproducing inequality and injustice' (ibid.: 261). She writes on the racism and sexism of those who consider themselves progressive: 'I have called critical racism and critical sexism this: the racism and sexism reproduced by those who think of themselves as too critical to reproduce racism and sexism' (ibid.: 155). She writes on being based within an institution: 'To be complicit should not become its own reproductive logic: that all we can do is to reproduce the logics of the institutions that employ us' (ibid.: 263). It is only ever problematic social forces that are 'reproduced' or seek to reproduce themselves in this rhetoric. A tendency towards sameness is imputed to bad things and the work of good scholars is to intervene in reproduction, to stop things being the same. There is no accompanying sense that there might be progressive social forms, structures and worlds that we might also want, explicitly, to 'reproduce'. But as we saw Silvia Federici (2012: 12) claim earlier, 'a movement that does not learn to reproduce itself is not sustainable'. Minority populations and movements, arguably more than any, cannot cede the logic and rhetoric of reproduction when it is us who most acutely need structures to enable our maintenance and durability. Surely it is too much to allow bad things to have the monopoly on reproduction.

Reproduction line

Perhaps the most vivid imaginations of the centrality of reproduction to progressive and utopian worlds come in the form of fiction that has been about exactly this. Indeed, for representation that is less dismissive of reproduction, we arguably have to look to writing not governed by the protocols of engaged cultural studies or queer theoretical criticism. For example, the thought and fiction of Charlotte Perkins Gilman frequently imagine worlds structured around reproduction – imagined as a systematising process of replication – to be ones that encourage broad social progress and transcend forms of compulsory heterosexuality. As

I have argued elsewhere, Gilman's founding philosophy was one in which the rationalisation of reproduction would free women from the assumption that motherhood and child-rearing are their natural calling, assumptions which indentured them to compulsory heterosexuality and nuclear family units (Nichols 2019). The society Gilman imagines in *Herland*, for example, is organised almost solely around the creation of the next generation and the protection of the social good on its behalf, around reproduction, sociality and the reproduction of sociality. Herland is a nation exclusively of mothers: every one of them acknowledges the 'Crowing Office' (Gilman 1999a: 198) of reproduction and child-rearing. Motherhood to the Herlanders is a 'lode-star', the 'highest social service' and the 'sacrament of a lifetime' (ibid.: 222). They value their world primarily 'as a cultural environment for their children' (ibid.: 227). Children are the 'most precious part of the nation' (ibid.: 232). Gilman's case, then, it might be suggested, hardly provides any critical perspective on Edelman's account of reproduction.[3] I want to suggest, however, that by in some ways embodying Edelman's reproductive futurism, but also by showing how this is not necessarily in the service of a heterosexual order, Gilman is the first author I will address in this chapter to offer a counterpoint to Edelman's polemic. Far from upholding heteronormativity, turning reproduction into a production line for making more humans has a role in unpicking it.

Consequently, perhaps more significant than the importance assigned to reproduction is the Herlanders' understanding of its role in creating a kind of systematic uniformity. Reproduction in Herland is copying. The parthenogenetic, asexual mode of reproduction means that the Herlanders quite literally give birth to versions of themselves. Life in Herland is therefore 'just the long cycle of motherhood' (ibid.: 198) and this figure of the cycle encapsulates the circularity, repetition and sameness that also characterise the rest of Herland. The first woman to realise her parthenogenetic potential is revered as 'Queen-Priestess-Mother' in her lifetime (ibid.: 196). The five daughters she bears are hailed as 'Daughters of Maaia, Children of the Temple, Mothers of the Future' (ibid.: 195) and initiate a process defined by regularity: each of them goes on to bear five more daughters, who in turn bear five more. They are 'One family, all descended from one mother!' (ibid.: 196). Consequently, none of the inhabitants of Herland have surnames, which are markers of familial division or difference: 'Why should we,' one Herlander asks incredulously: 'We are all descended from a common source

– all one "family" in reality' (ibid.: 211). They are 'all moved by precisely the same feelings, to the same end' (ibid.: 168). They value similarity: the explorers' principal guide in Herland (her name is Somel) tells the story's narrator Van that they like him 'the best' because 'you seem more like us' (ibid.: 222). In *Herland*'s sequel, *With Her in Ourland*, the same Herlander recognises that they are an 'isolated homogenous people' (Gilman 1999b: 299). Theirs is a 'homogenous, well-ordered life' (ibid.: 363). The Herlanders even look the same. 'They all wore short hair', we are told (Gilman 1999a: 174), and 'nondescript clothes' (ibid.: 168). The women of Herland, it seems, do not need tight plaid shirts and moustaches to be 'clones'. Not just female, Terry complains that the Herlanders are 'Fe-Fe-Females' (ibid.: 215). The inexplicable stutter in this word which leads to the repetition in the locution seems to echo the principle of repetition on which Herland is based: a fe-fe-female is someone who seems to take reproduction too literally as a process of engineering uniformity.

This homogenous life is liable to seem excessively flat, rational and boring to some. One Herlander recognises that life in Herland might seem 'monotonous' when contrasted with the possibility in a two-sexed world of 'far greater movement, constant change' (ibid.: 260). There is no difference and no conflict based on class hierarchy in Herland. 'There were no adventures because there was nothing to fight' (ibid.: 189). They have 'no kings', 'no priests', 'no aristocracies', only 'sisters' (ibid.: 198). Van notes the prevalence of theatrical productions, which, as we saw in the last chapter, are themselves art-forms based on imitation, copying or reproduction, but that they take this relation to sameness a bit too seriously: the 'drama of the country' is 'rather flat' because of the absence of conflict (ibid.: 231). They have 'no theory of the essential opposition of good and evil' (ibid.: 233) and so life in Herland can only be boring and dull (like the coming out stories discussed in the Introduction).

Part of the problem in Herland is that it often seems that there is nothing more to achieve. Although the utopian genre is sometimes imagined to be forward-looking and so to be based on a teleological model of time, the worlds presented are often worlds of static perfection: worlds in which there is nothing to change, but only perfection to reproduce. Herland, as we have seen, is in a state of 'perfect' cultivation (ibid.: 159). The roads in Herland are 'perfect' (ibid.: 164, 184). 'Physiology, hygiene, sanitation, physical culture' have all been 'perfected' to effect the 'perfect' living conditions (ibid.: 208). They give their children the 'perfect' care and training (ibid.: 209). The clothes they wear are 'perfect' (ibid.: 215). The Herland civilisation is 'all-too-perfect' (ibid.: 246). As Terry complains, 'Here it's all done' (ibid.: 231): he prefers 'Something Doing' (ibid.). Whereas, for Edelman, the idea of an end to the constant differential movement of signification that would finally offer meaning present in itself is an impossibility, Gilman's utopias present worlds in which such stasis is achieved. Whilst some critics have tried to suggest a corrective to Edelman's anti-futurist polemic by arguing for the importance of utopian imaginings (Muñoz 2009), Gilman's utopian novels show that utopias themselves are static societies that do not need to idealise a future time because they have already achieved perfection.

Crucially, this stasis or flatness also manifests in the Herlanders' rationalisation of sexual life. They have no sense of sex-distinction or what the explorers feel to be its necessary erotic attraction. They have no sense that they should treat the male explorers differently: 'It's as if our being men was a minor incident' (Gilman 1999a: 174), says Jeff. Consequently, they are given the same clothes as the Herlanders to wear (ibid.: 171). Moreover, the Herlanders cannot imagine sex as anything other than blankly instrumental, as being for anything other than reproduction. Van tells Ellador that their approach seems 'practical' and '[p]rosaic', '[m]erely a means to an end!' when compared to the 'sweetest, highest consummation of mutual love' (ibid.: 263). Terry calls them '[s]exless, epicene, undeveloped neuters!' (ibid.: 266). But the Herlanders cannot understand why anyone would have sex when reproduction is not possible. Often, this rational mindset is contrasted with the 'personal' relations in the rest of the world. As Van relates, to the Herlanders the 'limitations of a wholly personal life were inconceivable' (ibid.: 230). To his chagrin, his wife Ellador will talk only in terms of '"[w]e" and "we" and "we"': it is 'hard to get her to be personal' (ibid.: 253).

If there is something akin to factory production about the impersonal reproduction in Herland, this is partly because the Herlanders are likened to factory workers. They are 'Conscious Makers of People' (ibid.: 205) and in order to do this efficiently they specialise child-culture, in the way that Gilman recommends in *Women and Economics*, as if it were any other industry seeking optimisation. That is, whilst it is expected that every woman will bear children – with the population increasing with geometric precision fivefold every generation – it is left to the best-qualified women to look after the children and ensure their development to a common standard. In *Herland*, people specialising in child-culture are likened to 'spinners and weavers, farmers and gardeners, carpenters and masons' (ibid.). It is a line of work like any other. Following Rohy, we could describe the reproduction in Herland as a form of both semiotic and genetic reproduction: the transmission of ideas to ensure the continuity of certain ways of thinking as well as of genetic material. In Gilman's earlier utopian novel *Moving the Mountain*, this process of 'far more efficient motherhood' is called 'Humaniculture' and is practised only by those certified by the 'Department of Child Culture' (Gilman 1999c: 76). They must look for efficient ways to achieve the 'lateral transmission' (ibid.: 101) of social information. They do this by making learning 'ceaseless and unconscious' such that the children grow up 'among such carefully chosen surroundings as made it impossible not to learn what was really necessary', 'gathering by imitation and asked instruction' (ibid.: 120). In *Herland*, too, the children are taught 'continuously but unconsciously' (Gilman 1999a: 228). This process of instruction means that the explorers are 'educated swiftly' in the ways of the country (ibid.: 176). The language is 'not hard to speak' and very 'easy to read and write' (ibid.: 175). Consequently, there is the 'same high level of intelligence' across the whole population (ibid.: 202): 'what one knew, all knew, to a very considerable extent' (ibid.).

Motherhood, reproduction and child-rearing are more like an integrated system rather than something left to the apparently natural instincts of women assigned a particular role within compulsory heterosexuality and the nuclear family. In *Herland*, reproduction is a matter not of personal gain but of collective social service. It is not the role of the mothers in Herland to obsessively defend and protect their own children, but rather to care for all children equally. All the Herlanders are 'co-mothers' (ibid.: 234). Motherhood is approached as more than a 'mere personal function', but is 'highest social service' (ibid.: 222). In Herland, they are 'a unit, a conscious group; they thought in terms of the community' (ibid.: 214). When Ellador visits Van's America, she says that women need to 'make a long jump' from the 'narrowest personal ties to the widest social relation' (Gilman 1999b: 374). A structure that encourages these personal relations is the proprietary family. Ellador again: Americans need 'to *think in terms of the community*' whereas now they 'only think in terms of the family' (ibid.: 336, original italics). Rather than in the family, or in its conventional domestic bastion (the home), care and support are everywhere in Herland: 'It was like reflected lighting instead of a lamp on the center table; it was like an evenly steam-heated house, instead of one with an open fire in each room' (ibid.: 327). Herland is the dramatisation of the system that Gilman recommends in *Women and Economics*, in which freeing women from their compulsory roles as mothers and wives within heterosexual nuclear families allows them greater freedom and facilitates a wide range of forms of social progress.

Gilman's interest in systems speaks to her Progressive Era context and the scientific management that was prevalent at the time. Katherine Fusco has recently provided an account of the progressive affordances of Gilman's interest in systems such as those promoted by Frederick Winslow Taylor. Fusco argues that, whereas for many Taylor's name is a byword for unacceptable systems of social control, for Gilman social standardisation offers a means of eliminating the wastefulness of sex differentiation. Consequently, Gilman's preference for a 'radical subjugation of people to systems' (Fusco 2009: 424) is a way of eliminating the sex-distinction that, for her, is attendant on individuality. Gilman is engaged in a project for the 'elimination of difference in the name of efficiency' (ibid.: 426); or, in other words, an embrace of efficiency for its elimination of sex differences. Gilman refuses the logic of contemporary labour laws that figured women as lesser persons by confining them to the role of mothers, but she does this, Fusco suggests, by making the mother the paradigmatic figure of efficiency. Turning motherhood into an efficient system of production is a way to make women central to the workplace. For Fusco, the subjugation of the Herlanders and others to a system of scientific management therefore has feminist consequences. But we can also push this further to suggest that Gilman's system of motherhood – the reproduction line of Herland – also has a role in denaturalising what might otherwise seem to be transcendently necessary: the institution of compulsory heterosexuality.

Whereas, following Edelman, we might be inclined to view compulsory heterosexuality as a kind of instrumentalism, in so far as it justifies itself by the fact that it leads to something (children), Gilman's instrumentalisation of reproduction actually has a role in unpicking the institution of heterosexual marriage. The same cool rationality is applied across the country: deciding what is allowed to remain in Herland is a matter of ascertaining its usefulness. When the explorers tell the Herlanders about the dogs that they keep in America, the Herlanders want to know if they are 'useful' (Gilman 1999a: 190). The men say that they 'don't keep dogs for their *usefulness*. The dog is "the friend of man," we say – we love them' (ibid., original italics). The idea of utility carried through to relationships apparently meant to be based only on love is alien to the explorers, but central to the Herlanders. They want to teach the explorers only what is 'useful' (ibid.: 188). They dress the way they do only because it is 'always useful' (ibid.: 216). This emphasis on utility is as strange to the explorers as the Herlanders' sense that sex can only ever be for reproduction. Whereas, in the previous chapter on aestheticism, usefulness was imagined to get its value from its relation to difference, for Gilman it is a way of reducing individual difference. Gilman's emphasis on usefulness makes people into instruments in the social machine. It has a cool rationality and a de-individualising quality that makes the male explorers baulk. Indeed, usefulness was a motivating force throughout Gilman's life. In the final chapter of her autobiography, as justification for her suicide, she writes that 'when all usefulness is over, when one is assured of unavoidable and imminent death, it is the simplest of human rights to choose a quick and easy death in place of a slow and horrible one' (Gilman 2011: 333). She would rather be dead than useless. Even Gilman's fiction, which is not expository but imaginative writing, has an instrumental function: it is didactic and transformational rather than literary. As she writes in her autobiography, her intention in writing was 'to express the idea with clearness and vivacity, so that it might be apprehended with ease and pleasure' (ibid.: 284–5). Similarly Nellie, in *Moving the Mountain*, imagines that 'Literature is the most useful of the arts – the most perfect medium for the transfer of ideas' (Gilman 1999c: 116). For Gilman, literature plays a role in the kind of efficient social reproduction that we also see the Herlanders perfect through their system of motherhood and child-rearing.

In Gilman's utopian thought and fiction, then, worlds that orient themselves around reproduction become worlds also defined by sameness. This is, of course, not to contradict anything in Lee Edelman's account of reproductive futurism, in which he also strongly associates reproduction with a 'tenacious will to sameness'. But, following Rohy, we can see the problem not as reproduction itself but rather as the socially dominant institution of heterosexuality that has taken reproduction as its own. That is, we can try to disaggregate reproduction from the problematic social forces that can attend it. Fairly soon after their arrival in Herland, one of the male explorers attempts to describe the situation in the America from which he has come. He explains to the Herlanders that poverty often leads to increased reproduction and consequently to a decrease in living standards and prosperity. 'Reproduction is in inverse proportion to individuation' (Gilman 1999a: 200) is his sociological mantra. This neat formula is a way of associating a certain socio-economic class with sameness out of control, a dehumanising need to breed, a compulsive fecundity. It is intended to differentiate the rationalised reproduction of Herland from the thoughtless breeding that is imagined as the scourge of the American underclass. Ultimately, though, it describes the state of affairs in Herland too. In so far as individuation implies difference, reproduction is indeed in inverse proportion to it. As with Edelman, reproduction involves a 'tenacious will to sameness' but actually taking the sameness and systematicity in reproduction seriously becomes a way, paradoxically, of refusing the claim of the institution of heterosexuality.

Fe-fe-females

Whilst I do not intend to draw direct lines of influence between the authors, many of Gilman's concerns return in lesbian feminist speculative thought from later in the twentieth century. For example, the distinction that Gilman draws between reproduction as, on the one hand, the continuation of life and social forms, and, on the other, the shibboleth of an oppressive social institution (i.e. heteronormativity), is one that, as I will discuss below, we see in separatist fiction and discourse. While some scholars have debated Gilman's lesbianism or queerness, others are less equivocal: Val Gough (1995: 197) writes that the 'Herlanders are clearly lesbians as conceived by the utopian separatist lesbianism of the late 1970s'. But whether or not we decide to call Gilman's vision a lesbian one, we can certainly link her with later speculative fiction writers and imagine her as part of a tradition of thinking about same-sex communities and their links with other forms of socially valuable sameness.[4] In this section, I will explore four novels that take different approaches to imagining women-only worlds, but that share many of Gilman's concerns: Joanna Russ's *The Female Man* (1975), Sally Miller Gearhart's *The Wanderground* (1978), Suzy McKee Charnas's *Motherlines* (1979) and Nicola Griffith's *Ammonite* (1993). All of these novels present worlds that are structured around forms of reproduction. On the one hand, this is biological: all the worlds imagine a way for women to create more of themselves through technological or biological innovations, like cloning or parthenogenesis. On the other hand, forms of social reproduction are also key: particularly in *The Wanderground* and *Ammonite* the worlds are built around ritual rememberings or involve the collective sharing of memories and knowledge across vast distances of time. The novels demonstrate the crucial role of sameness in separatist lesbian feminist imaginations: that an awareness of what we should reproduce is as important as convictions about what we should not. Certainly, deciding on a set of values that are without problem is a difficult task. Arguably this is a factor in why dystopia is more popular than utopia in speculative feminist fiction today. Nevertheless, to stand any chance at all, minority movements and causes do need to reproduce their structures and values. Compulsory heterosexuality does not have the monopoly on reproduction, but to make sure this remains true, as these novels recognise, we need to make sure that non-heterosexual worlds also reproduce themselves.

Arguably it is *Ammonite* that has the ambition to get at a new form of reproduction most clearly at its centre. The novel is the story of Marghe, a woman whose primary motivation is to uncover the 'reproductive secret' (Griffith 1993: 21) and 'reproductive puzzle' (ibid.: 46) of the planet colloquially known as Jeep. The planet has been identified by the anonymous 'Company' as potentially rich in lucrative natural resources, but the problem is that the planet is also home to a virus that kills nearly all men. Marghe is nominally there to test out the viability of a vaccine, but is more personally invested in finding out how the women on Jeep are able to reproduce (which they do) without men. It eventually becomes clear that the virus is what allows the women to do this: it 'integrates with human cell DNA, a bit like a retrovirus' (ibid.: 48–9) and gives them the ability to control their autonomic nervous systems and stimulate their own bodies' reproductive capacities. As Marghe thinks, when she is fully exposed to it: 'The virus lived in [her body] now, in every pore, in every cell, every blood vessel and organ' (ibid.: 250). Like other viruses, it replicates through the cells of human bodies and its role in the novel is to associate reproduction with viral replication.[5] Moreover, some of the women and their daughters are biological replicants: like 'identical twins' (ibid.: 118). The ammonite that gives the novel its title becomes a symbol of Marghe's induction into the reproductive ways of Jeep. After forgoing her vaccine and allowing the virus into her body, Marghe is visited by her mother (who was, as Marghe is now, an anthropologist), who hands her the ammonite explaining that the word ammonite comes from the name *Amun*, the Theban god who became the 'complete one' after he 'acquired the power of fertility formerly invested in Min, the ancient Egyptian god of reproduction' (ibid.: 258). Marghe herself takes on the name 'Marghe Amun' (ibid.: 259): the name and the symbol of the ammonite show that it is through becoming part of this means of reproduction that Marghe herself becomes fully integrated in a replicating system.

Some of the other novels are more emphatic about the sameness that emerges in the populations of women because of the means of reproduction that they have developed. In *Motherlines*, for example, the Riding Women are organised into biological lines of identical sisters; each line ultimately stems from one mother. They are effectively groups of clones. Alldera, the woman who escapes from captivity in the Holdfast at the beginning of the novel, is inducted into the ways of the Women and is at first surprised to see them walking around camp in 'identical pairs, trios, or even more' (Charnas 1981: 48). They are 'lean replica[s]' (ibid.: 20) of each other: 'women who looked like older and younger versions of each other' (ibid.: 48). Within each motherline traits are 'repeated from individual to individual and from generation to generation' (ibid.: 55). They have 'identically patterned minds and bodies' (ibid.: 239). In *The Female Man* the regularity that emerges in the all-female population of the world of Whileaway comes from the highly regularised process of child-rearing: at five years old all children are removed from their mothers and gradually assimilated into the workforce. Their training is largely in 'how to run machines' (Russ 2010: 50), they learn 'gymnastics and mechanics' (ibid.), they 'run routine machinery' (ibid.: 51) and 'fix machinery' (ibid.). This exposure to the regularity of machines also influences the regularity that emerges in the population. The Whileawayans are 'impenetrably formulaic' (ibid.: 31): there is considerably less variation among them than in the other worlds the novel represents. As Whileawayan Janet Evason explains: 'we are not only smarter on the average but there is much less spread on either side of the average' (ibid.: 141). But this sameness adds to social cohesion: it 'helps our living together,' Janet explains (ibid.). In *Herland*, as we have seen, the regularity in the population emerges similarly though both biological and social replication.

The grip that sameness has on these novels' imaginative worlds also carries through to historical accounts of lesbian separatism. For example, the historian Greta Rensenbrink has discussed at length and in detail how lesbian separatists in America in the 1970s and 1980s were often drawn to the idea of parthenogenesis – the process of asexual self-copying – for the promise it offered of establishing and perpetuating a world without men. Rensenbrink surveys pro-parthenogenetic commentary in lesbian separatist periodicals such as *off our backs* (1970–2008), *Amazon Quarterly* (1972–75), *DYKE* (1975–79) and *Tribad* (1977–79). However, she focuses in particular on a newsletter called *Daughter Visions* (1981), devoted entirely to exploring and sharing ideas about the possibility of parthenogenesis. As well as debating scientific methods for the actual physical achievement of asexual reproduction, Rensenbrink suggests, the contributors to *Daughter Visions* were also often attached to this idea for the imaginative possibilities that it offered of a strong and continuing women's culture (Rensenbrink 2010). Other historians have noted the significance of imaginative literature to building a picture of a world brought about by parthenogenesis. Dana Shugar (1995: 121–86), for example, devotes a chapter of her account of mid-century American lesbian separatism to discussing the novels that I also discuss in this chapter: *The Wanderground* (1979) and *Motherlines* (1978), which both imagine innovations in human reproduction as crucial to the conceptualisation of utopian women's communities. These novels and the lesbian separatist thought behind them help to show the urgency of keeping things the same when what has been established (the conditions that are to be reproduced) is designed to ward off injury. In *Motherlines*, the men who would upset the regularity of the Riding Women, the 'long and slow and repetitive' rhythms of their lives (Charnas 1981: 40), are presented clearly as 'world killers', 'desert makers', 'torturers and thieves by nature' (ibid.: 8). In *The Wanderground*, the risk that men pose is rape. This becomes particularly apparent in the long chapter set in the 'Remember Rooms' where the Hill Women's collective memories are honoured and re-experienced. They remember 'Cunt Hunts': 'small bands of men, usually three or four at most, packed up what gear they would need and set out for the day or the weekend to see what womanflesh they could find in the hills' (Gearhart 1984: 160). This threat is also made palpable in *Herland* though the character of Terry, who is ultimately expelled for raping his Herlandian partner.

Given the reality of these threats, the novels also share an attachment to the feasibility of the means of reproduction that they explore. Many of the novels share an interest in the practical explanation of the empirical means through which the method of reproduction they explore is achieved. The effect of this is to make it seem as if these methods are possible – that the apparent necessity of heterosexual sex for human reproduction can be questioned. In *Ammonite*, for example, reproduction amongst the journeywomen is witnessed and described by Marghe in terms taken from biological science. During the 'deepsearch' that she shares with her lover Thenike, Marghe 'sees' the virus running through Thenike's DNA like an 'electrum thread' (Griffith 1993: 260) which, once plucked, causes reproductive cells to divide:

> She reached out again, and the thrumming electrum strand that was the virus coiled and flexed and the cell divided. Marghe searched her memory of those long-ago biology lessons: mitosis. But altered, tightly controlled and compressed by the snaking virus until it resembled a truncated meiosis. Chromosomes began their stately dance, pairing and parting, chromatids joining and breaking again at their chiasmata, each with slightly rearranged genetic material. But the chromatids did not then separate again and migrate to the cellular poles in a second anaphase, they replicated: this daughter would be diploid, able to have her own daughter. (ibid.: 267–8)

As the reference to biology lessons and the technical vocabulary make clear, this form of reproduction takes place in relation to empirically verified scientific accounts of the process of human reproduction. The effect is to make a different way of reproducing seem genuinely possible, while undermining the necessity of the existing account of how human biology works, to corroborate a sense articulated earlier in the novel that Jeep is 'a place where the human template of dual sexes had been torn to shreds and thrown away' (ibid.: 60).

There is a distinction that this fiction draws, then, between reproduction as, on the one hand, the continuation of life and social forms, and, on the other, the imprimatur of an oppressive social institution (i.e. heteronormativity). Rensenbrink (2010) also finds this distinction in the commentary and correspondence associated with *Daughter Visions*. It was important for the women writing in and to this periodical that the process of cell division that is the basis for reproduction be distinguished from the meeting of male sperm and female ovum: this was the scientific rationale behind women's faith in discovering methods by which cells could be made to divide without men. Other commentators and periodicals put forward similar positions. For example, in 'Radical

Reproduction: X without Y' Laurel Galana (1975: 130) surveys the then recent scientific research on forms of reproduction without men including 'gynogenesis' where an external stimulant is required to make an egg cell reproduce as well as parthenogenesis where the egg cell requires no external stimulant to make this happen. The article discusses experiments that have proved that these forms of reproduction are possible in toads and frogs and other animals (ibid.: 128, 131) and generally has a tone of scientific practicality about it, employing diagrams (ibid.: 127) and drawing repeatedly on the accounts of scientific experts. These forms of reproduction are very much presented within the realms of empirical reality, with a scientific realism whose explanatory power is that it doesn't depart entirely from established knowledge. This is key for showing that reproduction can be scientifically conquered: that it has no necessary, natural transcendent relation to a heteropatriarchy that marginalises and subjugates women. These accounts make reproduction seem like a technical and explicable system, rather a natural or transcendent necessity.

Moreover, these novels often denaturalise the link between reproduction and heterosexuality by explicitly associating procreation with lesbian intimacy. In *Herland*, it is affection between women that leads to reproduction: it is as the Herlanders become 'more and more mutually attached' (Gilman 1999a: 195) that they spontaneously conceive. Similarly the women associated with *Daughter Visions* imagined 'sensual connection and touching' to be crucial aspects of parthenogenetic conception (Rensenbrink 2010: 314). In *Ammonite*, it is through intimate 'linking' and 'deepsearching' that women on Jeep 'quicken together' (Griffith 1993: 133). It is only the most intense and intimate connections that allow the women to also share each other's genetic material. When Marghe and Thenike do this, the description is explosively orgasmic: they feel 'a fierce energy building between them, heating and shrinking, pulling them in, like a star about to go nova' (ibid.: 262). In *Motherlines*, the journeywomen use their horses' semen, not to provide genetic material but simply to stimulate the splitting of their ova in a form of gynogenesis. During a 'Gather' where the journeywomen ritualistically do this, a woman's 'sharemothers' – those with whom she will raise her child – lie with her 'to encourage and caress her so she would be moist and open to her stud' (Charnas 1981: 154). The broader effect of presenting reproduction as a technical and systematic process for generating sameness is to denaturalise the association between the gestation of human animals and the social institution of heterosexuality. This is carried through into the way in which these works present a closer relation between explicitly lesbian sex and intimacy and the stimulation of the process of replicating human genetic material.

Of course, *reproduction* can refer to more than just biological process. It is also needed in the realm of social knowledge to enable the maintenance and continuation of established ways of life. In *Herland*, as we saw above, education is as important as the biological means through which new life is created. The daughters who are born also undergo systematic training and socialisation so that the harmony of the land can be maintained. In *Ammonite*, the virus that enables the journeywomen to reproduce also links them into a long history of collective experiences and memories. While the journeywomen believe that the virus on Jeep enables them to reproduce, they also link it 'with their retention of languages and customs already dead a thousand years before they left Earth' (Griffith 1993: 122). The virus therefore does not only ensure its own biological reproduction through the infection of its host cells, but also acts as a form of collective memory that passes down culture and social information too. When Marghe is infected with the virus, she begins to know things she previously would have had no way of knowing and realises that she has access to memories that are not her own: 'suddenly she knew why the women of this world used ancient Greek words and Zapotec words and phrases from Gaelic; languages dead for hundreds of years' (ibid.: 293). The women of Jeep also trust their memories to characters known as 'viajeras': as Thenike, Marghe's lover and the viajera whose life we come to understand most fully, says: 'We travel and tell news, we sing songs and spin stories; we lead pattern singings and deepsearch, we heal broken bones and old resentments, but mostly we remember' (ibid.: 205). The world of the Hill Women in *The Wanderground* is ritualistically constructed around the need to remember and pass on memories. Similarly to the world of Jeep, the responsibility for remembering is entrusted to dedicated 'remember guides' who lead the women through the ritualistic rememberings that happen in the dedicated 'Remember Rooms', a quasi-religious and spiritual centre for the Hill Women (Gearhart 1984: 138). All of the memories of the women are stored in the Remember Rooms, so that they do not lose understanding of what life was like before women escaped from the City to live peacefully in the Wanderground: 'Lest we forget how we came here' (ibid.: 23). The novel also draws a link between the various forms of reproduction, social and biological. At the Remember Rooms, the remember guides Alaka and Nova 'enwomb the entire group' (ibid.: 140) as they lead everyone through the collective memories. The novel therefore draws an equivalence between birthing as biological reproduction and the passing on of memories.

As in Gilman's worldview, reproduction in these novels is presented as a system rather than a natural necessity. For Gilman, applying a managerial rationality to human reproduction turns it into a manufacturing process rather than the bedrock of heteronormativity. In the later novels, the invention of new ways to create human life shows that heterosexuality is not as vital to the process as some might claim. In all of the novels, the reproductive systems create systematic uniformity. Biological reproduction is often imagined as a process of cloning. Social reproduction ensures that the worlds that are established stay the same through the passing on of social and cultural knowledge. Reproduction of all kinds is taken to involve the perpetuation of established lives and social forms. Running through all of these novels is the recognition that worlds where women can be safe require work to establish and maintain. This work of maintenance is precisely *not* in the service of a heterosexual order. On the contrary, it is in the service of safeguarding lesbian worlds. Moreover, the novels are not driven by the theoretical imperative to understand all forms of reproduction to be involved in upholding a privileged heterosexual order. The novels recognise, more than theoretical scholarship tends to, that it is not just bad things that need to reproduce themselves.

Genus homo

The theoretical co-ordinates that are most widely available to engaged scholars today have made the tendency towards sameness of the communities in these novels seem instantly politically suspect. Attachments to sameness can seem to preclude openness to transformation and attention to social differences and are more often imagined to characterise reactionary rather than progressive social forces. Certainly, the kind of second-wave feminism from which these novels emerged has been critiqued on the grounds that it has been focused on a narrow and insulated concept of women, separated from considerations of other social differences such as race, class and sexuality. While it is clear that there have been and are enduring fissures within feminism that centre on race and other social differences, there are none the less sources and moments in the history of feminism that help us challenge this narrative. In her Introduction to *For Lesbians Only: A Separatist Anthology* (1988), Sarah Lucia Hoagland challenges what she perceives to be a widespread assumption that lesbian separatism is structurally racist because it seeks separation from non-white men. Hoagland (1988: 8) quotes the separatist of colour Anna Lee: 'The ideology of separating from males is racist only if one accepts that males define ethnic community' (8). Moreover, recent scholars have sought to return to previously rejected or maligned aspects of queer culture to see what productive energies in the present they can help to stimulate or encourage. Elizabeth Freeman (2010: 62) neatly encapsulates one view of a certain kind of feminism when she evokes 'essentialized bodies, normative visions of women's sexuality, and single-issue identity politics that exclude people of color, the working class, and the transgendered'. Freeman seeks to unearth the unexamined radical affordances that may none the less exist within a feminism that also may involve all of these things. Unsurprisingly, of all the writers I address in this chapter, it is Gilman who is least influenced by the kinds of intersectional frameworks with which late twentieth-century engaged scholars are very familiar. For example, a key way in which she justifies her systematic and systematising form of reproduction is by suggesting that it has a role in improving racial stock, a position of hers which is accompanied by a broader belief in the eugenic perfectibility of humanity, and embroilment in various racial and nationalistic problematics. I do not have an interest in defending Gilman's politics, but I would like to examine how key scholarly accounts of Gilman and her racialised politics also rely on the kind of theoretical assumptions that guide, say, Lee Edelman. For some critics, as I will explore, all forms of reproduction represent a problematic attachment to homogenisation. But I want to explore how this has as much to do with certain expected critical protocols as with anything inherently reactionary about the idea of keeping things the same. Moreover, ceding reproduction entirely is to miss out on some of its importance affordances, and a blanket ban on all forms will not help us understand which ones result in consequential social exclusions or disempowerment.

    A number of scholars have noted Gilman's place in the context of early feminist discourses in America which often valorised women's role in motherhood and biological reproduction via racist, eugenicist and nationalist rhetorics.⁶ This has built on work that has read Gilman in relation to the racial panics of her time and the work of other scholars who have noted that Gilman's general social evolutionism — her insistence on a rhetoric of upward evolution in society — mires her in a language that is similarly racist.⁷ Gilman was only one of many early feminists to imagine that figuring women's role in reproduction as intrinsic to the success of 'the race' was a way to make them a part of an endeavour of public significance. As Gail Bederman (1995: 122), amongst others, notes, the rhetoric of women's importance in this endeavour was an 'explicit attempt to revise antifeminist ideologies of civilization by making women central to civilization'.⁸ However, whilst it may have been a tactic for women's emancipation, a way to insist on women's integral role in the success of 'the race', the rhetorics they employed appealed to popular racial nationalisms. Therefore, critics have come to associate Gilman with 'racism' (Hausman 1998: 503), 'nativist elitism' (Ganobcsik-Williams 1999: 23), 'white supremacism' (Bederman 1995: 122), '*maternalist racial nationalism*' (Weinbaum 2004: 62, original italics) and, most recently, 'eugenic reproduction' (Nadkarni 2014: 44).

Certainly critics are right to identify Gilman's racism, both throughout her career and across the genres of her writing. In *Herland*, as the male explorers observe, the women are 'of Aryan stock': 'They were "white," but somewhat darker than our northern races because of their constant exposure to sun and air' (Gilman 1999a: 193). It is specifically white values that the Herlanders uphold and perfectly reproduce, over and against what the visiting men identify as the 'savages' that live in the surrounding hills (ibid.: 227). By preventing apparently unfit mothers from reproducing, the women of Herland have also been able to 'train out, to breed out, when possible, the lowest types' (ibid.: 217), as the explorers' guide Somel gladly tells them. As Weinbaum (2004: 80) notes, 'Throughout *Herland* the ethos of purified reproduction is described in nationalist terms and Herlandian maternalism translated directly into racial nationalism'. Elsewhere in her writing Gilman imagines a programme of compulsory education and training not dissimilar to the one practised in *Herland* as a means to reintegrate an apparently errant African American population into the protocols of white bourgeois respectability (Gilman 1991). Not stopping at the black population, the world of *Moving the Mountain* has enacted a process of 'Compulsory Socialization' for all immigrants who come to America as a way of assimilating them to white American values (Gilman 1999c: 55). This brings a new and more sinister dimension to the idea of manufacturing people addressed above.

In elaborating these racial dynamics, however, critics have tended less to throw Gilman's work out entirely than to think about what her racial politics may have helped her to articulate. A number of scholars have drawn equivalences between race and gender to suggest that Gilman's interest in racial assimilation can be seen as of a piece with the breaking down of dichotomous gender identity. Alys Eve Weinbaum (2004: 100), for example, has suggested that it is through racial terms that Gilman is able to articulate a mode of queer desire in *Herland*: when the gender division, which is analogised to a racial division in the novel, between Van and Ellador seems to disappear is when they become intimate, such that the pairing cannot properly be conceived as a fully heterosexual one. Others such as Lisa Ganobcsik-Williams (1999: 24) and Louise Newman (1999: 136) have argued that it is Gilman's complete commitment to the erasure of all social barriers (between genders, races and classes) that leads to her interest in racial assimilation in so far as the possibility of eradicating racial differences through assimilation also provided hope for the possibility of eradicating the excessive sexual or gendered differences that Gilman imagined were holding back social progress.

Gilman's interest was in working towards ways of understanding human life as broader and more generic than the differences that seemed to define people. For example, in *Women and Economics*, her repeatedly articulated goal is to enable women to leave behind their emphatically gendered feminine roles in life and to become not women but human. The distinction she often draws here is between 'sex' and 'race'. 'Race' therefore provides Gilman with a vocabulary for articulating a broader structure within which individual differences are no longer significant: an impersonal structure in which one is no longer an individual with the markers of one's 'sex', but part of a race. In *Women and Economics*, the 'race' that she talks about is the human race: what she often refers to as 'genus homo' (Gilman 1998: 9, 11, 28). Of course, Gilman's 'homo' is the Latin not the Greek, 'human' not 'same', but through this phrase she nevertheless articulates a broad sameness or collectivity. Being 'undeniably over-sexed' (ibid.: 28) (too different) gets in the way of women's being properly 'homo' (the same). Gilman's distinction between 'sex' and 'race', then, is of a piece with other distinctions that she draws throughout her work and some of which we have seen. 'Sex' is associated with the personal, individual, various, non-reproductive, inefficient and gendered. 'Race' is associated with the social, collective, preservative, reproductive, organised and human.

Of course, to assume that a structure like 'race' as she articulates it could non-violently transcend human differences is a form of idealism that jars with the theoretical co-ordinates that underwrite most contemporary engaged cultural criticism. One thing that some critics seem to be reacting against in accounts of Gilman's racism is this kind of idealised sameness, which often enters their analyses most pertinently through the concept of reproduction. Alys Eve Weinbaum, for example, as we have seen, argues that a lot of Gilman's writing is based on an idealised image of a racial nation and a desire for a 'pure' genealogy of the perfected nation and its citizens (as in *Herland*). According to Weinbaum, the history of feminist scholarship on Gilman is similarly engaged in constructing a 'pure' genealogy for feminism by imagining Gilman as an ideal feminist foremother and not taking full account of her more problematic racial politics. What Weinbaum (2004: 65, 105) twice calls a 'truly liberatory' feminism needs to take account of processes of racialisation. Suggestively, the activity that she criticises amongst feminist critics is repeatedly described as 'reproduction'. A theory of feminism as originating in the intrinsic goodness of women is 'implicitly reproduced' by Gilman scholars who do not account for her racial politics (ibid.: 62). She intends to examine how such a theory of feminism is 'constructed and reproduced' (ibid.: 64). A 'Gilman publishing boom' in the years of the early twenty-first century perpetuates the 'reproduction' of this narrative of feminism (ibid.: 88). In place of this reproduction, Weinbaum seeks to intervene in this scholarly history as a means of making it, in the words of the animating figure for her study of transatlantic thought, 'wayward'. The effect of her rhetoric is to displace reproduction on to the feminist scholars from whom she distances herself. Whilst surely seeking to reproduce a 'truly liberatory' feminism, Weinbaum never figures herself in relation to reproduction. Her own critical enterprise is never described as requiring 'reproduction': it is only ever about intervening in reproduction, about reproduction becoming 'wayward'.

For Weinbaum, all reproduction is bad, caught up in the problematic logics of racism. In tracing what she calls the 'race/reproduction bind' (ibid.: 5) through modern transatlantic thought, she argues for the complete 'inextricability of the connection between race and reproduction': they are a 'conceptual unit' and cannot be 'analytically separated' (ibid.). Just as racism requires the fantasy that race is reproducible, so 'reproduction is a racialising force' (ibid.: 37). However, whilst it does seem to me that, as Weinbaum writes, the 'interconnected ideologies of racism, nationalism, and imperialism rest on the notion that race can be *reproduced*' (ibid.: 4, original italics), it seems less apparent that any form of reproduction will always be tied to a celebrated or anxiously defended racial formation, particularly, drawing on arguments I made above, where the form of reproduction in question is not biological. It seems possible to me that what will be reproduced will not always be questionable or undesirable: as I suggested previously, and as we learn from Silvia Federici, Weinbaum's 'truly liberatory feminism' needs mechanisms of reproduction to be successful. As other scholars have noted (such as Lisa Ganobcsik-Williams and Louise Newman above), Gilman's interest was in a world in which racial boundaries ceased to be effective, or in which reproduction could work to effect a standardised and homogenised 'race'. In itself, this idea of reproduction does not need to carry in it any particular racial formation: it can just as easily signal the dissolution of all particular racial formations into one that perhaps does not bear any relation to any one of those particular formations. The fact that Gilman's Herlanders are observed by the visiting men to be of 'Aryan stock' does not mean that attachments to reproduction as in Gilman's fiction will always and necessarily be so tied to such hegemonic formations. Moreover, as discussed above, there are many forms of reproduction – not all of them biological – which will have no discernible or logical relation to any racial formation at all.

In many ways, Weinbaum's theoretical co-ordinates are like Edelman's: like him, she is unable to embrace a reproduction that would run smoothly: the idea that 'racial "purity" can be reproduced is a ruse' (ibid.: 59). Just as in Edelman's argument the reproduction that reproductive futurism thinks it wants will always be disrupted by what queers are made to figure, so in Weinbaum the idea of reproduction being anything other than wayward is only ever, can only be, an impossibility, a 'ruse'. Asha Nadkarni's more recent account of Gilman's eugenic feminism is highly indebted to Weinbaum's earlier study. Nadkarni (2014: 210) argues for a feminist reading practice that is open to 'radical alterity' which would be 'non-eugenic, because non-reproductive'. Anything reproductive here is also problematically eugenic. Nadkarni's 'radical alterity' resembles the 'radical difference' as which Edelman calls on queers to understand themselves and it is no surprise that she also suggests that her account is in line with his (ibid.).

Although her analysis is not about how Gilman's racism is caught up in her maternalism, Susan Lanser performs similar critical moves. Lanser (1989: 423) reads the second-wave feminist consensus about 'The Yellow Wall-paper' that takes it as a 'universal woman's text' for the way in which it obscures the consideration of issues around other social differences, such as race. Lanser seeks to look at what it might mean to read the text in the context of the obsession with race and immigration at the time of its writing. She associates the abject colour yellow in the story with ideas like 'yellow peril', or the imagined takeover of American cities by immigrants. In the way that Jane in Gilman's story cannot abide the yellow of the wallpaper, feminist critics have, for Lanser, been unattuned to the racial overtones of Jane's disgust. Lanser's intervention is therefore into what she calls the 'reproduction' of the narrator's reliance on a universalised white womanhood: the repetition of this critical stance is repeatedly evoked as 'reproduction'. The feminist critics Lanser surveys are described as 'reproducing' the narrator's 'relentless pursuit of a single meaning on the wall' (ibid.: 420). Lanser highlights changes in feminist criticism to include women of colour and lesbians as the background for the period in which the standard feminist reading of the story was 'produced and reproduced' (ibid.: 423). Providing another celebratory feminist reading is again to 'reproduce the narrator's reading' (ibid.: 425). This reproduction, tellingly, is built on the 'repression of difference' (ibid.: 435). Notably, the 'good' reading practices that Lanser recommends are never described in terms of reproduction: they are not reproductions of the critics like Barbara Smith or Adrienne Rich whom she celebrates for bringing respectively race and lesbianism into academic feminism. Lanser herself admits only to having 'produced and perpetuated' the feminist reading of Gilman's story (ibid.: 420): she has never 'reproduced' it.

Reproduction helps to evoke an abject critical routine that must be intervened in: it is a very effective metaphor for describing perpetuation so as to implicitly critique it. There is something especially persuasive in the rhetorical energies that reproduction generates. To admit that there are reading practices that one may also want to reproduce (such as those of a 'truly liberatory' feminism) by emphatically relating them to forms of reproduction is to cede too much rhetorical force. In so far as reproduction – or making more of the same – is what is articulated as the principal problem, then the articulation of 'genus homo' can only ever be a problematic endeavour. But perhaps if we acknowledge that sameness per se need not be a problem, then the search for 'genus homo' in itself need not seem so bad after all, allowing us, perhaps, to focus more precisely on the causes and effects of social exclusion. I do not want to argue that Gilman's work is not racist or ethnocentric. Rather, I want to note the ways in which a concern with racism can get displaced on to a concern with reproduction. By dismissing all reproduction we lose sight of its necessity within progressive thought. We also arguably lose analytic purchase on what forms of reproduction can perpetuate racial disempowerment (such as racial eugenics), and those which do not have to (such as structures for maintaining progressive cultures and worlds).

Re-re-reproductive

In this chapter, then, we have seen the centrality of forms of reproduction – of maintaining both biological life and social forms – to the imaginative worlds of a number of lesbian feminist writers from across the twentieth century. A dominant view in contemporary queer theory is that reproduction is intrinsically linked to heteronormativity. But the authors I have addressed in this chapter refute this by presenting worlds structured around forms of reproduction which are none the less emphatically lesbian. More recent queer scholarship has begun to offer different accounts of reproduction, recognising that it can happen through signs and social forms as much as biology. The authors above also show this: they do not just effect innovative biological means to reproduce, but structure the worlds they imagine around social reproduction too. They therefore help to offer a counterpoint to queer theoretical accounts whose firm commitment to specific theoretical models leads them to dismiss all forms of reproduction. My own investment in my coherence to myself, in the continuation and stability of my own psyche, the work I do on a daily basis to persist in my own being: these do not necessarily uphold, support or propagate heteronormativity. The future I want is for myself, not for any Child, fantasmatic or historical.

It is only adhering in an unreconstructed way to the theoretical co-ordinates that we find in the work of someone like Lee Edelman – theoretical co-ordinates that take difference to be the only fundamental truth of the world – that all forms of reproduction can be imagined as the source of an intrinsically reactionary or misguided sameness. Scholars of twentieth-century race who have explored Gilman in particular also embrace a similar theoretical underpinning in which any form of reproduction – because it evokes a problematic sameness – is to be avoided. But although critics rely on the negative associations of reproduction to make clear what is wrong with the social institutions of heterosexuality and chauvinistic racial formations, there is no necessary connection between these entities. Or, to articulate the same point from the opposite direction: without the social institutions of heterosexuality that have built up around it, without the chauvinistic racial formations that can seek to continue through it, reproduction does not stand alone as a problem. Rejecting heterosexual privilege and racism are not necessarily reasons that we should oppose the sameness in reproduction. Indeed, if we do want to oppose homophobia, racism or other forms of social abjection and exclusion then perhaps we would do well to disaggregate these social forces from the idea of reproduction per se, and try not to forget that worlds without these forms of abjection also require efforts of reproduction.

Notes

1 Even those, such as José Esteban Muñoz (2009: 92) or Jack Halberstam (2005: 1), who have argued against Edelman's anti-futural arguments have none the less still opposed themselves to reproduction.
2 For scholarship that reads these texts, or a selection of them, together see: Freibert 1983; Fitting 1985; Bartkowski 1989; Shugar 1995
3 For an account of *Herland* that critiques it on the basis that it embodies Edelman's reproductive futurism see Evans 2014.
4 As some scholars have done, we could certainly chart the intense same-sex relationships that Gilman enjoyed throughout her life. These relationships took a variety of forms, from earliest childhood crushes (Etta Talcott (Gilman 2011: 18)), to sustained adult friendships (Martha Luther (Gilman 2011: 47)), to those with whom she enjoyed both erotic and affective connections (such as Adeline Knapp (Lane 1990: 158–81; Allen 2009: 51–57))
5 Given the context of the novel's publication in the early 1990s, it would be difficult not to think about HIV/AIDS in relation to the virus it represents.

In so far as the virus in *Ammonite* is crucial for the women on Jeep, one reading is that the novel undercuts prevalent homophobic accounts of HIV/AIDS.

6 See, for example, Berg 2002: 5, 23, 29; Newman 1999: 132–57; Seitler 2008: 175–98; Valverde 1992; Weinbaum 2004: 61–105
7 See, for example, Lanser 1989; Bederman 1995; Ganobcsik-Williams 1999; Hausman 1998.
8 For similar arguments see Berg 2002: 18; Newman 1999: 9–10; Seitler 2008: 183, 197.

3

Normative

Should it be especially noteworthy for queer theory that what has been credited with a major role in inventing certain forms of lesbian identity is a middle-brow novel? Historians and literary critics such as Jeffrey Weeks (1977: 101), Sonja Ruehl (1982), Alan Sinfield (1994: 3) and Laura Doan (2001: 1–30) have all argued that Radclyffe Hall's *The Well of Loneliness* (1928), and the furore that its obscenity trial caused, were central to making available a distinct modern English lesbian subjectivity.[1] The geographical reach of this identity beyond England meanwhile is borne out by testimony from lesbian lives. In *The Coming Out Stories*, for example, a number of contributors describe formative, if often aversive, encounters with the novel (Stanley and Wolfe 1980: 44, 116, 156, 200–1, 218). One of the contributors displays a more common preference that we see in the cultural history of sexuality for avant-gardes and outlaws, scorning *The Well* in favour of 'Genet and Gide' (ibid.: 116). Hall's novel, by contrast with these figures, sticks with a formal register that eschewed experimentation in favour of appeal to the middle-class mainstream. Moreover, despite its fame and central role in lesbian identity formation, *The Well* was far from singular during the period of its publication. It takes its place alongside a range of middle-brow novels which similarly present same-sex relations between women in an accessible, realist style: Rosamond Lehmann's *Dusty Answer* (1927), G. Sheila Donisthorpe's *Loveliest of Friends!* (1931), D.L. Loddon's *Do They Remember?* (1934), Mary Renault's *The Friendly Young Ladies* (1944) and Dorothy Bussy's *Olivia* (1949). Whilst their ideological positions vary, all of these novels present lesbian relations in a frank and distinctly ordinary register. Furthermore, some of the novels (some of the ones I deal with in more detail below) explicitly demand that their lesbian characters be seen as ordinary and normal.

In this chapter, I explore some of this 'lesbian middle-brow' writing, in order to investigate the hostility that queer theoretical work often aims at norms, normality, normativity and normalisation. For example, Hall's oeuvre includes a number of stories about queer characters who perpetuate the values of a dominant order even as this may sometimes seem to lead to their exclusion, isolation and misery. Both thematically and formally, then, Hall's work stands in tension with contemporary queer strategies and ambitions. To take only the most famous example, in *The Well*, Hall's (1994: 438) lesbian protagonist Stephen Gordon has an 'inherent respect of the normal' and spends the entire novel endeavouring to win acceptance within the terms of a dominant culture. She demonstrates an early deference to the heterosexual domestic bliss of her parents at Morton, her family's country seat in Worcestershire. She longs to be of useful war service when her nation needs her. She works hard not only for literary recognition but so she can be accepted as a useful and worthwhile contributor to society. At the end of the novel, she surrenders her lover Mary Llewelyn so that Mary can have a more normal and supposedly fulfilling life with Stephen's former suitor Martin Hallam. Stephen surrenders her own happiness because of her unshakeable belief in the correctness of dominant culture.

Heather Love has provided the most recent game-changing reading of *The Well* as part of her project to focus attention on what might seem useless or abject in the context of affirmative queer history and politics. As we have seen in the previous chapters, Love's project in *Feeling Backward* is to linger over queer representations of a wide range of negative affects as a way of restoring our attention to aspects of queer life that positive political strategies – which she associates with the politics of gay pride – may have obscured. Rather than dwelling only on what is recuperable or redeemable in the terms of our current political moment, queer scholars should attend to the 'specificity and density of the historical past' (Love 2007: 104), which, for queers, has often meant loss and pain. This, in turn, is imagined to help us tune in to the ongoing and enduring effects of marginalisation and exclusion. Integral to this project, *The Well* is addressed as a fiction 'singularly out of step with the discourse of gay pride' (ibid.: 100): the novel, Love argues, offers scenes of misery and trauma for Stephen that are unpalatable for modern readers, culminating in her abject display of deference to heterosexual norms in the surrender of her lover into the arms of a biological man. But rather than reject the novel, as previous readers have done, or seek to redeem it in some way by foregrounding its gestures towards a brighter picture, Love's position is that we should recognise that the negativity it represents may have something to say about the continuing effects of social exclusion. Love suggests that Stephen's misery might help us to see how not everything is necessarily great with our current situation.

Love's approach is explicitly anti-redemptive and has been an important counterpoint to many scholars who have attempted to make Hall's novel seem significant by distancing it from the dominant norms that in most ways it seems to support.[2] However, I want to highlight how Love's project achieves its own kinds of redemption through its citation of a queer scholarly tradition that has consistently repudiated norms and normalisation. That is, Love's reading of *The Well* is part of the broader project of *Feeling Backward* which is to resist the kinds of affirmative political projects that she repeatedly associates with the normalisation of gay life. Love critiques the 'rising tide of gay normalization' (ibid.: 10), praises Lee Edelman's *No Future* as the 'most important recent response [...] to gay normalization as a social phenomenon' (ibid.: 22) and suggests that surveying queer abjection is the best way of '[r]esisting the call of gay normalization' (ibid.: 30). For Love, as for others, the social phenomena now widely associated with 'gay normalization' — gay marriage, increased media visibility, corporatised gay prides — are problematic because of how they exclude the seemingly less palatable aspects of queer life. The 'politics of gay pride will only get us so far,' she argues (ibid.: 147), because of how Pride has 'become a code name for assimilation and for the commodification of gay and lesbian identity' (ibid.: 153). The combined forces of marriage, increased visibility and gay pride come together under the banners of 'normalization' and 'assimilation', which rather than making everyone the same actually facilitate social exclusion. At the same time, Love recognises *The Well*'s 'glorification of normative heterosexuality' (ibid.: 101), as well as Stephen's deference to 'masculinist, aristocratic, nationalist norms' (ibid.: 102), and her alliance 'with the values of the normal world' (ibid.: 104), but this does not affect the broader project of using the novel as part of an effort to resist gay 'normalization'. Ironically, Stephen Gordon's desire for normality comes to seem valuable in part as a means of resistance to contemporary forces of gay assimilation.

Such stances against the forces of normalisation and normativity are canonical and field-defining in queer theoretical writing. As Robyn Wiegman (2012: 339) has written recently, a decisive commitment to anti-normativity in queer theory is the 'primary political gesture of the field'. Opposing newly formulated manifestations of normativity continues to be a focus of contemporary queer scholarship: as I will detail below, chrononormativity, metronormativity and transgender normativity are all social forces recently added to the sights of queer work. But there have always been alternative visions within queer scholarship and no necessary reason that this anti-normative stance should have become so central. For example, Judith Butler's work has always been committed to the necessity of norms for providing meaningful shape to social life, even as these norms must remain open to re-signification and change. Scholars such as Biddy Martin (1997) and Susan Fraiman (2003) have insightfully highlighted the gendered politics of ordinariness, where queer work frequently genders its avant-garde anti-normative subject as male, and conservative ordinariness as female or feminist. Specifically literary scholars such as Karma Lochrie (2005), Julian Carter (2009) and Hugh Stevens (2010) have also highlighted queer subjects' insistent affective investments in ordinariness and normativity. Scholars such as Sharon Marcus (2007) and, more recently, Elizabeth English (2015) have shown the very plain and normal registers in which desire between women has entered English literary history, whether all over the culture of Victorian public life or in the pages of early twentieth-century genre fiction. Nevertheless, the greater part of queer theoretical work has followed a different trajectory in taking it as axiomatic that normativity, figured as a force of pernicious homogenisation, must be opposed at all costs.

In doing this, queer scholarship has taken up Michael Warner's (1993: xxvi) influential suggestion that queer work should oppose all 'regimes of the normal' in so far as heterosexuality inflects a wide variety of aspects of social conformity beyond the conventionally sexual. For Warner, opposing normativity in this way was an important means of making the study of sexuality integral to the study of all kinds of social phenomena. Such a universalising argument helped to define queer theory as its own field with its sights set not only on a sexual minority but on a range of assumptions and institutions that uphold sexual hierarchies. Warner gives the example of a state that devolves the care of its elderly to their children, which disadvantages those who do not procreate, a constituency still represented in the majority by lesbians and gay men (ibid.: xiv). Warner suggests that a narrower minority-ethnic model of scholarship focused on the direct treatment of queer people misses moments like this in which non-heterosexuals are deprivileged. However, across Warner's work we can trace how this argument about how a particular sexual formation ('heterosexuality') undergirds a wide array of what passes for normal life transforms into stark rhetorical lines in which the 'normal' and its cognate ideas have come to represent forms of conformism or conventionality which, we are to understand, are problematic *because* they are forms of conformism. There is a slippage in Warner's thinking, and arguably even more so in the work it has inspired, which moves from a recognition that a wide range of forms of social conformity uphold heterosexual values, to *any kind of conformity* upholds heterosexual values. No embodiment of a norm can escape its relation to what is politically and socially suspect, a rhetorical imperative driven, it seems to me, by the received scholarly wisdom that all forms of sameness are bad.

However, in recent work scholars have begun to question queer theory's anti-normative commitments. For example, in recognising, as quoted above, that anti-normativity is the 'primary political gesture' of queer studies, Robyn Wiegman has also sought to demonstrate how the field is, paradoxically, normalised by its commitment to anti-normativity. For Wiegman, demonstrating one's anti-normative credentials becomes a way of showing that one understands what it means to belong to the field of queer theory, but may not always work to desired queer political ends. More recently, Wiegman has also been at the centre of efforts to imagine what, in the title of a special issue of the journal *differences*, she and co-editor Elizabeth Wilson call a 'Queer Theory Without Antinormativity'. Contributors to this volume explore many subjects, including the queer theoretical misinterpretation of Foucauldian models of normativity (Wiegman and Wilson 2015; Jagose 2015), the socio-political complexities that a strong anti-normativity may obscure (Wiegman 2015) and the unacknowledged debt of queer studies to earlier sociological models that imagined homosexuality as an ordinary part of the social fabric (Love 2015). In a way, this special issue systematises an ambivalence towards strong anti-normativity that has threaded through earlier work by the queer scholars that I cited above. Yet I would add to these analyses an account of how far they too are driven by the specific protocols of engaged Anglophone criticism. Indeed, the title of

Wiegman and Wilson's Introduction to the *differences* special issue – 'Antinormativity's Queer Conventions' – makes it clear that part of their problem with anti-normativity is that it has become too samey or too much of a 'convention'. In her individual contribution, Wiegman also figures queer theory's commitment to anti-normativity in terms of *habit* (Wiegman 2015: 51), *limitation* and *impasse* (ibid.: 66). Here, anti-normativity is a problem because it constitutes a blockage or restraint: it threatens to keep queer theory too much the same.

My contribution to this debate is to suggest that, even if queer theory has been staunchly anti-normative, phenomena that one might associate precisely with the normative have none the less played a crucial role in queer history, particularly in making available certain kinds of queer identity. Hall, for example, was both instrumental in developing and publicising modern lesbian identity and firmly placed in middle-class culture and attached to conservative social values. In the early stages of her writing career, she published books of poetry that were staunchly anti-modernist in their adherence to traditional forms, strict metrical arrangements and sentimentally pastoral imagery. But her novels, too, embodied the kind of sometimes melodramatic realism which scholars have associated with the emergence in the early twentieth century of distinctly 'middle-brow' literary production marketed at a discerning mainstream. Indeed, as some critics have suggested, it is precisely the middle-brow appeal of Hall's writing that led to the furore of *The Well*'s obscenity trial in 1928. Had she been more high-brow or avant-garde, critics suggest, then Hall's presentation of inverted life might have gone unnoticed and arguably we would have very different accounts of the making of modern lesbian identity (Whitlock 1987).

Moreover, in terms of content, Hall's novels also frequently present lesbianism in a desired or accepting relation to normality. Stephen Gordon, for example, longs to be like everyone else, to have her desires respected and valued, and to imagine a world in which inverts like her are not excluded from the 'so-called normal': she is an assimilationist *avant la lettre*. She also longs to cultivate pride for herself and her partner Mary and even, at one early point, wants to marry her lover Angela Crossby (Hall 1994: 204). Pride and marriage, as we have seen and will see at various points below, are both aspects of the normativities that continue to be the principal antagonists of queer theoretical work. Whilst we can recognise the damage that a commitment to some of these ideas can do to a character like Stephen, we can also see that this damage does not lead Stephen to abandon any prospect at all of the 'normal'. The damage comes from the inability of the current configuration of the normal to accommodate Stephen's pride and desires for marriage, from arbitrary processes of social exclusion: from difference, not sameness. It is the affective toll of having to deal with such exclusion that is captured in Hall's earlier novel *The Unlit Lamp* (1924), which I discuss in more detail below. The novel offers a portrait of a person unable to bear the emotional upset of breaking with convention. Joan Ogden longs from an early age to escape her routinised life in the seaside town of Seabourne and the overbearing influence of her mother. She makes plans to study medicine at Cambridge and form a domestic partnership with her former governess Elizabeth Rodney in London, but neither of these plans comes to fruition because Joan feels that they would too much upset the status quo – the peaceful usualness or normality – of her life with her mother by the sea. When her mother dies, she finds another position as a carer for an elderly relative, creating for herself an almost identical situation.

But, as indicated above, Hall's work was not entirely singular in its presentation of desire between women. In the penultimate section below, I also turn to Mary Renault's *The Friendly Young Ladies* (1944) as a novel not only written by a recognised author of 'middle-brow' works but that frequently explicitly draws attention to the ordinariness of the same-sex female relationship of Leo Lane and Helen Vaughan, the ladies of the novel's title. Indeed, it is only the heterosexual characters in the novel who tend to grasp for images of the radicality of queerness. Building on work on the 'feminine middlebrow' (Humble 2001), alongside theoretical work that has examined how ordinariness and conventionality are often figured as feminine in apparently politically radical contexts (Martin 1997; Fraiman 2003), I suggest that we might also think in terms of the 'lesbian middle-brow', or a form of distinctly ordinary writing by women in which lesbian desire came into view in this period. Sticking to a framework that opposes the normal, the conventional and the ordinary arguably makes us miss out on a key moment, in terms of literary representation, when desire between women was expressed in a very ordinary fashion. The challenge that these novels offer, then, is manifold: they are distinctly ordinary in formal terms and yet have been instrumental in the history of queer identities, and, at the same time, they outline for us some of the legitimate reasons that queer people have had for wanting the relief of feeling normal and show us for whom an image of queers as exotic can sometimes be more satisfying.

The literary writers addressed in this chapter, I argue, offer various ways of putting pressure on the commitment to anti-normativity in queer theory and criticism. Despite the revelatory quality of Love's arguments in *Feeling Backward*, by using a novel like Hall's *The Well of Loneliness* in a project emphatically opposed to normalisation it would seem difficult for us to do justice to the 'specificity' and 'density' of Stephen's affectivity, which frequently takes the form of a longing for the normal. Moreover, the framework provided by queer theory does not do sufficient justice to the role of what might seem hopelessly normative in establishing specifically lesbian identities. Of course, queer theory has been uniquely damning about any form of identity whatsoever. Scholars such as Leo Bersani (1995) and David Halperin (2012) have examined how this anti-identitarianism embodies a subtle homophobia, a gay-aversiveness manifest in a preference for what seems to exceed sexual identity categories. Following scholars such as Biddy Martin and Susan Fraiman, we can arguably also see a specific aversiveness to women and femininity in this opposition to normativity. But, of course, queer theory's more urgent and explicit imperative has been to oppose sameness in all its forms. This is what has made anti-normativity so irresistible and so utterly definitional for queer scholarship. Driven by this imperative, queer theory has offered us a framework insensitive to the actual contours of queer history and a skewed understanding of what queer culture was, is and should be.

What do norms want?

Manifestations of normativity continue to be important antagonists for queer theoretical writing. Wiegman and Wilson (2015: 1) describe how queer scholars have opposed these in forms such as '[h]eteronormativity, homonormativity, whiteness, family values, marriage, monogamy, [and] Christmas'. But we could certainly add other forces to this list too. Elizabeth Freeman (2010: 3) has formulated the concept of 'chrononormativity': a name for the way that 'naked flesh is bound into socially meaningful embodiment through temporal regulation'. Similarly, Scott Herring (2010: 6), via Jack Halberstam, has elaborated the concept of 'metronormativity': the name he gives to the force of 'lesbian and gay metropolitan norms', 'compulsory forms of urbanization' in lesbian and gay lives, and what 'help[s] support, sustain, and standardize the idealizing geographies of post-Stonewall lesbian and gay urbanism' (ibid.: 16).³ Susan Stryker and Aren Aizura (2013: 4) have also more recently begun to explore what they call 'transgender normativity', formed, seemingly, by analogy with the earlier 'homonormativity', by which they mean a form of transgender subjectivity that accrues legitimacy by 'replicating many forms of racism, xenophobia, and class privilege'. Normativity, then, shows little sign of surrendering its position, within the collective queer imagination, as the name for what perpetuates undesirable forms of social exclusion.

This continued chronicling of the forms of normativity against which queer analysis should position itself of course owes something to Michael Warner's (1993: xxi, xxvi) influential formulation of 'heteronormativity' and his insistence that queerness should necessarily be figured in a relation of hostility to 'regimes of the normal'. Warner's early work was part of efforts in the 1990s to set a direction for queer theory, to outline some of the ways in which the new rubric that it offered was necessary and important. For Warner, the concept of 'heteronormativity' provided a means to describe how a wide range of social institutions are grounded in presumptive heterosexuality. Trying to forge viable lives for non-heterosexual people, then, was a matter not simply of asserting the validity of a sexual minority but of rethinking the defining institutions of social life: 'gender, the family, notions of individual freedom, the state, public speech, consumption and desire, nature and culture, maturation, reproductive politics, racial and national fantasy, class identity, truth and trust, censorship, intimate life and social display, terror and violence, health care, and deep cultural norms about the bearing of the body' (ibid.: xiii). The new embrace of 'queer' was valuable because it represented an 'aggressive impulse of generalization' (ibid.: xxvi), an opposition to a 'wide field of normalization' (ibid.: xxvi). The very 'critical edge' of queer came from 'defining itself against the normal' (ibid.). Warner's work, then, was crucial to universalising efforts in the early years of queer theorising that sought to give scholarly work on sexuality wide-ranging significance and validity. Warner's injunction to aggressively generalise is an invitation to think about where seemingly non-sexual aspects of social conformity uphold heteronormativity.

In his more recent work, the 'normal' has come to be represented by a smaller range of phenomena. In *The Trouble with Normal: Sex, Politics, and the Ethics of Queer Life* (1999), Warner makes clear that it is a particular brand of gay sexual conservatism that he identifies as the 'normal' of his title. In this later work, then, 'the normal' is associated not just with what upholds a hegemonic heterosexuality, but with a specific set of orthodoxies espoused by more mainstream gay voices. He seeks to combat conservatives' strategies of sexual shaming by asserting the importance of a publicly accessible and freely circulated culture of sex that, for him, promises to be of benefit to all in its dismantling of the assumptions that ground 'normal' culture. Warner's position is part of what is now a familiar opposition between 'lesbian and gay conservative' positions (broadly speaking in favour of normalisation) and those that might be designated 'queer radical' (broadly speaking in favour of the 'most radical and disruptive vision of queer life' (Robinson 2005: 89)). These lines of debate have become so familiar that they have their own chronicle in Paul Robinson's *Queer Wars: The New Gay Right and Its Critics* (2005). Robinson outlines the main tenets of this new gay conservatism, which include distancing the gay movement from its historical association with the left, from its historical association with gender nonconformity; and from its association with sexual permissiveness and promiscuity (ibid.: 2). There are also a few key political issues which have come to be seen as dominating the gay conservative agenda, like gay marriage (which we have already seen mentioned by Love) and the right of openly gay people to serve in the military, which 'signal the desire of gays to enter into the most traditional structures of our society' (ibid.: 6). There are particular phenomena, then, that the 'normal' of Warner's title names: for example, to name a few more, a sense that the political battles for gay people have been fought and homophobia superseded, the implicit critique of those who spend any part of their lives in the 'gay ghetto', and particular prescriptions about the value of monogamy and marriage which stigmatise public sex.

Perhaps more significantly, the normal has been associated strongly with forms of sameness. For Warner (1999: 75), those aligned with the normal seek to bring a form of limiting prescription to the 'diversity of what we call sexuality'. But for him sex should be taken to be 'as various as the people who have it' rather than 'tidy, normal, uniform' (ibid.: 35). Normalisation leads to stultifying 'conformity' (ibid.: 178) rather than encouraging the 'unpredictability of sexual variance' (ibid.: 218). For Warner, the 'embrace of normal' means having the will to 'blend, to have no visible difference and no conflict' (ibid.: 60). Herring (2010: 14) mobilises an equally suggestive rhetoric: 'metronormativity' enforces a set of values 'to which rural-identified queers must assimilate'; it describes the force of 'dominant versions of metropolitan queer stylistics' that 'often work internally to intimidate, to normalize, and to box queers into urbane habitus formations' (ibid.: 21); all must perish in its 'homogenizing wake' (ibid.: 22). Assimilation, normalisation, 'boxing in', homogenisation: it seems that a certain rhetorical authority is established by associating normalisation with sameness, even as the primary problem with it is that it creates exclusions, hierarchies and difference. The transition in the queer understanding of normativity is embodied in the prefixes that have come to be attached to it in queer work (metro-, chrono-, transgender-, even homo- (Duggan 2002)), which draw attention to conformism or assimilation, but not explicitly to how this is a problem because of the dominant sexual formation ('heterosexuality') that it takes for granted. Writing with Lauren Berlant, Warner has disputed the contention of, for example, Biddy Martin that their position is against all norms, ordinariness and averageness, reprising the argument that they are against these ideas only in so far as they uphold heteronormativity. But at the same time, they cannot conceive of any idea of the average that would not be a problem in this way: 'This deceptive appeal of the average remains heteronormative, measuring deviance from the mass' (Berlant and Warner 2003: 175). For them, there is no form of sameness ('average', 'mass') that could escape its relation to the dominance of heterosexuality. An arguably curious upshot of Warner's 'impulse of generalization' – particularly when generalisations assume a certain sameness or stability in what they point to – has been the dissemination of the idea that the proper domain of queerness is bringing difference to bear on the homogeneity of norms in all contexts and that what norms do is make things the same. There is a rhetorical satisfaction and appeal in figuring normalisation as a force of stultifying limitation that queerness as radical difference always opposes.

But it is this particular model of normalisation as something that can successfully be opposed which has come under scrutiny in recent efforts to rethink the defining anti-normativity of queer theory. For example, Wiegman and Wilson have drawn on Foucault to argue that normalisation is the radically inclusive medium of social life and so therefore cannot be escaped. For them, figuring norms in terms of 'domination, homogenization, [and] exclusion' (Wiegman and Wilson 2015: 2) achieves a certain kind of work in making norms seem clearly like what right-minded scholars should oppose. But norms actually operate through aggregation: they are achieved through taking account of *everybody* in a set. As they write, a 'norm is a wide-ranging, ever moving appraisal of the structure of a set; and this operation generates each of us in our particularity' (ibid.: 16). According to this understanding of normalisation, then, one cannot oppose norms because 'to stand against one part of a normative system would be to stand, comically, against oneself' (ibid.: 17). As Foucault (2003: 48) writes in his lectures about processes of normalisation given at the Collège de France in 1974–75, the 'invention of positive technologies of power' in the modern period has involved not 'rejection, exclusion, and so on' but rather 'inclusion, observation, the formation of knowledge, the multiplication of effects of power on the basis of the accumulation of observations and knowledge'. Crucially, then, he writes, partly ventriloquising George Canguilhem: '[t]he norm's function is not to exclude and reject. Rather, it is always linked to a positive technique of intervention and transformation, to a sort of normative project' (ibid.: 50). Normalisation is a pervasive force that structures all meaningful social interaction: it works by structuring all forms of life, not by selecting between those who are and are not normalised. Similarly, it is not something that can be opted out of or into: it is just non-negotiably the case, as the very medium of social life.

Wiegman and Wilson are not the only scholars to have formulated models of normativity and norms in which wholesale subversion or opposition becomes problematic. For example, in her contribution to the special issue, Annamarie Jagose details misunderstandings of Judith Butler's work which imagine Butler as licensing a model of anti-normativity that stands in full opposition to norms. Partly, Jagose argues, this is down to Butler's own account of subversion in certain parts of *Gender Trouble*, but to take only this version of normativity from Butler's work is to ignore her commitment to a more Foucauldian model of normalisation in which it is not possible to stand outside of all norms and all constraints but only to manipulate them strategically (Jagose 2015: 42–4). For Butler (2004a: 7), norms are crucial to any subject's self-understanding: 'One only determines "one's own" sense of gender to the extent that social norms exist that support and enable that act of claiming gender for oneself'. It is crucial for social survival, however, to expand the reach of those norms when they seem to shut down possibilities for life, to make use of the fact that norms are not fixed but mobile negotiations 'open to resignification' (ibid.: 27–8). As Butler (1997a: 99) puts it elsewhere, the fact of this instability enables the 'possibility of a re-embodying of the subjectivating norm that can redirect its normativity'. It is a similar understanding of the importance of norms that underwrites Biddy Martin's (1996: 69) critique of 'radical anti-normativity' in early queer formulations. For Martin, a staunch opposition to norms suggests that they are fixed and inevitable, whereas she wants to argue, as does Butler, that they are open to re-signification and change. Moreover, Martin notes how, in the context of early field-forming debates about the relation between feminism and queer theory, a radically anti-normative queer position is often figured in opposition to a feminism that is imagined as outdated and too closely tied to identity. Radical anti-normativity, Martin suggests, figures itself in opposition to the 'fixed ground or maternal swamp of woman-identification' (ibid.: 46), and associates itself with the fluidity of queer desire, figured in relation to the 'universality of man' (ibid.: 47). In other words, the evocation of norms as inevitably problematic is a rhetorical foil to make them seem 'stagnant and ensnaring' (ibid.: 46) in the face of a heroically mobile masculinised desire. Martin suggests that this need to stand apart from convention ignores the fact that queer scholars are also average people in the world, unavoidably attached to and imbricated with its material conditions.

However, I am less interested here in advancing any particular account of how norms operate empirically in the world than in thinking about the critical authority that is established through associating them with sameness. For example, in the chapter of her book *Object Lessons* in which she explores anti-normativity in queer theory, Wiegman investigates what blindnesses institutionalised queer studies needs to sustain in order to keep anti-normativity as the authentic sign of queerness. The particular example she gives is of her own investment in gender transitivity as the hallmark of non-normative queerness, which gives way, as she very effectively describes, under the realisation that transitivity cannot be sustained in any logical way as the mark of specifically queer gender. She shows that the move to claim gender transitivity for queerness is a way of demonstrating allegiance to a field, a way of satisfying an institutional demand, when that institutionalised field has imagined transitivity as its defining feature, a way of making use of the authority that comes from asking the questions that the field teaches us to ask, rather than a way of necessarily providing a queer-positive analysis. She writes that 'the critical authority derived from critique belongs not to the critic but to the questions she learns to hone' (Wiegman 2012: 318).

Wiegman and Wilson also address the self-licensing nature of queer theory's opposition to normativity. They argue that figuring norms in terms of *domination* and *exclusion* makes sure in advance that standing against norms 'becomes politically and critically irresistible' (Wiegman and Wilson 2015: 11) as these ideas appeal so strongly to commonsense notions about what is problematic. The title of the chapter of *Object Lessons* in which Wiegman explores anti-normativity in queer scholarship is 'The Vertigo of Critique', but what I would suggest gives queer critique its thrilling 'vertigo' is the compelling satisfaction it provides of opposing queer difference to a normative sameness. Wiegman (2012: 309) actually addresses this rhetorical satisfaction, as she mimes the thought processes that initially inspired her desire to write about the queerness of transitive gender: 'This tactic promised to let me share pleasure in the way that the queer pursuit of gender transitivity rendered heteronormativity and its dedication to dimorphic gender the monotonous height of monotonous sameness'. Hence, the rhetorical satisfaction of linking queer desire with mobile transitivity comes from opposing a caricatured sameness. And yet, in their own exploration of the character of norms, Wiegman and Wilson seek to make them seem more interesting or compelling by distancing them from this 'monotonous sameness'. They argue for a model of norms as radically inclusive of difference: for them, norms range over every person in a set, even as the contents of that set begin to shift and mutate, collecting this difference together to form an average. As they put it, 'we must keep in mind that what is "hetero" about them [norms] is not their insistence of the rule of two (man and woman; normal and abnormal), but their barely containable, ever mobile hetero-geneity' (Wiegman and Wilson 2015: 17). Rather than fixed and limiting, they argue, norms are dynamic and variable accounts of entire sets. There is no desire in Wiegman and Wilson's Introduction to think about why sameness is often imagined to be necessarily problematic. Although Wiegman and Wilson do recognise that figuring norms in a certain way is a means of generating authority, their account nevertheless suggests that norms become interesting only when their operation can be viewed in relation to difference.

In surveying this work on the position of normativity within queer theory, then, I've wanted to highlight what does not feature that strongly in the existing accounts: that it is sameness in particular that anti-normative positions take such satisfaction in opposing. Even those most concerned with interrogating the strong commitment to anti-normativity in queer theory, such as Wiegman and Wilson, seek to make norms interesting by associating them with difference. There is no sustained interrogation of how it is a taken-for-granted distaste for sameness specifically that gives authority to the rejection of norms. From this section, then, it should be clear that there are reservations that we might raise about the strong opposition to normativity simply from a reading of the theoretical scholarship. But I also want to go on to survey how literary writers can offer further ways of encouraging us to reconsider the opposition to normativity in queer theory. For one thing, novels such as Hall's dramatise the role of the normal and the ordinary in the invention of modern lesbian identity. But by looking at the work of early and mid-twentieth-century lesbian middle-brow writers, I am also keen to bring out how they encourage us to understand why some queers might see value in being the same as everyone else. At the same time, in the penultimate section below, I want to go on to foreground a connection that the work of these writers makes available between ordinariness, convention and desire between women.

'Inherent respect of the normal'

Aside from her role in the formation of modern lesbian identity, Hall also expressed a philosophy that, from our current perspective, we might be inclined to call assimilationist. *The Well*, for example, is Hall's call for inverts to be accepted in the same way as everyone else. Whilst the novel's protagonist Stephen Gordon is clearly differentiated by many, and seems to rail against the institutions of the 'so-called normal' that exclude her and make her feel worthless, the primary issue she has with these institutions is that she is forbidden access to them (Hall 1994: 303). As we will see, even though the forces of the 'so-called normal' world are damaging and harmful for Stephen, she remains deferent to that world: rather than resisting the 'normal', she resists exclusion from it. Richard Dellamora (2011: 213) reads the novel as an activist text that makes a case for the recognition of gay marriage and recognises the similarity that Hall's novel has to 'directions pursued at present in the gay and lesbian politics of liberal reform'. This 'liberal reform' agenda is the one that Warner criticises as the 'normal', that Love opposes as 'normalization' and that they both associate with social exclusions. For Hall in *The Well*, though, there is no necessary link between the normal and social marginalisation, it is only the extant arrangement of normal life that renders the world so difficult for her.

Of course, on the one hand, it cannot be denied that the novel works to set Stephen apart, to render her different or abnormal: a tragic case of non-coincidence with the dominant. Her friend Jonathan Brockett, for example, gladly exclaims that he has 'no doubt whatever' that she is 'abnormal' (Hall 1994: 242). But those around Stephen are not able to appreciate her 'abnormal[ity]' in the same campy way that Brockett does. Her queerness forces on her the kinds of social exclusion that lead to Stephen's isolation and alienation. Mrs Antrim thinks her 'very unusual, almost – well, almost a wee bit unnatural' (ibid.: 70). Stephen's neighbours, we learn, 'feared her': 'it was fear that aroused their antagonism. In her they instinctively sensed an outlaw' (ibid.: 108). Ralph Crossby calls Stephen a 'freak', and thinks her 'appalling': 'that sort of thing wants putting down at birth,' he declares (ibid.: 150). Even Angela, Stephen's lover, can jump on her abnormality as a means to discredit her: she calls her a 'pervert' and a 'degenerate creature' (ibid.: 200). Talking with Violet Antrim about her wedding to Alec Peacock, Stephen thinks with grievance about the 'pitiful thousands' who stand outside the reach of such 'blessing' (ibid.: 190). Stephen must fret that the conditions of the world she lives in are such that, for Mary, entering into a relationship with her would make Mary's life considerably more difficult. Stephen imagines telling her lover the 'cruel truth' of heterosexism: 'If you come to me, Mary, the world will abhor you, will persecute you, will call you unclean' (ibid.: 302).

Often, Stephen is able to channel a certain defiance in the face of this conservatism that targets her for disapproval and censure. Growing up at Morton, she dislikes the long formal dinners because they are 'firmly conservative in spirit, as conservative as the marriage service itself, and almost as insistent upon sex distinction' (ibid.: 75). Overwhelmed with Violet's wedding-talk, Stephen '[m]ust realize more clearly than ever, that love is only permissible to those who are cut in every respect to life's pattern; must feel like some ill-conditioned pariah, hiding her sores under lies and pretences' (ibid.: 190). She foams at what she perceives to be the hypocrisy of the world:

> Yes, it was trying to get her under, this world with its mighty self-satisfaction, with its smug rules of conduct, all made to be broken by those who strutted and preened themselves on being what they considered normal. [...] They sinned grossly; even vilely at times, like lustful beasts – but yet they were normal! (ibid.: 256)

This indignation that is born in Stephen, then, might make it seem as if she embraces the abnormality assigned to her. When she eventually makes the turn to her 'people', the invert community in Paris, out of 'her fear of isolation for Mary', she is 'made very welcome' because 'no bond is more binding than that of affliction' (ibid.: 360). In Paris, she thinks with stirring indignation that there are 'many another exactly like her in this very city, in every city; and they did not all live out crucified lives, denying their bodies, stultifying their brains, becoming the victims of their own frustrations': 'They had their passions like everyone else, and why not? They were surely entitled to their passions?' (ibid.: 302). All this doubtless makes her more open to Brockett's warning to 'be a bit careful of the so-called normal' (ibid.: 350), to distrust it and defy it.

But she embraces the community in Paris, not in any sense for its defiant queerness or for how it thwarts convention, but as a step towards achieving what she feels to be normal. Joining the community of inverts in the French capital is a step towards repairing her internalised sense that we see throughout the novel that she is a 'curious creature' (ibid.: 98), 'lonely and discontented' (ibid.: 99), a 'freak' (ibid.: 101), 'some kind of abomination' (ibid.: 152) and 'cursed' (ibid.: 217). The small set headed up by Valerie Seymour provides an environment in which everyone there can feel 'very normal and brave' (ibid.: 356). Seymour's strategy, which Stephen endorses, is that they should all feel self-worth and self-respect: 'they should all cultivate more pride, should learn to be proud of their isolation' (ibid.: 413). Contrary to Heather Love's antiredemptive approach to abjection, for Stephen and Valerie, and other characters, the only way to deal with their abjection is to make it good. This is Stephen's nurse Puddle, for example: 'For the sake of all the others who are like you, but less strong and less gifted perhaps, many of them, it's up to you to have the courage to make good' (ibid.: 208). It is only, paradoxically, as a concession to Mary's being a 'perfectly normal young woman', in Brockett's words, who 'can't live by love alone' (ibid.: 350), that Stephen consents to explore the 'garish and tragic night life of Paris' (ibid.: 384), as a means of finding Mary some company. It is, perhaps ironically, only Stephen's sense of 'sick misery at her own powerlessness to provide a more normal and complete existence' for Mary (ibid.: 384) that leads her to pursue a social life in the Paris subculture at all. At the same time as she indulges in this subculture, though, 'her vision stretched beyond to the day when happier folk would also accept her' (ibid.: 360).

Consequently, she is often disappointed with her friends' inability to embody the normality that she wants. She cannot decide, for example, whether her friend Jonathan Brockett 'attracted or repelled her'; she finds him 'curiously foolish and puerile' and feels a 'queer little sense of outrage creeping over her when she looked at his hands' (ibid.: 227–8). On Brockett's introducing Stephen to Valerie Seymour, Stephen observes that 'his voice took on the effeminate timbre that Stephen always hated and dreaded' (ibid.: 245). She is also annoyed that Valerie is interested in her, not because she is a 'decent human being with a will to work, with a well-trained brain, with what might some day become a fine talent, but rather because she was seeing before her all the outward stigmata of the abnormal' (ibid.: 247). Stephen's true distaste emerges in a famous scene at a bar called Alec's. Alec's is the 'meeting-place of the most miserable of all those who comprised the miserable army. That merciless, drug-dealing, death-dealing haunt to which flocked the battered remnants of men whom their fellow-men had at last stamped under; who, despised of the world, must despise themselves beyond all hope, it seemed, of salvation' (ibid.: 393). Stephen recoils from the 'haunted, tormented eyes of the invert' (ibid.).

However, Stephen's distaste for individuals also turns into a distaste for the situations into which they have been forced by an exclusionary normativity. For example, she decries the fact that because of her inversion the young Dickie West has been 'shut away from so many of the pleasures that belonged by right to every young creature' (ibid.: 412). 'But here, as in all the great cities of the world, they were isolated until they went under; until, in their ignorance and resentment, they turned to the only communal life that a world bent upon their destruction had left them; turned to the worst elements of their kind, to those who haunted the bars of Paris' (ibid.: 412–13). Stephen defers to the values of the society that she also blames for forcing inverts into this terrible 'communal life' in so far as she can only imagine being forced into it. She cannot see that there might be important pleasures in what it is that people get up to at Alec's:

> Bereft of all social dignity, of all social charts contrived for man's guidance, of the fellowship that by right divine should belong to each breathing, living creature; abhorred, spat upon, from their earliest days the prey to a ceaseless persecution, they were now even lower than their enemies knew, and more hopeless than the veriest dregs of creation. For since all that to many of them had seemed fine, a fine selfless and at times even noble

emotion, had been covered with shame, called unholy and vile, so gradually they themselves had sunk down to the level upon which the world placed their emotions. (ibid.: 393)

In some sense, it is a dramatisation of the positions we see today amongst lesbian and gay conservatives and queer radicals: conservatives decry 'ghettoisation' and the rituals of queer subcultural life in the same way that Stephen does. For Stephen, the 'shame' with which the denizens of Alec's have been covered is not in any sense, as it is for Love, to be embraced. But Stephen's despair is born of the fact that the prevailing social conditions will not allow inverts any place other than Alec's; she is not opposed to the idea of prevailing conditions per se. The phrase that is used to designate those conditions – the 'so-called normal' (ibid.: 303, 350) – indicates a distaste not for the normal but for an inauthentic 'so-called' version of it. What she criticises is an exclusionary version of the normal that does not allow people like her to participate. Indeed, when her feelings of exclusion are so dramatic ('abhorred', 'spat upon', 'unholy', 'vile'), it is perhaps not difficult to understand why she would seek for herself and others some relief from this disapproval.

Stephen therefore believes that she has to work hard to show her worthiness in the context of the values of the normal world. 'She had her work, work that cried out to be done [...]. She must show that being that thing she was, she could climb to success over all opposition' (ibid.: 255). Stephen longs for success within the terms of pre-existing norms. Adolphe Blanc is another figure who encourages Stephen's normalising endeavours. He is 'of all men the most normal abnormal' (ibid.: 355). He notices Stephen's discomfort in Alec's and agrees that the people there are 'terrible' because 'they are those who have fallen but not risen again' (ibid.: 394–5). Stephen, by contrast, has the power to change things: she has a duty to educate the 'so-called just and righteous' outside the walls of Alec's (ibid.: 395). Only the 'normal invert' can know the 'whole truth': 'The doctors cannot make the ignorant think, cannot hope to bring home the sufferings of millions; only one of ourselves can some day do that' (ibid.). Stephen takes this duty on board, 'I have faith in my writing, great faith; some day I shall climb to the top and that will compel the world to accept me for what I am. It's a matter of time, but I mean to succeed for Mary's sake' (ibid.: 433). Valerie Seymour, too, is very encouraging. She thinks Stephen has the 'nerves of the abnormal' combined with the 'respectable country instincts of the man who cultivates children and acres': 'But supposing you could bring the two sides of your nature into some sort of friendly amalgamation and compel them to serve you and through you your work – well then I really don't see what's to stop you' (ibid.: 414). If only the values of the normal could be made to incorporate Stephen's 'nerves of the abnormal' then this would obviate the drama of exclusion that she experiences.

Indeed, Stephen consistently upholds the values of the society she maligns, far more than she rails against them. She has, for example, a 'curious craving for the normal', unshaken by her exile from Morton after her mother finds out about her relationship with Angela Crossby, that leads her to write about 'quite simple people, humble people sprung from the soil, from the same kind of soil that had nurtured Morton' (ibid.: 213). When Martin Hallam comes back into her life, Stephen is glad to have 'the friendship of a normal and sympathetic man whose mentality being very much her own, was not only welcome but reassuring' (ibid.: 424). Stephen and Mary stop going to the Parisian bars so much, which Stephen had initially agreed to do as a concession to Mary's normality, because the 'thoroughly normal' Martin offers 'recreations that were really much more to Mary's liking' (ibid.: 424). Indeed, when her neighbours scorn her, she can partly see their point of view:

> The strange thing was that she understood her neighbours in a way, and was therefore too just to condemn them; indeed had nature been less daring with her, she might well have become very much what they were – a breeder of children, an upholder of home, a careful and diligent steward of pastures. There was little of the true pioneer about Stephen. (ibid.: 106–7)

Stephen acutely envies the people she sees in Lady Massey's copies of *The Tatler* and *The Sketch*, partly because of their reproductive credentials: 'in her heart she must envy these people. Must envy these commonplace men and women with their rather ridiculous shooting-sticks; their smiling fiancés; their husbands; their wives; their estates, and their well-cared-for, placid children' (ibid.: 373). Stephen admires the procreative heterosexuality of her servants:

> Adele and Jean, the simplicity of it [...] they loved, they married, and after a while they would care for each other all over again, renewing their youth and their love in their children. So orderly, placid and safe it seemed,

this social scheme evolved from creation; this guarding of two young and ardent lives for the sake of the lives that might follow after. (ibid.: 400)

She compares herself to the generations of Gordons who have lived at Morton before her: 'Surely never was [an] outlaw more law-abiding at heart than this, the last of the Gordons' (ibid.).

What gives Stephen one of her greatest feelings of normality though is her relationship with Mary. Mary is, of course, by all accounts, a 'perfectly normal young woman' (ibid.: 350). Martin Hallam's aunt takes a fancy to her as a girl she thinks 'excessively pretty' in contrast to the 'freakish and masterful-looking Stephen' (ibid.: 422). According to Martin, Mary's 'normality' is 'her danger' because she is 'all woman' and so less resilient than Stephen in the face of the demands of the normal world (ibid.: 431). He also believes he 'know[s] how she clung to what he could offer, how gladly she turned to the simple things that so easily come to those who are normal' (ibid.: 437–8). It is to give Mary a more 'normal' life that Stephen undertakes her own normalising endeavours, and then it is the very deference to normality that attracts her to Mary that also prompts her to give Mary up. It is the final price she pays for her 'inherent respect of the normal which nothing had ever been able to destroy' (ibid.: 438). She chooses to surrender Mary to Martin, who she feels can give her the 'perfect thing which she had divined in the love that existed between her parents': 'children, a home that the world would respect, ties of affection that the world would hold sacred, the blessed security and the peace of being released from the world's persecution' (ibid.).

At the end of *The Well*, after Stephen has severed her ties with Mary in the hope that her former lover will find more normal fulfilment with Martin Hallam, Stephen is confronted with a vision of apparitional inverts. The 'quick, the dead, and the yet unborn' alongside 'those lost and terrible brothers from Alec's' with 'marred and reproachful faces' all accuse her of failing them: 'you have taken our strength and have given us your weakness!' (ibid.: 446). The amassed inverts fault her for the deference to normality that has made her surrender Mary. Reading this scene, Love very powerfully evokes a parallel between Stephen's turning away from the other inverts and queer critics' rejection of Stephen because of her complicity with negative representations of queers: both Stephen and queer critics, Love argues, must come to an appreciation of their forebears' weaknesses. 'The miserable army reproaches Stephen for taking only the strength and not the weakness of these subjects' (Love 2007: 126). In this scene, though, Stephen is not (or is not only) in the position of the affirmative critic judging queer figures from the past for their failures to live up to the criteria of contemporary politics, but is rather the one who is herself chastised for giving the inverts *her* 'weakness'. She is the weak one here for having chosen normality. If, following Love, we refuse to refuse the weakness of queer figures from the past, then we must refuse to refuse Stephen's investment in normality. We must consequently refuse to insist that the only viable project within which to understand Hall's novel is one that opposes gay 'normalisation'.

'[H]itherto unsuspected respect for convention'

In Stephen Gordon, then, we see both the damage that deference to normality can do and the persistence of this deference in the face of such damage: we see that the normal world marginalises Stephen in some ways, but that she never surrenders the prospect of acceptance within its terms, which promise a sought-after and blissful 'release from the world's persecution'. Hall explores a similar dynamic in her earlier novel *The Unlit Lamp* (1924), in which convention is both deadening and apparently irresistible. Joan Ogden, the novel's central character, like Stephen Gordon, demonstrates a strong and unshakeable commitment to normality. Whilst this might be seen to manifest as her desire to establish some form of homonormative domestic arrangement with her former governess Elizabeth Rodney, which is akin to the normality that Stephen Gordon longs for in *The Well*, this normative coupling never comes off. This is due to Joan's more thorough deference to the normality that the relationship with Elizabeth would disrupt. She thinks of her plans to settle down with Elizabeth as '*unusual*': 'because it was unusual she had been embarrassed; a hitherto unsuspected respect for convention had assailed her' (Hall 1981: 247, original italics). Instead of breaking with convention, Joan continues to live with her demanding mother until, when her mother dies, as we have seen, she finds for herself an almost identical position caring for another elderly relative.

This is not to say, however, that she is not at all conflicted about this 'respect for convention'. Much of her time is spent railing against Seabourne, the small seaside town in which she has grown up, and the unambitious, small-minded and conventional people who live there. 'Centuries of custom, centuries of precedent! They pressed, they crushed, they suffocated. If you gave in to them you might venture to hope to live somehow, but if you opposed them you broke yourself to pieces against their iron flanks' (ibid.: 247). Indeed, in many ways she longs to get away from 'that monster tyrant: "the usual thing"' (ibid.). Seabourne is repeatedly figured as a monotonous and imprisoning force. For Joan's one-time love interest Elizabeth there is something about her brother's house in Seabourne that 'chained you, held you fast': 'They were velvet chains, they were plush chains, but they held' (ibid.: 41). She feels that by being in the house and in Seabourne she is allowing her life to be 'slowly and surely strangled to death': 'damn their tradition; another name for slavery, and excuse for keeping slaves!' (ibid.). Elizabeth's days in Seabourne had a 'dreadful monotony' (ibid.: 259). But such is the power of the chains that even Elizabeth feels drawn back there. Trying to live an independent life in London, she nevertheless hears a voice telling her to 'Go back, go back, go back! There is something sweeter than ambition' (ibid.: 179).

Seabourne is a place in which the days are 'colourless and flat' (ibid.: 103). In the years leading up to Joan's seventeenth birthday 'nothing occurred in the nature of a change': in Seabourne, 'she had grown accustomed to monotony, but the past two years seemed to have been more monotonous than usual' (ibid.: 115). The death of Colonel Ogden, Joan's father, gives way to 'years of monotonous uncertainty' (ibid.: 157). It is not a hopeful uncertainty: 'like everything else that came under the spell of the place, it was dull' (ibid.: 157). The seasons in Seabourne go by 'monotonously' (ibid.: 183). For Joan, after her final break from Elizabeth, Seabourne is a place in which the 'queer days succeeded each other like phantoms' (ibid.: 258). It is a place in which twenty-year-old aspects of the town are still 'spoken of as "New"' (ibid.: 265). It is 'always the same': the 'same dull streets, the same dull shops and the same monotony' (ibid.: 270). After being diagnosed with pneumonia Joan's sister Milly cannot bear the thought of having to stay at the family home, 'If she stayed at Leaside she was sure she *would* die, but not of consumption, of boredom!' (ibid.: 216, original italics).

In Joan's mind, however, the monotony of Seabourne is also tied up with the monotony she feels in relation to her mother. Mary Ogden has a 'fear of independence for Joan' (ibid.: 86). Joan experiences her mother both as a form of intolerable and burdensome sameness and as someone from whom she cannot stand the idea of being separated. In Joan's mind, Mrs Ogden, like Seabourne, is 'always the same' (ibid.: 141).

When Joan returns to Seabourne, Elizabeth tells her that her mother is 'just the same as usual' (ibid.: 145). After her husband's death, Mrs Ogden 'allowed herself to be a little monotonous' (ibid.: 172). But there is something in this sameness that attaches to the mother that Joan also cannot bear to leave: she tells Elizabeth that she 'can't bear to hurt things, especially things that seem to lean on me' (ibid.: 119).

> If she left her now it would be with the haunting knowledge of having left a woman who either would not or could not adapt herself to the changed circumstances; who would harbour a grievance to the end of her days. Her mother's very devotion was a weapon turned ruthlessly against her daughter, capable of robbing her of all peace of mind. (ibid.: 246)

As the novel progresses, it becomes clear that it is Joan too who cannot adapt to changed circumstances: 'Mrs. Ogden had become a habit now, and quite automatically Joan fetched and carried, and rubbed her chest and gave her her medicine; it was all in the day's work, one did it, like everything else in Seabourne, because it seemed the right thing and there was nothing else to do' (ibid.: 269). The final time that Joan is unable to bring herself to leave with Elizabeth, the reason she gives is that she cannot leave her mother: 'I can't leave her' (ibid.: 258). It is a move that makes her lose Elizabeth and all hope of ever breaking with the deadening normativity of Seabourne. It is the final replay of a recurring scenario in the novel. On her twenty-first birthday when Elizabeth gives Joan the lease to their flat in London, Joan still will not fully commit. Whilst she is adamant that she will leave Seabourne – 'I'm going before it's too late to go, before I get so deeply rooted that I can't free myself' (ibid.: 169) – Elizabeth recognises that there is something in Joan preventing her from moving on: 'You're quite free except in your own imagination, and your mother is not ill except in hers' (ibid.). 'You're the veriest self-deceiver, Joan! You think you're staying on here because you can't bring yourself to hurt your mother. It's not that at all; it's because you can't bear to hurt yourself in the process' (ibid.). *The Unlit Lamp*, then, in some sense emblematises Biddy Martin's suggestion we encountered above that stifling conformity and normativity are associated with the 'maternal swamp of woman identification'.

There are, however, influences in Joan's life that promise to help her escape the clutches of Seabourne. Joan herself is keen to leave the town and pursue medical studies at Cambridge. Several people around her encourage her ambitions. Richard Benson, the younger son of another

Seabourne family, for example, warns Joan not to let herself be 'bottled' by the town and its inhabitants, not to get 'all cramped up and fuggy' (ibid.: 60). Perhaps the keenest anti-Seabourne influence in her life, however, is Elizabeth, who repeatedly tries to persuade Joan to live with her in London, with initial success, but ultimate failure. Elizabeth believes in Joan's potential, telling Mrs. Benson that she's been 'fighting, fighting, fighting to get out, to be herself' (ibid.: 79):

> Joan's young and clever, and sensitive and dreadfully worth while. Surely she has a right to something in life beyond Seabourne and Mrs. Ogden? Joan has a right to love whom she likes, and to go where she likes and to work and be independent and happy, and if she can't be happy then she has a right to make her own unhappiness; it's a thousand times better to be unhappy in your own way than to be happy in someone else's. (ibid.: 80)

Joan's escape from the clutches of Seabourne is glossed here in terms of 'be[ing] herself' or of extracting herself from the homogenous morass of time spent in her home town. Joan 'ache[s] to get away; to leave the house and never set foot inside it again, to leave Seabourne and try to forget that such a place existed' (ibid.: 242). She goes so far as to argue with her mother: 'I can't go on living in Seabourne and never doing anything worth while all the rest of my life; you've no right to ask it of me!' (ibid.: 245). She thinks that she '*must* swim against the current; it was ridiculous, preposterous that because she did not marry she should be forced to live a crippled existence' (ibid.: 247, original italics). 'I've a right to my life, and I shall go in August. I defy precedent. I'm Joan Ogden, a law unto myself, and I mean to prove it' (ibid.: 248), she resolves to herself. 'I'm going to be free at last' (ibid.: 253), she thinks, as the date approaches for her to finally go up to Cambridge, aged twenty-three.

As ever, however, Joan's plans to leave Seabourne are sabotaged. Sometimes, it is external factors that jeopardise her plans (such as her father's investment of her inheritance in spent mines), but more often it is a conviction or imperative that comes from her which keeps her in Seabourne. Her triumphant chant as a twenty-three-year-old ('Freedom, freedom, freedom!' (ibid.: 253)), for example, is accompanied by 'something in her [that] shrank and weakened' (ibid.). Joan feels 'afraid' when she hears the news about the inheritance that will make her independent. When Joan's sister Milly falls ill, Elizabeth sees that this is another 'ready-made excuse' for Joan to stay in Seabourne (ibid.: 230). As the final time that Elizabeth tries to make Joan come away with her approaches, Joan can see that Elizabeth thinks she will 'go back' on her again: 'You won't mean to do that, but so many things happen don't they? I think I'm getting superstitious' (ibid.: 249).

Joan's ultimate fidelity, then, is to remaining the same and not defying precedent in the way that her domestic partnership with Elizabeth promises or threatens to. She is, in the apt phrase of one of the girls that Joan overhears in the hotel grounds when on holiday with her mother, a 'pioneer that's got left behind' (ibid.: 284). Rather than escaping with Elizabeth, Joan lives a life that she purports to hate: in close proximity to a dependent and draining mother. Even when her mother dies, Joan does not want her life to change: 'All this thinking was a terrible effort – if only she had had enough money to keep Leaside, she felt that she would never have left it. She would gladly have lived on there alone […]. After all, Seabourne was comfortably familiar, and in consequence easy. She shrank with nervous apprehension from any change' (ibid.: 309–10). She eventually ends up looking after her cousin Rupert at Blintcombe, his seaside home: 'In fact, it would be just Seabourne under a new name, with Cousin Rupert to take care of instead of her mother' (ibid.: 314). Despite her apparent regret about it – 'I was bottled, after all,' she says to Richard Benson when they unexpectedly meet (ibid.: 288) – Joan chooses the monotony that Seabourne represents. Rather than breaking free from 'that monster tyrant: "the usual thing"' (ibid.: 247), Joan installs herself in a near-identical house to Leaside, in a near-identical arrangement to the one she so hated with her mother.

What are we to make of Joan Ogden? On the one hand, the novel might be seen as a cautionary tale about what can happen if one never manages to break free of the 'usual thing' that stifles and restricts. On the other hand, though, the novel is a keen portrait of the difficulty (in Joan's case it is so difficult that she cannot manage it) of moving outside of conventional channels. Joan's exasperated self-questioning in the moment of anxiety that is produced in her by the thought of setting up a home with Elizabeth rather than a 'husband' paints a picture of the affective toll that breaking with conformity can take: 'Then it was only by submitting to precedent that you could be free? What she was proposing seemed cruel now, even to herself; and why? Because it was not softened and toned down by precedent, not wreathed in romance as the world understood romance' (ibid.: 247). Whilst submitting to precedent is not a transcendent freedom, a freedom that lets one realise the most personal desires and ambitions that one has (it is not a freedom that would allow Joan to 'be herself'), it is nevertheless a freedom from censure, from violence and disapprobation: the 'cruel[ty]' that the world imposes on those who are defiant.

In her account of how anti-normativity normalises the field of queer theory, Wiegman (2012: 339–40) is adamant that she does not want to propose a definitive solution or fix to this situation, but the one thing she does suggest is a more careful historicisation of queer people's investments in certain kinds of normativity. For example, she suggests that a queer investment in marriage might be a way of healing some historical injuries that arose as part of the AIDS epidemic, in which, say, intimate partners were denied access to their dying or dead loved ones because of the absence of legal ties. Whilst a critic like Warner might dismiss this as false consciousness, another, like Elizabeth Freeman (2007: 497), is able to 'take seriously people's longing for that relief, for the privilege of being ordinary'. Not everyone has the capability, inclination or resources (emotional and financial) to disrupt convention. In a way, we might even choose to see that, if anything, queer people are the *most likely* to want to feel ordinary. Or, in logical terms, queer people are those who have good reason to want to feel normal as we are often the ones who have felt particularly acutely the consequences of not being deemed normal. It is indeed hard to resist, as both Stephen Gordon and Joan Ogden show, the lure of 'being released from the world's persecution'. Moreover, the fact that something is ordinary is no logical grounds for rejecting it. The idea that queer people should never countenance feeling normal, that their role is only ever to disrupt and interrogate the sameness of normality, is the one that Hall would seem to question. As with Stephen Gordon, if we want to do justice to the specificity of Joan Ogden's affectivity, we have to refuse to imagine that the 'usual thing' is only ever there to be got over, disrupted or subverted.

'[S]adly ordinary'

We have seen, then, that Hall's lesbian novels thematise queer attachments to normality and convention. But as I have hinted above, the formal association of this work with ordinariness in terms of genre, style and status is also significant for the Anglophone history of sexuality. As critics have recognised, for example, *The Well*'s status as a middle-brow and accessible novel is what created the furore around its subject matter. Moreover, it was the novel's apparent lack of literary quality, rather than its lesbian content – though in many ways the two are linked, as I discuss below – that many commentators picked up on. Virginia Woolf, herself firmly placed in the high-brow cultural circle of the Bloomsbury Group and damning about middle-brow culture (she wrote that she would stab with her pen anyone who called her 'middle-brow' (Woolf 1942: 119)), disparaged Hall's *Well* because of the quality of its writing (Doan 2001: 10). Hall's biographers have similarly recognised that she was generally 'no stylist', writing 'clumsy prose' (Souhami 1998: 64). Attempts by some critics to redeem Hall's status and associate her with lesbian high modernism (Whitlock 1987; Winning 2001), would seem to fail up against Hall's tendency to stick with traditional genres and styles that were squarely middle-brow: neither avant-garde nor aimed at the low-brow masses. But we could associate Hall with a separate tradition of writing in this period in which various women writers used the medium of middle-brow fiction to represent desire between women. Building on work by scholars such as Sharon Marcus and Elizabeth English which has located literary intimacies between women in highly ordinary places – in various aspects of nineteenth-century public discourse (Marcus 2007), or in early twentieth-century genre fiction (English 2015) – I suggest that we understand Hall as part of a 'lesbian middle-brow'. Later in this section, I turn to Mary Renault's *The Friendly Young Ladies* (1944) as a novel from this tradition that also repeatedly makes explicit equivalences between lesbianism and ordinariness.

Feminist literary scholarship and feminist theory have both been interested for some time in what avant-garde positions would seem to devalue, whether that is middle-brow fiction or the ordinary everyday routine activities of social reproduction. Feminist literary scholars who focus on the early twentieth century in both the UK and the US have noted how the kind of accessible fiction aimed at the growing middle-class reading public in this period was and is often associated with femininity, which is why it has often been overlooked and denigrated (Humble 2001; Botshon and Goldsmith 2003; Harker 2007). This literary scholarship also relates to more theoretical work on how conventionality and ordinariness have been gendered as feminine. For example, in *Cool Men and the Second Sex* (2003), Susan Fraiman provides a number of detailed analyses of contexts in which apparently left-leaning, 'cool' men articulate their transgressive projects in opposition to a conventionality that is often implicitly figured as female. In her chapter on queer theory, she writes that queer theoretical scholarship by the likes of Lee Edelman and Eve Sedgwick 'tends unconsciously to position women, gender, femininity, and feminism as normative "other" to its antinormative project' (Fraiman 2003: 129). For example, in his argument about reproductive futurism, Fraiman argues, Edelman does not allow female bodies to appear as anything other than the vehicles for heterosexual reproduction's conservatism. The fluidity that queer scholars often celebrate is frequently opposed to a 'form of constraint figured as maternal' (ibid.: 122). Fraiman's is a more detailed and substantiated version of Biddy Martin's critique, which we encountered briefly above, in which she suggests that radical queer visions often evoke feminism as fixed and limiting. As Heather Love (2015: 91) writes in her contribution to 'Queer Theory without Antinormativity', the 'field of queer studies has been riven almost from the beginning by gendered debates about the relationship between antinormativity and the ordinary'.

Building on this work, I also want to think about how, in the history of Hall's reception, ordinariness itself has been associated with queerness and specifically with lesbianism. For example, in her detailed account of the reception of *The Well* in the months immediately after its publication, Laura Doan suggests that there was something that contemporary reviewers saw in Hall's treatment of homosexuality that made it seem, at least in aesthetic terms, distinctly average: 'The explosive topic of the novel effectively turned Hall into a one-book author and stole from her the "literary"' (Doan 2001: 12). Far from engendering what Doan calls a 'mythic moral panic' (ibid.: 1), Hall's novel was generally well received by the mainstream press, but criticised on aesthetic grounds: it was *too usual*, or, rather, not distinguished enough to merit celebration. In the words of W.R. Gordon writing in the *Daily News and Westminster Gazette*, it was 'sadly ordinary' (Doan and Prosser 2001: 65). Indeed, what makes it 'ordinary' from the perspective of literary criticism is its focus on an 'issue' and commitment to achieving a practical effect in the world, or in other words its explicit commitment to lesbianism. Other commentators at the time also suggested the conceptual links between middle-brow culture and the sameness associated with homosexuality. In a suggestive turn-of-phrase from her oft-cited polemic against 'Middlebrow' culture, Virginia Woolf (1942: 118) worries about the homogenising effects of middle-brow ascendancy: 'what will become of us, men and women, if Middlebrow has his way with us, and there is only a middle sex but no husbands or wives?' While this may be a flippant moment in the essay, it clearly associates middle-brow culture with the erasure of the difference between the sexes: with the sameness that brings about the sad eclipse of heterosexuality.

Given this figurative relation to the erasure of heterosexuality, perhaps it is no surprise that in more subjective or material terms middle-brow works should be vehicles for representing non-heterosexual intimacies between women. Indeed, various scholars have suggested that many distinctly ordinary registers, including middle-brow realism, have been prominent vehicles for representing desire between women in particular. According to Heather Love (2015: 91), 'Intimacies between women have a privileged place in the elaboration of the concept of a queer ordinary'. To support this claim, Love cites Sharon Marcus's account of the centrality of relations between women – platonic, sexual, marital – to the structure of Victorian gender. Marcus (2007: 13) shows that in Victorian England 'female marriage, gender mobility, and women's erotic fantasies about women were at the heart of normative institutions and discourses'. Using a method she calls 'just reading' (ibid.: 2), Marcus shows that these relations were not hidden or secret, but rather there on the surface of texts for all to see. The more recent work of Elizabeth English has highlighted the hitherto unexplored role of genre fiction in lesbian modernism. English (2015: 15) argues that 'conventional and popular genre fictions' actually offered a means for authors to write frankly about intimacies between women in the early twentieth century, at a time when more realist depictions such as Hall's *Well* were subject to censure. My argument here is not to adjudicate which form of writing (either genre fiction or middle-brow realism) provided the readiest vehicle in this period for representing lesbian desires, but to join with English and Marcus in attesting to the importance of the non-avant-garde in the history of lesbian sexuality.

There is perhaps no lesbian middle-brow work that associates lesbianism with ordinariness more strongly than Mary Renault's *The Friendly Young Ladies* (1944). It is a novel which occupies the 'solid center ground of the feminine middlebrow' (Hinds 2009: 301) and in which it is only the heterosexual characters (whom we are invited to imagine as misguided) who glamorise and sensationalise the lives of the novel's lesbian couple Leo (Leonora) Lane and Helen Vaughan who see themselves in very ordinary terms. For example, many years after Leo leaves home her younger sister Elsie is inspired to try to find her by a mixture of dissatisfaction with her family life in Cornwall and the influence of a handsome young doctor Peter Bracknell who himself shows an interest in Leo and in living an unconventional or nonconforming life. Elsie had been only young when Leo left home and there has been an air of mystery and secrecy around Leo's reasons for leaving and her current whereabouts. As Elsie says to her sister, she was aware that there had been 'something queer' about the situation (Renault 2005: 88). Meanwhile, the sheltered and naive Elsie has become very unhappy with the 'routine of domestic comfort' (ibid.: 1) with her parents in Cornwall and the 'familiar cycle' (ibid.: 2) of family life. Her dissatisfaction is partly due to her taste for adventure. Early on, we learn that she is a 'great reader of romances' as well as 'popular biographies and the yellow press' (ibid.: 16). Throughout the novel, her tendency is to see crime, intrigue and catastrophe in what more readily appear as very ordinary events, such as a man sitting in her carriage on the train (ibid.: 53). Indeed, in various contexts, 'Elsie was unwilling to dismiss any risk that could add to the glamour of the situation' (ibid.: 227).

This tendency of Elsie's is exacerbated by the arrival of Peter, who initially comes into her life as the substitute for their usual family doctor. He listens to some of her concerns about her stifling family situation and encourages her to seek an alternative life by finding Leo. Through Peter's influence, Elsie formulates an idealised image of the glamorous bohemian life her sister leads, determining that Leo must be living with an artist (ibid.: 44). Recognising Peter's investment in a certain kind of unconventional life, Elsie seeks to find Leo, partly as a means of impressing, and hopefully winning the affections of, the doctor. When she finds Leo living on a houseboat with her female companion (though Elsie never recognises Helen as Leo's lover), she writes to Peter to assure him that Leo 'lives a very Bohemian life' (ibid.: 104). She brags to him that her sister is 'interested in all sorts of queer things' (ibid.: 224). When Elsie finds out that Leo is not a 'serious' writer, but instead writes genre fiction under the pseudonym Tex O'Hara, she is concerned that Peter might not be so interested (ibid.: 106). Peter, too, is clearly very excited and intrigued by the prospect of the kind of bohemian life that he imagines Leo leads. When he finally meets Leo and Helen, he is 'delighted' and convinced that his sojourn with them will be 'even more original and interesting than he had supposed' because they are both 'so untypical, so different from the conventional idea' (ibid.: 157). In conversation with Leo, Peter himself makes it clear why he likes her: because she is 'separate [...] from the herd' (ibid.: 195).

However, Leo and Helen's own sense of themselves contrasts starkly with the image of them that Elsie and Peter cling to. Indeed, more than anything else both women imagine themselves as emphatically 'ordinary'. For example, Leo is very quick to correct Peter's idea of her:

> For another thing, I don't feel separate from the herd, if by the herd you mean ordinary people and not public mobs, as I suppose you do. I like them. Why should they pamper oddities, anyway? It's they who are in charge of evolution. They think it's better not to be odd, as far as they bother to think at all, and they're quite right. There are shoals of women made up pretty much like me, but a lot haven't noticed and most of the rest prefer to look the other way, and it's probably very sensible of them. If you do happen to have had your attention drawn to it, the thing to do is to like and be liked by as many ordinary people as possible, to make yourself as good a life as you can in your own frame, and to keep your oddities for the few people who are likely to be interested. (ibid.: 196)

Aligning herself with 'ordinary' people, Leo recognises, a bit like Stephen Gordon and Joan Ogden, the value that can come from not seeming 'odd'. Indeed, it is not an effort for Leo to understand herself as normal: 'her way of life had always seemed to her natural and uncomplex, an obvious one' (ibid.: 181). To treat her life with Helen 'with drama or pathos would have been in her mind a sentimentality and a kind of cowardice' (ibid.). When Peter describes her and Leo's relationship as 'unusual', Helen counters that, on the contrary, it 'seems quite ordinary to us' (ibid.: 239). Leo and Helen, then, reject the attempts of Peter and Elsie to make them seem anything other than ordinary. As Elsie recognises at one point, she has to repress the desire to describe the women with terms such as 'artistic' and 'bohemian' because she detects in both Helen and Leo 'a curious lack of enthusiasm when they were uttered' (ibid.: 134). More than anything, the novel works to present Leo and Helen not as extraordinary bohemians but, in the words of one character, Mr Hicks, 'A couple of real nice, friendly young ladies' (ibid.: 221).

The Friendly Young Ladies, then, is a novel with a lesbian relationship at its centre which is not only written in a highly ordinary ('middlebrow') register but also works to set up lesbianism in particular in relation to this ordinariness. More than anything else, what threatens to disrupt the ordinariness of Leo and Helen's life is the arrival of straight people. Elsie brings Peter, who in turn causes sexual and romantic intrigue with both of the friendly young ladies. Leo's heterosexual dalliance with Peter in turn prompts overtures from her neighbour Joe who, it turns out, has harboured romantic feelings for her for a while. Even as Leo briefly considers leaving Helen for Joe, there is no clear resolution at the novel's end. As Leo begins to pack some things to leave, she experiences again the satisfaction that the peaceful domesticity with Helen has given her: she 'retast[es], with the intolerable sharpness of finality, five years of happiness, contentment which, to the part of herself that it satisfied, had been complete' (ibid.: 305). Sure enough, the novel ends with Leo ignoring Peter's knock at her door with the strong implication that she will resume her ordinary life with Helen.

In her brief account of the novel in the context of a larger argument about how disappointment is coded as feminine in middle-brow novels, Hilary Hinds (2009: 302) writes that 'Elsie's ordinariness is set against the extraordinariness of her androgynous, bohemian, and rebellious sister Leo'. For Hinds, the novel codes femininity in terms of disappointing ordinariness, from which Leo is saved by her female masculinity. Yet, I would argue that Hinds's position owes more to the expectation of such a contrast than to the novel itself, which as we have seen actually labours to make us see Leo as very ordinary. While it may make sense within the general terms in which homosexuality has been understood as an extraordinary deviance to see the characters divided along the lines that Hinds imagines, the novel itself insists on Leo and Helen's ordinariness. Indeed, it is the heterosexual people in the novel who idealise Leo as bohemian. We might even suggest that this is what Hinds does: she is herself in the position of Elsie and Peter glamorising someone whom she makes out to be more bohemian and extraordinary than she is.

In the 'Afterword' to the 1983 Virago edition of her novel, Renault implies that it was written, in part, in response to Hall's *Well*. Renault (2005: 310) writes that she found Hall's novel 'irresistibly funny': for her, it carries 'an impermissible allowance of self-pity, and its earnest humourlessness invites irreverence'. She suggests that queer people should steer clear of stridency and self-pity, which she sees in Hall's work. But Renault's disparaging remarks do not take sufficient account of the similarities between her novel and Hall's. Of course, where Leo succeeds in feeling normal, Stephen fails, or is made to fail by the lack of acceptance around her, but this does not change the fundamental desire that they share, or the middle-brow register in which this desire for ordinariness is expressed. On one level, we can associate middle-brow writing with sameness in so far as 'middle-brow' seems to get so much of its ability to discredit from the way it conjures blandness and homogeneity. As we have seen, Woolf associates the middle-brow with the end of difference and heterosexuality. On another level, it can be associated with femininity, particularly as ordinariness and conventionality have so often been gendered female. But beyond these formal associations of the middle-brow, ordinary and conventional with the feminine or with the sameness that homosexuality has also been seen to embody, the fiction thus classified itself often seeks to represent desire between women as normal or as ordinary. The 'lesbian middle-brow', then, is a term we could use to name a tradition of fiction that occupies the formal position in many accounts of something that is too normal or samey, but that also explicitly thematises the ordinariness of lesbianism. Within the field of literary representation, the dominant framework provided by queer theory can have the effect of erasing this tradition of distinctly ordinary fiction that registered desire between women particularly clearly. It is this tradition that links lesbianism and ordinariness that we risk missing out on, or passing over, if we leave the categorical queer theoretical opposition to normativity unquestioned. And why would it be bad to miss out on this fiction? On the one hand, because it shows us that an image of queers as wildly transgressive can actually, as we see in the character of Peter Bracknell, be more satisfying to heterosexual than to non-heterosexual people. On another hand, though, harking back to Stephen and Joan, this fiction tells us that being the same as everybody else – and thus freed from persecution – is something many have been entirely justified in wanting.

'Like to like!'

Perhaps it is in this last respect that these novels can be of most interest to a queer theory defined by its opposition to norms, normality, normativity and normalisation. In their status as imaginative literature, arguably, they humanise this desire and show its affective stakes. Radclyffe Hall's protagonist in *The Well of Loneliness*, for example, repeatedly displays a desire to be 'like' the dominant rather than opposed to it. She is sad to have been 'never quite like all the other children' (Hall 1994: 104). She tells her father early in her life that she longs 'to be someone like Nelson' (ibid.: 22). At the balls and formal occasions that Stephen seems to hate so much, she feels conflicted about her peers: 'While despising these girls, she yet longed to be like them' (ibid.: 74). Stephen gets on so well with Martin Hallam because when they are together they are 'like two men' (ibid.: 99). She even comes to see an element of promise in the prospect of some kind of queer community in Paris: 'There was many another exactly like her in this very city, in every city; and they did not all live out crucified lives' (ibid.: 302). She can support them, however, only because she is able to convince herself that they are really 'like everyone else' (ibid.: 302). For Stephen's governess Puddle the thought of Stephen becoming a part of the community of inverts in Paris is unbearable: 'Like to like. No, no, an intolerable thought!' (ibid.: 244). Indeed, an ominous refrain is sparked off in Puddle's mind when Stephen tells her of her plans to move to the French capital: 'Like to like! Like to like! Like to like!' (ibid.: 250). So, whilst, on one hand, likeness is ominously (at least ominously for Puddle) associated with devolution into subculture, at the same time, being like everyone else, or assimilating into a larger field of normality, is Stephen's goal and ambition in the novel. For Stephen, 'like to like' does not need to be so bad, as long as the likeness taken on is not going to exclude and alienate her. Moreover, being 'like' others offers the possibility of simply not constituting an aberration. Stephen's is a model of subjectivity that is fundamentally about likeness. Stephen looks to others, and principally others in positions of normative authority and value, for ways in which she might be more like them.

Jonathan Flatley (2010a: 73) has recently written about the relation of 'liking' – 'positive emotional engagement' – to being 'like' or 'alike' something – the apprehension that 'one thing is similar to, resembles, or imitates another'. He sees Andy Warhol as providing an emblematic case of combining the two in his obsessive collecting habit (that is, his liking a lot of things) and those collections' tendency towards similarity, because 'collections are, almost by definition, organized along lines of likeness' (ibid.: 80). Warhol's practice is glossed as an 'attempt to imagine new, queer forms of emotional attachment and affiliation, and to transform the world into a place where these forms could find a home' (ibid.: 72). Likeness, or similarity, is, for Flatley, imagined to be the 'condition of possibility' for the 'affective affiliation' that would make such queer forms possible (ibid.: 73). But we arguably also see this in less celebrated figures. So, in *The Friendly Young Ladies*, as we saw above,

Leo Lane's advice is to 'like and be liked by as many ordinary people as possible'. Leo's positive emotional engagement with ordinary people ('I like them') is manifest in her also wanting to be similar to them (as we have seen, she insists on her own ordinariness). In another essay, Flatley links the capacity to like, and to like likeness, to Eve Kosofsky Sedgwick's notion of reparative reading. The 'reparative, mimetic' mode of reading that Sedgwick endorses is one that does not censure imitation, whereas the 'suspicious mode of attunement to which we are most accustomed in the academic profession' is one that is all about outlining one's difference, originality and innovativeness (Flatley 2010b: 227). However, Flatley is very clear that 'likeness' is not to be confused, not to be imagined as too much like, sameness. Instead, 'likeness', as he understands it, constitutes a 'third term aside the same-different binary' (Flatley 2010a: 73); it 'make[s] room for a conception of queer sexual attraction [...] that tries to move beyond the homosexual (love of the same) heterosexual (love of the different) distinction itself' (ibid.: 76). So, 'likeness' is definitely *unlike* either sameness or difference: it becomes curiously, even paranoiacally, distinct.

In this chapter, I have not wanted to distance likeness from sameness. Stephen Gordon, Joan Ogden, Leo Lane and Helen Vaughan all in their own ways seek to be the same as (that is, 'like') others who are deemed normal, usual or ordinary. In this, I have suggested, they can be the occasion to reflect on queer theory's opposition to the sameness in normativity. For Heather Love, as for other queer theoretical scholars that we saw above, normalisation and normativity effect damaging forms of social exclusion. Certainly, we can see this at work in figures like Stephen Gordon and Joan Ogden who have what seem like their chances at happiness and fulfilment ruined by a commitment to the normal. But this commitment is nevertheless apparently unwavering. Stephen, for example, continues to defer to the 'so-called normal' world, even as it damages her. What we see then is a resistance not to normalisation – she remains committed to the idea of the normal – but to forms of exclusion. It is not the normal per se that Stephen opposes, only how she is not enabled to live the life that she wants within the existing conditions that it offers. Joan Ogden, similarly, gives us an object lesson in how difficult it can be for some queers, already the bearers of cultural disapprobation, to lead lives of nonconformism. Leo Lane and Helen Vaughan show us that queerness as an anti-normative force can often seem more exotically appealing to straight people than to queers.

I do not suggest, then, that Stephen, Joan, Leo, Helen or Hall should necessarily encourage us to embrace any particular standard *as* normative, but am asking instead, following their example, what, necessarily, would be so bad if we did.

Notes

1 Scholarship that has read the novel in relation to the development and emergence of trans identities has not displaced *The Well*'s reputation as a central work in the history of lesbianism (Prosser 2001).
2 For examples of such readings see Halberstam 2001; Hemmings 2001; Winning 2001.
3 'Metronormativity' first appears as a concept in Halberstam 2005: 36–8. I cite Herring in the main body of the text instead of Halberstam because a critique of the concept is the crux of his entire book.

4

Reductive

Despite being the author of at least one 'gay classic' in his first novel *City of Night* (1963), John Rechy has often talked about not wanting to be known only as a gay writer (Warrick 1996). In an interview from 1986, for example, he suggests the power of artistic creativity to refuse this kind of categorisation: the 'imagination knows no limit', he says, in the face of attempts to 'label' gay writers and keep them 'in a box' (Pally 1986: 53). As if describing gay identity in terms of the undeniably unappealing 'limit' of labels and boxes were not enough to persuade us against it, he goes on to discredit those who would celebrate writers like him as 'gay' writers by asking a question whose rhetorical force is apparently similarly indisputable: 'Are we to be reduced to one collective mass?' (ibid.). For Rechy, at this moment, being 'reduced' is imagined to be self-evidently problematic, but several of Rechy's readers have noted how he and his work effect exactly the reduction from which he distances himself. Stephen Adams (1980: 105) suggests that Rechy's preoccupation with gay male promiscuity in works like *City of Night* succeeds only in 'reducing life to the merely physical'. Ricardo Ortiz (1993: 124n17) calls Rechy's quasi-pornographic prose in his second novel *Numbers* (1967) 'hyper-reductive'. One of Rechy's fans who meets the author at a conference is disappointed because he wears a 'skin-tight T-shirt and jeans', embodying the fact that 'everything among gay men is reductive to sex and the way you look' (qtd in Casillo 2002: 248). However, Rechy and his readers importantly share a sense that what has a peculiar power to bring about forms of reduction is gayness, whether in the label of gay writer, the depiction of gay male sexuality or Rechy's self-presentation as a gay man.

But why do the emphatically gay aspects of Rechy's work and personality seem so reductive? Certainly, to some commentators, any attachment at all to a particular social identity is liable to seem problematic in this way. Scholars have noted this dynamic in which minoritised positions are imagined as restrictive or ghettoising, whereas the particularities that define a dominant or majority position are afforded apparently universal validity.[1] However, I am also keen to investigate the links between the formal qualities of reduction and specifically gay identity. Reduction leads to an implicitly problematic decrease in complexity, a loss of individuality and difference, the homogenisation that Rechy's phrase 'one collective mass' portends. Within the form of sexual definition that foundational queer theoretical texts have held to be fundamental to even the least sexual aspects of modern Western culture, reduction embodies the misguided attachment to sameness that has also defined homosexuality.[2] I suggest that the tacit hierarchies of difference over sameness, hetero over homo, that structure modern Western epistemologies, are at work in the assumption that reduction is implicitly undesirable. That Rechy finds focus on the gay aspects of his writing to be more reductive and limiting than anything else is therefore suggestive. In a 1995 interview, Rechy disavows the content of works such as *The Sexual Outlaw* (1977) and *Rushes* (1979), in addition to *City of Night* and *Numbers*, which are all preoccupied with the sex lives of gay men, hoping that one day his work 'will be viewed beyond subject matter' (Castillo and Rechy 1995: 123). Echoing this sentiment in a Foreword to *Beneath the Skin: The Collected Essays of John Rechy* (2004), publisher Don Weise is keen to stress that Rechy has written 'on a wide array of issues beyond gay sex' (Rechy 2004: xiii). Rechy's biographer Charles Casillo (2003: n.p.) sympathises with Rechy's bitterness at often being 'reduced by critics to a series of labels'. Whilst there are other 'labels' that have attached to Rechy and that he protests against, including the label 'Chicano', nevertheless the label that he most emphatically rejects is that of 'gay writer' (Castillo and Rechy 1995: 113). Whilst he claims that 'All categorization that limits the artist is negative' (ibid.: 118), 'gay' in particular comes to stand in for that limitation. Whilst gay identity is certainly not the only phenomenon that can limit, Rechy figures it here as particularly well-suited to aligning with the formal properties of limitation: keeping things confined, restricted, the same.

In this chapter, I argue that Rechy's writing frequently performs and embodies the limitation and reduction he decries and is therefore a helpful staging ground for pushing back against the presumptions at work that allow him and many others to imagine that these concepts are necessarily problematic. For example, despite his attempts to disavow the fact, and as some of his readers recognise, Rechy's fiction is frequently limited to the representation of gay sex worlds. *City of Night* is built around the sexual experiences of a nameless and transitory male hustler, travelling through the worlds of casual sex and sex work in America's big cities. *Numbers* tells the story of its protagonist Johnny Rio's obsessive counting of the sexual contacts he makes on a ten-day cruising spree. The semi-fictional *The Sexual Outlaw* details its narrator's sexual exploits over one sex-filled weekend. Bringing into question any account of Rechy's writing career as a steady broadening away from gay themes, his more recent novel *The Coming of the Night* (1999) details the sexual preoccupations of several unconnected gay men on one day in Los Angeles in 1981 and their improbable convergence in a portentously fatal orgy. Jesse, the character who is effectively killed by sex at the story's end nevertheless speaks the truth of the novel and its thematic limits: 'And sex was everywhere!' (Rechy 1999: 5). The worlds Rechy presents repeatedly see people reduced to anonymous numbers or body parts, sexual activity reduced to a policed repertoire of acts, and their geographical spread reduced to gay bars, orgy rooms and cruising spots. Moreover, Rechy's work comes from a broader genre in queer culture, which is that of the 'stud file' or the chronicle of sexual partners and activities: accounts of the ways of relating through serial sex that have been a significant part of queer history. We could trace this from the original 'stud file' of Samuel Steward maintained from 1924 to 1974 (Spring 2010: xiii), through fiction of gay liberation such as Renaud Camus's *Tricks* (1978) and *Queens* (1984) by Pickles, to post-AIDS accounts like Jane DeLynn's *Don Juan in the Village* (1990), to non-fictional works on the impact of gentrification such as Samuel Delany's *Times Square Red/Times Square Blue* (1999), right up to current-day versions of the genre such as Brontez Purnell's *The Cruising Diaries* (2014). By presenting an intimate relation between queer sexuality and forms of reduced or limited relating, this work encourages us to pause over the assumption that reduction is self-evidently problematic and to ask what that assumption might have to do with the queer sex that is the focus of these accounts.

Assumptions against reduction work powerfully in a number of contexts, many of which we have encountered throughout this book. Used to indicate improper simplification, or an unintelligent indifference to the finer points of an issue or situation, casual evocations of reduction like those of Rechy's readers also relate to philosophical critiques of reductionism. By seeking to understand all phenomena only via recourse to the same explanatory principles (such as, in Stephen Adams's words, the 'merely physical'), this critique goes, reductionism flattens the apparent 'fullness of reality' (Jones 2000: 16). Less analytic philosophical traditions, like post-structuralism, have associated reductionism with a metaphysics of presence unattuned to the fundamental absence at the heart of signification which generates a differential force that makes reduction to self-sameness or identity impossible. Equating this differential force with the apparent complexity of sexuality, queer theoretical work has used post-structuralist terms for articulating how sexual lives always remain irreducible to the norms that govern them. For some scholars, however, post-structuralist accounts of non-identity have proved inadequate for describing the play of specifically social rather than metaphysical difference, leading to calls for intersectional analyses capable of accounting for the effects of the interplay of multiple social affiliations (Crenshaw 1989; 1991). As I discuss below, some queer theoretical scholarship has imagined intersectional frameworks to be the best guard against what this scholarship figures specifically as forms of reductionism in the single-axis identity politics of contemporary queer liberalism. Rejecting reductionism in all of these ways has been an important means for scholars and activists in various contexts to signal a commitment to values like complexity, variability and difference, often imagined as the route to social change, over and above simplicity, stasis and sameness. In queer theoretical writing, a too-strict fidelity to identity and its accompanying reductionism is just one headline aspect of the sameness that we have seen in the preceding chapters rejected in ideas like normativity, reproduction and the useless status quo.

Whilst there are clearly very good reasons that scholarship has opposed these ideas, I have also suggested that drawing the battle lines against the sameness they embody is often taken to constitute its own justification. As we will see in this chapter, reductionism is frequently imagined to speak for itself as a problem. Post-structuralists see it as a mistake to 'reduce' *différance* to identity, sociologists accuse post-structuralists of 'reducing' material differences to the play of textuality. The way in which reductionism can be levelled from apparently competing positions suggests that it can also be used as a rhetorical shorthand, a way to frame, rather than simply describe, those with whom one disagrees. Accusations of reductiveness are moves to obtain the rhetorical high ground by situating oneself on the side of creativity over inertia, dynamism over stasis, variation over fixity, complexity over simplicity, of difference over reduction's sameness. In other words, it is only because one presumes the value of ideas like creativity, complexity and difference that reduction can stand alone as a problem. We all know exactly how we are supposed to feel about reduction: it is because of the approval and agreement that ideas related to difference tend to generate that one can rely on reduction's capacity to seem inarguably undesirable. Queer scholarship has provided persuasive terms for understanding this implicit preference for difference over sameness in relation to the homo/hetero or same/different split that structures understandings of sexuality. To what extent is it the associations of reduction with the denigrated sameness of the homo that, paradoxically, give it such rhetorical force in queer scholarship and beyond?

In what follows, I explore this question by placing John Rechy's writing in conversation with the work of queer theorists, with a particular emphasis on the work of Leo Bersani. Because he has also asserted the potential value of sameness and reduction, Bersani provides an important starting point for understanding the rhetorical work that reduction achieves in queer theory. Specifically, as we have seen, he has looked to the definitional sameness of homosexuality – what he calls 'homo-ness' – as a model for forms of relating not based on the defensive assertion of individual differences. For Bersani, access to these new ways of relating is explicitly facilitated by modes of reduction which subjects enter into by abandoning their individuating features, such as in, among other things, anonymous gay cruising. Yet, at the same time he evokes other phenomena explicitly as forms of reduction, like 'identity', which appear abject in the context of his argument because they seem to thwart the homo-ness he endorses. I do not have any interest in proving Bersani wrong – his anti-redemptive work is foundational and enabling for the argument I make here – but instead I examine one of the ways in which his rhetorical terrain gestures toward apparently irredeemable forms of sameness despite advocating for homo-ness in the context of his larger argument. I am interested, then, less in evaluating the heuristic 'sameness' that Bersani attaches to new, less individualistic or less differentiated modes of relating than in the other kinds of sameness he rejects to give comprehensible rhetorical shape to his work. I argue that Rechy's fiction helps to focus critical attention on the forms of sameness that remain abject even in the work of those, like Bersani, who have explored the potential value of sameness. That is, Rechy remains irredeemably reductive. If Rechy's imagination of gay male sexuality in relation to modes of reduction would seem to align him with the kinds of de-individuating reduction that Bersani has celebrated (such as in cruising), then it is also the case that Rechy's fiction does not refuse the forms of irredeemable sameness that Bersani does. By in some ways exemplifying the terms currently available for understanding sameness and reduction in queer theory, I suggest, Rechy's work is also in a position to focus attention on the other forms of sameness that those terms reject. To put this another way, while queer theoretical work has opposed certain forms of reduction, queer representation and history have none the less been quite reductive in precisely these ways.

For example, in place of characters entering into a Bersanian correspondence of forms, Rechy's sex worlds are peopled by casts of starkly reduced identitarian types: queens, scores, youngmen, etc. Perhaps most typifying of all, though, is the unrelenting expectation of a certain kind of conventional masculinity among Rechy's hustlers and sexcruisers. In the same interview in which he decries being thought of as a 'gay writer', Rechy also valorises 'stereotypes'. 'It was the "flaming queens" who most often resisted arrest during raids, including at the Stonewall Inn. Inspected closely – on the various battlefronts – gay, Chicano, black, feminist "stereotypes" often reveal themselves to be the earliest sources of confrontational rebellion' (Castillo and Rechy 1995: 116). The recurrence of these types exemplifies the structure of habitual return in Rechy's writing. He often redeploys a series of biographical anecdotes and personal observations, creating an oeuvre out of repetition and reduction rather than limitless creativity and variation. Repeatedly we read of characters – the nameless narrator in *City of Night*, Johnny Rio in *Numbers*, Jim Girard in *This Day's Death* (1969), Manny in *The Fourth Angel* (1972), Jim (or Jerry or John, as he also calls himself) in *The Sexual Outlaw*, Endore in *Rushes* – who share Rechy's biographical experiences, whether it be particular sexual encounters, his tendency to exercise obsessively or his opinions on the prevalence of S/M sexual practices amongst gay men in the US in the 1970s. What is significant is not that what is repeated may have a basis in autobiographical fact, but that it is repeated and consolidated.

By in some ways exemplifying key terms currently available for understanding sameness and reduction in queer theory, I suggest, Rechy's work is also in a position to focus attention on the other forms of sameness that those terms reject. In making this argument, I am continuing the work of several critics who have recognised the less conventionally progressive facets of Rechy's fiction, its limited, complicitous and normative aspects (Pérez-Torres 1994; Ortiz 1995; Arnold 2011). However, this is at odds with most current scholarship on Rechy, which has tried to imagine him and his work in various ways as productive, indenturing his writing to a generally positive, progressive political story of non-normative or otherwise malleable gender and sexual identity (Christian 1997: 25–54; Johnson 1998; Gove 2000: 41–80; Foster 2006: 91–110; Moon 2006; Heise 2011). In a related vein, other critics have located Rechy's political potential in his apparent rendering of identities formed along multiple axes of oppression, such as race, ethnicity, gender, sexuality and class (Bruce-Novoa 1992; Saldívar 1997: 95–129; Libretti 2004; Aldama 2005; Alvarez 2007: 97–120; Vázquez 2011: 101–33). Both approaches (focusing on either subversive or intersectional identities) share assumptions with theoretical projects that have opposed themselves to reduction in the form of 'identity' or single-issue political organising. The imperative to move beyond single-issue organising echoes in many respects the consensus to move beyond the gay content of Rechy's writing that we saw above: this demand celebrates the move beyond an apparently limiting or reductive focus on sexuality alone. This is the approach of David William Foster in his reading of Rechy's novel *Bodies and Souls* (1983), which he celebrates because it has apparently moved beyond the direct representation of gay characters in Rechy's earlier novels to a representation of forms of sexual non-normativity strewn across the entire urban landscape of LA. His choice of title is apt for evoking the blockage as which a focus only on sexual identity is often imagined: 'John Rechy: The Limits of Exuberant Queer' (Foster 2006: 91).

Rechy's writing, though, stands in tension with these attempts to recuperate it. Despite the scholarly and critical imperative to avoid limitation, or else to move beyond sexual identity, Rechy and other authors of sexual seriality show us that queer culture has frequently embodied the reduction that scholars have found problematic. Rechy's refusal of the label of 'gay writer' as a limiting reduction also stands in tension with the way in which we have seen him valorise stereotypes.

Equally, his resistance to this single-axis identity also gives way to a recognition that it may in some sense be necessary: 'it's impossible to reconcile problems that deal with homosexuality with those of other minorities' (Castillo and Rechy 1995: 114), he says. There is a tension, then, between Rechy's professed desire not to be reduced to the status of 'gay writer' and his belief in the power of stereotypes, between his not wanting to be a stereotype himself and his assertion of their power, between the position he outlines in his interviews and his repeatedly reductive writings. In tracing the reductiveness of Rechy's writing, I continue in the mode of the previous chapters, which has been to build on anti-redemptive queer theoretical work by figures like Heather Love, Jack Halberstam and Kadji Amin. Continuing in this vein, I examine the ways in which Rechy's writing performs the kinds of reduction we have seen him and others decry. In this chapter, the reductiveness ascribed to Rechy by his readers is not therefore grounds for dismissal or recovery, but instead an opportunity to pause and consider what exactly makes such reduction so implicitly undesirable.

Too unlimited

Anti-reductionism has had a significant place in queer theoretical texts. As we saw in the Introduction, for example, Judith Butler's work in *Gender Trouble* involves subverting the 'reductive efforts of univocal signification' (Butler 1999: 132) that would limit the possibilities for gendered life. Of course, it is 'identity' and, in the case of this early work, stable gender identity, that renders this form of reduction. The particular issue with how stabilised identity threatens to reduce or thwart less predictable forms of gender, however, develops into a general structure to which Butler returns throughout her work. This structure becomes a way of articulating the importance of remaining irreducible to the norms that limit any form of living, not so as to do away with those norms but to imagine strategies for their expansion. Butler often returns to the idea that subjects cannot transcend the social realm on which they necessarily depend, such that liveable lives require certain kinds of constitutive norms or limitations. However, the forced consolidation through repetition of a given set of norms also allows for the possibility of subversive re-signification when this process encounters what cannot be subsumed within it: at the 'limit of what is familiar, parochial, and already known' (Butler 2004a: 38) at the 'limits of what is knowable' (ibid.: 27) at the 'limit of the thinkable, the narratable, the intelligible' (ibid.: 165). Whilst these limits make the conditions for recognisability, liveable lives are not entirely reducible to them: limits can be 'expanded, destroyed or reworked' to create new possibilities (ibid.: 38).

This structure of the enabling, non-reductive limit, then, appears across Butler's work. In *Gender Trouble* and *Bodies that Matter* (1993), the iterative consolidation of both sex and gender is inescapable but not fully determining. Gender play is 'regulated by heterosexist constraints though not [...] fully reducible to them' (Butler 2011: 178). The 'structuring presence of heterosexual constructs' in queer sexuality does not mean that it is 'reducible to those constructs' (Butler 1999: 158). In *The Psychic Life of Power* (1997), power produces the subject, but this 'does not mean that the subject can be *reduced* to the power by which it is occasioned' (Butler 1997a: 16, original italics). In her contributions to *Contingency, Hegemony, Universality* (2000), Butler even turns her attention to universalism, an arena often associated with dehumanising reductions, in order to suggest that the claims to universality of those previously excluded from the universal will help to keep it 'irreducible to any of its determinate modes of appearance' (Butler, Laclau, Žižek 2000: 3). When invoking universality, as elsewhere in her work, 'we can – and must – push the limits' (ibid.: 41). Butler makes anti-reduction into the defining position of her writing: limits are enabling only when they are not reducible to themselves.[3]

What I think we see in Butler's work, then, is a movement from specifically targeting the reductionism of certain social identities to a broader commitment to the capacity of phenomena to exceed the terms through which they are commonly understood. As in other thinkers encountered in the previous chapters, there is a general refusal to accept a broad 'logic of identity' that would reduce things to what they are and deny the possibility that they might become other than themselves. The effort becomes one of resisting all 'reductive efforts of univocal signification', making a commitment to the intrinsic mulitivocality of phenomena. In this, Butler's work puts to political use the terms of a post-structuralist tradition that, as we saw in the Introduction, has articulated irreducibility as a metaphysical inevitability. For Derrida (1978: 281), for example, the nature of the system of differences that is the upshot of signification is problematically 'neutralized or reduced' by any imposition or commitment to 'self-identity'. To 'conceive of structure on the basis of a full presence which is beyond play' is to perform a 'reduction of the structurality of structure' (ibid.: 279). This system of differences, which, of course, in another canonical instance Derrida (1982: 8) calls 'différance', is 'irreducibly polysemic' and 'irreducibly nonsimple' (ibid.: 13). For Derrida (2002: 24), a crucial aspect of the logocentrism that he critiques is the 'reduction of writing' or the 'reduction of the exteriority of the signifier'. For Derrida in these instances, there simply (or rather, non-simply) is just a system of differences, which are irreducible in the sense that they always elude attempts to reduce them to self-identity. Drucilla Cornell (1992: 1) has sought to mobilize this insistence on the impossibility of self-identity to ethical ends in her description of deconstruction as the 'philosophy of the limit'. For Cornell, the quasi-transcendental limit to the self-presence of any system or structure allows for keeping open the question of what lies beyond that system so that it remains radically contingent and alterable. The quasi-transcendental limit therefore helps to elude the bad 'limit' or 'reduction' that a stable centre would effect.

Like Derrida and Cornell, Butler similarly articulates a necessary irreducibility that keeps limits from becoming limiting. In terms of the norms that govern sexual life, this is what at one point she calls the 'irreducible complexity of sexuality' (Butler 1999: xxvi). Butler often returns to the idea that nothing can exist fully outside a normative frame for understanding, in the way that there is no biological sex that is before the discursive organisation of gender. But the facticity of sex that is rejected reappears in the guise of the apparently equally factic complexity that always eludes full capture at the hands of the norm. As with Derrida, Butler's anti-reductionism is based on the pre-discursive necessity of this irreducible complexity. Nothing exists outside of the frame of its articulation, apart from the 'irreducible complexity' of phenomena, which is apparently non-discursive, non-negotiable and inarguable. Assumptions in favour of difference are at work that make it seem more correct to imagine that phenomena in the world just are irreducibly complex. The corollary of an irreducibly complex world is the impossibility of reduction: the impossibility of a limit that is limiting, or, in other words, a limit that stays the same.

Post-structuralist assumptions about the necessity of non-identity also influence scholarship that has focused on the way singular identities misrepresent the multiplicity of social positions that people inhabit. Indeed, as we also saw in the Introduction, reductionism is frequently what the post-structuralist-inflected politics of difference imagines itself to counteract. This criticism has often explicitly embraced difference as the value that can provide salvation from the reductionist and homogenising forces of a logic of identity that conceptualises subjects as present-in-themselves rather than as necessarily fractured by many social differences. For example, Iris Marion Young (1990: 3) writes that this 'politics of difference' can question the 'reductionism' of political theory and its 'tendency to reduce political subjects to a unity', to 'value commonness or sameness over specificity and difference'. Young critiques a 'logic of identity' that seeks to 'think things together, to reduce them to unity' (ibid.: 98). In the same year as Young, and in a similar fashion, Cornel West (1990: 32) is able to suggest that 'reductionism' is one of the 'deadly traps' against which the 'new cultural politics of difference' is able to militate (ibid.: 31). This new politics is presented as a matter of opposing sameness per se: it seeks to 'trash the monolithic and homogeneous in the name of diversity, multiplicity and heterogeneity' (ibid.: 19).

Similar rhetorical alignments enter more recent scholarship through continuing assertions of the importance of intersectional social analysis. For example, as we have seen earlier, central to David Eng's recent work on 'queer liberalism' has also been a call for a 'renewed intersectional approach' (Eng 2010: 41). For Eng, this renewal is an important means of combating the neoliberal political formation in which certain lesbian and gay subjects are afforded civil rights on the proviso that they conform to normative kinship arrangements. Intersectionality is intended to bring back to view the social differences that queer liberalism apparently attempts to flatten and, in particular, bring to light the processes of racialisation that attend liberal rights claims. Partly, this is to defend against reduction: intersectionality is imagined to guard against the 'ways in which heterogeneity is reduced to homogeneity' in the context of queer liberalism (ibid.). As with Young and West, heterogeneity seems to speak for itself here as preferable to being 'reduced' to homogeneity. As I discussed in the Introduction, though, the ways in which reduction and homogeneity are aspects of the operation of queer liberalism are not clear. Nor is it clear that embracing heterogeneity will lead to a more emphatic sense of the ways in which race in particular plays a role in public life. Embracing heterogeneity over reduction and homogeneity, however, certainly makes more sense within the established protocols of engaged queer scholarship.

This use of the shorthand that reductionism provides is, however, by no means confined to those who have championed intersectionality or the 'politics of difference'. Indeed, use of this shorthand unites a number of otherwise competing positions. For example, José Esteban Muñoz (2009: 31) can reprise his belief in the importance of intersectionality by decrying 'reductive left thinkers' who apparently refuse to take account of gender and sexuality in their analyses. At the same time, Amanda Anderson (2006: 2) discredits the kind of attention to social categories that motivates thinkers like Muñoz, as well as Eng and Young, by calling it 'sociological reductionism'. Another theorist convinced, as we have seen, of the validity of post-structuralist positions, Lee Edelman (1994: 9) has associated a 'logic of identity' with a dominant heterosexuality that effects a 'reduction of "différance" to a question of determinate difference'. At the same time, post-structuralist theory has been criticised by sociologists like Steven Seidman (1993: 135) for the way in which it threatens to 'reduce' social and material differences to the play of textuality. Indeed, throughout this book we have seen multiple thinkers evoke reductionism: almost no one, of course, has a good word to say about it. Jasbir Puar (2007: 213) writes that intersectional identities are attempts to 'capture and reduce' the 'threatening mobility' of assemblages. Janet Jakobsen (1998: 10) similarly identifies a 'reductive pluralism' that pretends to nurture difference, but really requires homogeneity from the subjects it claims to represent. Echoing Jakobsen, Mikko Tuhkanen (2002b: 5) writes that the treatment of difference in multiculturalism has 'often been reduced to a kind of careless consumerism of otherness'. Steven Epstein (1996: 157) argues that post-structuralist queer theory involves a 'reduction of complex cultural codes'. Diana Fuss (1989: 55) rejects a version of essentialism that is 'simply reductive'. Even Madhavi Menon (2008: 3), who has associated the privileging of difference in historicist methodologies with a broader privileging of heterosexuality, none the less argues that the alternative historical method she articulates ('homohistory'), whilst it 'echoes the "homo" of a homosexuality deemed narcissistic', nevertheless 'cannot be reduced to it'. Moreover, 'desire "itself" cannot be reduced to any one set of acts or identities' (ibid.). The crucial agreement in these instances is that forms of reduction are a bad thing. Whilst reductionism may be used to describe social and philosophical problems whose effects many, like Butler, have important reasons for combating, when it is allowed to stand as a problem on its own, it becomes a matter of rhetoric too. Accusing one's interlocutors of reductionism is a matter of attributing to them a mistaken attachment to a misguided sameness that deprives objects of their singularity and complexity.

However, in contrast to many of the preceding positions, for Leo Bersani's work it is often the associations of reduction with sameness that make it important. Throughout much of his writing, Bersani has sought to articulate modes of relating that do not involve defensively and anxiously differentiated selves. He has often suggested that a more effective way to target social violence is not to insist on the fundamental legitimacy of selves, but rather to refuse this form of redemption and embrace an abject communication with reduced or '"lower" orders of being' (Bersani 2010: 29). Bersani explores phenomena that do not uphold the dignity or importance of this subjectivity as salutary models for relations based, at least in heuristic terms, on sameness. The 'category of homosexuality' (Bersani 1995: 5), or what he prefers to call 'homo-ness' (ibid.: 7), provides one such model in so far as it is defined as a mode of relating to that which is in some way 'the same' rather than anxiogenically different. Not necessarily involving the annihilation of selves, homo-ness facilitates a process of 'self-extension' (ibid.). That is, homo-ness designates a universal correspondence of being within which the subject is no longer definitively differentiated but exists as a relay point in a constant mobility of minutely differing forms. In homo-ness, selves are not destroyed and do not entirely lose their difference, but are dissipated in a 'vast network of *near sameness*, a network characterized by relations of inaccurate replication' (ibid.: 146, original italics). In his co-authored work with Adam Phillips, Bersani calls this form of relating both 'impersonal intimacy' (Bersani and Phillips 2008: 27) and 'impersonal narcissism' (ibid.: 56) in so far as it involves finding and relating to parts of oneself outside of oneself: it involves investing in a self that is radically dispersed and therefore depersonalised. Often with co-author Ulysse Dutoit, Bersani has also found this way of relating modelled in various works of visual art and literature which map subjectivity by showing the 'ontological implausibility of individuality' (Bersani and Dutoit 2004: 153).

This form of connectedness in sameness is frequently explicitly related to reduction. Bersani (1995: 166) celebrates a scene in Genet's *Funeral Rites* in which a German soldier fucks a French collaborator because of how the act connects them to impersonal experience: 'they are reduced, or elevated, to a kind of objectless or generalized ejaculation'. Drawing an analogy between 'sociability' as described by Georg Simmel and gay cruising because of the ways in which they eschew the distinctiveness of personality, Bersani (2010: 47) recognises in both the possibility of happily 'being "reduced" to an impersonal rhythm'. Discussing Samuel Beckett, Bersani and his co-author Ulysse Dutoit (1993: 77) celebrate *Worstward Ho* as a 'reduced work', its use of 'rhymes and alliteration reduce the text itself to a linguistic "unlessenable least"' (ibid.: 83). The value of the Rothko chapel in Houston is that while in it the 'viewer's self can momentarily be reduced to the cognition of consciousness and the world [...] as nonoppositional' (ibid.: 140). In Alain Resnais's film *Mon Oncle d'Amerique* the 'ego is reduced to (or ennobled by?) a consciousness of itself as the moves of a cinematic composition' (ibid.: 179). Across his work, Bersani (2010: 47) suggests that in order to commune with otherness, to enter into commerce with the universal play of forms in homo-ness, we must embrace an ethics of reduction, be '*less than what we really are*': 'lessness is the condition of allness' (Bersani and Dutoit 2004: 165).

But Bersani's attempt to redeem reduction by positioning it alongside ideas like elevation and ennoblement does not prevent him from making use of its more familiar rhetorical associations. For example, he writes that 'homo-ness' is a 'mode of connectedness to the world that it would be absurd to reduce to sexual preference' (Bersani 1995: 10). Theories about the redemptiveness of art are 'essentially reductive and dismissive about both life and art' (Bersani and Dutoit 1993: 3). The Freudian ego creates boundaries that 'would reduce all that we contain [...] to the psychologically shaped space of a particular subjectivity' (ibid.: 139). The differences upheld in conventional forms of relating are reinforced by the 'reduction of the subject to an untroubled optical identity' (ibid.: 159). In heteroised relations the 'world [is] reduced to a specular image of the ego' (Bersani and Phillips 2008: 121). There is seemingly a propriety that must be maintained: Bersani's analysis must still be marshalled against apparently problematic forms of reduction even as it is able to celebrate other instances of it.

Despite his professed interest in the non-redemptive, these reductions are just one of a number of forms of irredeemable sameness whose rejection figures significantly in Bersani's work. As we saw in the Introduction, for Bersani (2010: 56), what contrasts with the 'inaccurate replication' that characterises homo-ness are 'exact replications', the expectation of which constitutes an 'impossible demand' for an absolute sameness or a final consolidation and stabilisation of forms. In a way that we have also seen in Derrida and Butler, this final reduction is an impossibility, it simply cannot take place. Moreover, moving away from identity, or exact replication, towards inaccurate replication is a better way to serve difference: it rearticulates difference as the 'nonthreatening supplement to sameness' (Bersani 1995: 7). Bersani's aversion to the exact replications in identity is the reason he thinks of homosexuality, or homo-ness, only in terms of its 'specificity'. Homosexuality is valuable as a model only in so far as it is an 'anti-identitarian identity' (ibid.: 101), in so far as it can be formulated as containing the mobility that always thwarts the process of exact replication. Whilst for Bersani there are certain kinds of 'reduced' being that facilitate the communication of forms, we can also be 'reduced' to a 'particular subjectivity', an 'untroubled optical identity' or a 'specular image of the ego'. It is not only in becoming anonymised that we are reduced, but also in being particularised or limited to an identity. Yet the latter sameness, the latter mode of being 'reduced' or '*less than what we really are*', is not something that Bersani can embrace. Reduction is celebrated only in so far as it facilitates the subject's 'limitless extensibility in both space and time', or, in other words, in so far as it constitutes some form of redemption rather than a reduction (Bersani and Dutoit 2004: 9).

Once more without feeling

Bersani has an ambition to embrace forms of reduction that seem hopelessly unappealing within conventional value-systems tied to individualism and difference. I want to begin my reading of John Rechy's writing by noting how it arguably shares this ambition to revalue reduction and, consequently, the ways in which Bersani's terms might provide a persuasive account of Rechy. When one of the scores from *City of Night* (nicknamed the Professor) refers to the hustler's streetlife as 'reduced [...] to the Essential' (Rechy 1963: 66), this does not have the effect of discrediting that life or making it seem less appealing to Rechy's protagonist. When one of the 'numbers' in *Numbers* criticises Johnny Rio's instrumental approach to sex – 'Everything reduced to the physical act! [...] Instead of the mind and the heart stimulated, it's the *penis!*' (Rechy 1967: 103, original italics) – this does not prevent him from continuing to accumulate anonymous sexual contacts. Similarly, when Jim, the narrator of *The Sexual Outlaw*, recognises that while out cruising there is '[a]lways the possibility of a soulless reduction of bodies to limbs and orifices' (Rechy 1977: 287), this is not grounds for putting on his shirt and going home. These instances describe a form of reduction that does not necessarily respect individuality, complexity or difference, but, as in Bersani's account, this is not necessarily unwelcome or problematic.

Many of the areas that Rechy explores in his fiction are phenomena that Bersani imagines to figure access to anti-identitarian homo-ness. For example, Bersani has, at least in part, been interested in forms of gay cruising for the new modes of relating that they may facilitate. Sexual seriality within cruising has also been Rechy's preoccupation: his sense that he 'wanted all the characters [in *The Sexual Outlaw*] to be defined only through their sexual journeys' applies equally for characters across his oeuvre (qtd in Casillo 2002: 252). Certainly, in *The Sexual Outlaw*, the protagonist's life for the three days we have access to his movements is entirely preoccupied with preparing himself for and then participating in the sexhunt in Los Angeles. During sex with one man, Jim feels 'as if the universe itself were gathering into their bodies, their mouths, their cocks' (Rechy 1977: 131). In *Numbers* Johnny Rio is only really interested in hunting for sex in Los Angeles's Griffith Park: 'This is what I'd like to do all my life!' (Rechy 1967: 248), he thinks. Rechy's novel *Rushes* barely allows any space to the world outside of the cruising bar that gives it its title, and certainly not to the world beyond the purview of the casual sex culture it houses. (Strictly speaking, the novel begins outside the bar, during Endore's approach to it, and finishes in the orgy room next door.) As the night draws on, Chas, the novel's most aggressive sexhunter, declares gladly: 'All is sex now' (Rechy 1979: 192). For Bersani, fiction that is generically very similar to Rechy's in this regard exemplifies the terms for understanding sameness that he sets out. In Guillaume Dustan's *Dans ma chambre* (1996), for example, Bersani writes that '[t]ireless sexual promiscuity makes for a connectedness based on unlimited bodily intimacies' (Bersani and Phillips 2008: 37). Because this connectedness takes place solely on the level of sex instead of on the basis of individuality or personality, Dustan's novel presents a 'universal relatedness' based in the 'felicitous erasure of people as persons' (ibid.: 38).

As in Bersani's reading of Dustan, the people in Rechy's novels are often erased as individual persons. Assessing a day's hunting, Jim in *The Sexual Outlaw* wonders not how many people he has made it with but: 'How many hands? How many mouths? How many cocks? How many assholes?' (Rechy 1977: 107). During sex, the narrative focus is on individual parts: 'They press together again, cock on cock, hands sliding up and down, around, front, back; mouth on mouth, mouths on nipples, mouths on cocks, on balls, thighs on thighs, mouth on mouth' (ibid.: 131). In an orgy room there are only 'hands, limbs, mouths, bodies': 'it doesn't seem to matter whose cock, whose ass, whose body' (ibid.: 265). Men are 'reduced to shadows' and 'shadows reduced to mouths in alleys and parks' (ibid.: 286). Rechy's novels are full of these anonymous 'shadows' looking for sex (Rechy 1963: 34), '[s]hadows within shadows' (Rechy 1979: 12) and 'hunting shadows' (Rechy 1967: 40). If they are not shadows, then they are 'male ghostforms' (Rechy 1963: 191), 'misty ghosts' (Rechy 1967: 144) or 'dark searching ghosts' (Rechy 1977: 81). Throughout *The Sexual Outlaw*, Jim 'swims through pools of flesh' (ibid.: 303) and flesh is also the dominant motif in *Rushes*. Outside the bar are a series of meat trucks, which by day carry 'denuded carcasses of cattle hanging on savage racks' (Rechy 1979: 12), but by night are used as venues for men to meet for sex. Similarly, the orgy room not far from the Rushes (appropriately called The Rack) is situated next to a 'wholesale meat company' and is itself a collection of body parts: a 'square concrete mouth' for an entrance that opens below the 'iron bones' of an old fire escape ladder (ibid.: 15). What excites Chas about the men in the Rushes is the collective impression they create of 'illumined flesh': 'meat, prime meat' (ibid.: 30). Whether shadows, ghosts, or meat, 'outlines' (Rechy 1977: 26), or 'lifeless manikin people' (Rechy 1963: 256) all are 'intimate nameless strangers joined for one gasping brief space of time' (ibid.: 34–5), with Rechy's 'intimate strangers' relating to each other in a way that arguably foreshadows Bersani's 'impersonal intimacy'.

In *Numbers*, people become a means to an end for Johnny Rio's personal sex quest. His sexual contacts occasionally have some defining or distinguishing characteristics (for example, the 'curly-haired guy wearing the sailor's cap' (Rechy 1967: 170), or 'the man who licked me all over' (ibid.: 126)). More frequently though, Johnny makes it simply with a 'youngman' (ibid.: 29), or with one aspect of him, as when it is a 'youngman's mouth' that 'pounces as if starved – sucking him expertly' (ibid.: 81). Johnny counts these youngmen just like the other things he heavy-handedly counts throughout the novel (the number of days he intends to cruise in LA (ibid.: 10), bugs on his windscreen as he drives towards the city (ibid.: 12–13), the number of cars he passes on the road (ibid.: 14), repetitions during exercise (ibid.: 90), rosary beads in reminiscences of childhood (ibid.: 125) and even parked cars in the cruising areas of Griffith Park (ibid.: 147)). The novel is preoccupied with Johnny's compulsive desire for more sexual partners, but it is only when he counts '*Twenty-one!*' that he becomes aware that he '*is* counting, accumulating numbers aimlessly' (ibid.: 190, original italics). In order to ameliorate his sense of aimlessly accumulating contacts, Johnny '[f]everishly' performs other calculations to justify the goal of 'thirty' at which he tells himself he will stop (ibid.: 190–1). To nobody's surprise though, this turns out not to be enough for him. '*Thirty-one!* Johnny counts automatically' (ibid.: 245, original italics), returning to counting as soon as he returns to cruising, until the novel ends on the victorious declaration of number '*Thirty-seven!*' with no hint that this is in any real sense an ending (ibid.: 256, original italics). The frantic accumulation means that 'Numbers race madly through his mind, tumbling over each other. One-hundred-and-12, 113, 114 ... 5117, 6118, 7119 ... Numbers, numbers, numbers, numb – ...' (ibid.: 249). Like his penis, which is 'so numb it feels soft between the other's lips' (ibid.: 250), Johnny is numb to the difference between the numbers, the repetition causing them to blur into one, to lose 'even their few vestiges of identity' (ibid.). The increase suggested in Johnny's oft-reiterated mantra of self-assurance – 'Just one more!' (ibid.: 246) – is also a lessening. In a reversal of the conventional minimalist wisdom, more is less. Johnny's numbers end up flattening into one and reducing into shadows, but this, as per Bersani, might be seen as a mode of relating not predicated on the violence of discrete difference.

For both Bersani and Rechy, we could say that the kind of cruising that gets Johnny his numbers is a means not to respect another's individuality but to experience oneself as part of a constantly shifting correspondence of forms. Repeatedly, Rechy's characters understand themselves as elements in a formal arrangement that exceeds them. Johnny Rio is in a 'curious trance' (ibid.: 19): he moves 'like one hypnotized, reacting to some awful demand beyond his consciousness' (ibid.: 73). To alleviate this sense of being in a trance he puts in place his arbitrary total of thirty sexual contacts, but, as we have seen, this total is not enough for him. Finally, he makes the realisation: 'There never was a reason, I'm just here and that's all' (ibid.: 255). It is at this moment that he feels an 'enormous craving whose demands are already multiplying, squaring themselves, burgeoning geometrically' (ibid.: 255).

For Jim, in *The Sexual Outlaw*, the sexhunt is a 'ritual' (Rechy 1977: 28) with 'beautiful abstract choreography' that is 'balletic' and 'symphonic' (ibid.: 71). Similarly, what obtains in the Rushes are 'balletic rites' (Rechy 1979: 158), an 'arcane ritual' (ibid.: 30). The ideas of rituals, formalised dances and mathematical form suggest experiences in which the subject is reduced to a necessary continuity or correspondence with the forms of the world around it, which both include and exceed it. As Johnny Rio recognises, they are 'just here and that's all'. As Jim thinks to himself in *The Sexual Outlaw*, the 'search is the end. Not the answer – the riddle. The ultimate life-hunt, without object. Everything is found in nothing' (Rechy 1977: 300). The point for Jim, as with Johnny, is that one simply *is* in the world, not separate from it or able to gain mastery over it.

Indeed, Bersani's terms arguably allow us to understand not only Rechy but also something broader and more enduring in queer culture. As well as Dustan, writers such as Steward, Camus, DeLynn, Delany and Purnell have similarly explored the tendency of queer people to have multiple sexual partners via both literary and non-fictional writing. In a theoretical register, Guy Hocquenghem (1993: 132, 131) accounts for this as the inherent errancy of homosexual desire which, freed from the 'Oedipal cloak of morality', shows what happens when 'polyvocal desire is plugged in on a non-exclusive basis'. The result: 'The essential effect of the gay movement is first of all its crude sexualisation of the social field' (ibid.: 144). For Bersani, this constant sex results in a felicitously impersonal kind of intimacy not invested in defensive individuality. In his earlier work especially, sex is the agent of the undoing of the self. Famously, he begins his essay 'Is the Rectum a Grave?' with the provocative statement that 'There is a big secret about sex: most people don't like it' (Bersani 2010: 3). The reason they do not like it, Bersani claims, is how it troubles the sense of secure selfhood that people are assumed to be attached to. In Jane DeLynn's *Don Juan in the Village* (1990), this dislike of sex takes on a slightly different meaning. The narrator of the novel has lots of sex – the novel is structured around a series of sexual adventures – but frequently does not enjoy it. She repeatedly reports not finding her partners attractive (DeLynn 1990: 5, 62, 78, 223), sometimes even finding them disgusting (ibid.: 83, 101, 121), often goes about sexual acts 'with a total lack of desire' (ibid.: 14), or lack of interest (ibid.: 137), or maintains relationships with people she does not enjoy having sex with ('Nor was our sex particularly good' (ibid.: 63)). The narrator proves Bersani right: she does not really like the sex that she frequently has. And yet she continues to have it. The effect, though, is not necessarily to reveal how sex engenders and advertises the self's evacuation, but rather to make sex into just another thing that one does. Through being serially disappointing sex is relieved of the pressure to be fantastic, fulfilling, affirming. In being reduced to just another act, the pressure on sex to be the bearer of exalted meaning (i.e. the 'Oedipal cloak of morality') is removed.[4]

To some extent some of these writers even share with Bersani a rhetorical reliance on irredeemable forms of sameness. In *The Sexual Outlaw*, for example, Rechy repeatedly imagines promiscuity to have revolutionary effects (Rechy 1977: 28, 71, 125) that work against the 'stagnant conformity' (ibid.: 206) and 'heterosexual imitation' (ibid.: 299) of marriage and monogamy. These forms of sameness also attach to those who take the sexual outlaw lifestyle in the wrong direction. Jim goes into one LA bar and is struck by the 'posturing studs in fascist uniforms', a '[x]eroxed pseudo-"butch" conformity' (ibid.: 246). The uniforms are 'unindividualistically standard': the men who wear them 'often resemble mannikins manufactured, with varying degrees of attention, from one iron mold' (ibid.: 256). In *Rushes*, Endore recognises that the bar's patrons look '[i]ncreasingly alike': 'there is a new conformity, a marked sameness among the men of this sexual army' (Rechy 1979: 19). Again, they are like 'mannikins' (ibid.: 94). Rechy also refers to these men in an interview: 'In their "macho" rigidity, they become very "gay"', as if it is the rigidity itself, the unwillingness to entertain the possibility of change or difference, that makes them gay (Castillo and Rechy 1995: 122). Misguided sexual outlaws, then, turn into archetypal gay clones. Outlawry becomes like monogamy or marriage and accrues the disapprobation repeatedly expressed through the way in which Rechy associates them with sameness. In an essay on 'The Outlaw Sensibility', he writes that the proper outlaw's lifestyle involves the 'constant questioning of limiting assumptions' (Rechy 2004: 151). In *Numbers*, whilst Johnny Rio imposes his total of thirty sexual contacts in order to do away with the 'horror of counting toward no limit' (Rechy 1967: 191), the limit he imposes on himself, as we have seen, is one that he feels compelled to transgress. Rechy and Bersani, then, share a conceptualisation of a reduction that eschews limitation, and both arguably embrace reduction only in so far as it can be imagined as preventing solidification into normative and identitarian positions.

Soulless reduction

Acknowledging the approaches to reduction that Bersani and Rechy share, however, I also want to bring into focus the irredeemable ways in which Rechy's characters become '*less than what* [they] *really are*'. That is, if Rechy's characters become less than themselves, I want to explore how this takes place through the imposition of limits rather than through their transposition into 'limitless extensibility'. By in some ways exemplifying Bersani's terms for understanding sameness and reduction, I suggest that the parts of Rechy's fiction that do not fit so well with those terms encourage critical examination of Bersani's work. For example, the way in which sex in Rechy's fiction becomes a limit rather than a conduit to mobile correspondence within a universal relatedness manifests through the formal reduction effected in a number of neologistic compound nouns. One of Rechy's earliest essays, 'The City of Lost Angels' (1959), yields the terms 'sexsounds', 'sexpose' and 'sexpicture' (Rechy 2004: 23, 30, 33). Elsewhere, we see 'sexmusic', 'sexmoney', 'sexscene', 'sexfantasy', 'sexdream', 'sexsharing', 'sexeyes', 'sexmoans', 'sexnervousness', '*sexnoises*', 'sexmutterings', 'sexdrawings', 'sexpleadings', 'sexrooms' (Rechy 1963: 11, 26, 36, 36, 41, 62, 123, 190, 194, original italics, 238, 254, 315, 315, 342), 'sexhunters' (Rechy 1967: 94), 'sexhunt', 'sextime', '[s]exsenses', 'sexflesh', 'sexsighs', 'sexbuyer' (Rechy 1977: 16, 26, 75, 139, 164, 249), 'nightsex', 'sexcruiser', 'sexmoments', 'sexturf' and '[s]exshadows' (Rechy 1979: 13, 24, 38, 95, 95). The extent of these compounds speaks not only to the way in which nearly anything (or nearly everything) in Rechy's work can be about sex but also to the particular formal reduction effected through the use of compounds. By compounding the ideas in each case, Rechy limits the horizons of the noun so that it is not modified by sex, but reduced to nothing beyond its relation to sex. In this way, constant sex for Rechy is a limitation, not necessarily a facilitator of limitless extensibility.

Moreover, amongst all the indifference to specificity and anti-identitarian anonymity of Rechy's sexworlds, there is one particular quality that his characters are frequently expected to unflinchingly embody: conventional masculinity. Playing a non-participatory role in sex – that is, mostly, only allowing themselves to get blown – permits Rechy's characters to exist within circuits of normative masculinity by distancing themselves from the homosexual scenarios they nevertheless seek out again and again. This is how Johnny Rio, in *Numbers*, describes his limited sexual imaginary:

> First, I have never *desired* another man, I'm aroused only by what another man *does* – and not by *him*; second, I have not reciprocated sexually with another man – nor have I ever let a man come on with me other than with his mouth – and of course his hands – on my body; and third, I've done it for the money. (Rechy 1967: 45, original italics)

Johnny recognises this as the 'Myth of the Streets': 'a curious myth which says that a man may go with other men, over and over [...] and still be "straight" (that is, heterosexual) as long as he doesn't reciprocate sexually' (ibid.: 45–6). The narrator of *City of Night* has to engage in a similarly limiting sexual repertoire: 'Sex for me became the mechanical reaction of This on one side, That on the other. And the boundary must not be crossed' (Rechy 1963: 59). Sex acts are carried out 'mutely, automatically' in 'unconcerned, mechanical gesture[s]' (ibid.: 363). Visiting a cinema known as a cruising location, in *Numbers* Johnny becomes bored of the films that have been playing: 'it seems he's seen the same scenes over and over' (Rechy 1967: 93). Yet, ironically, Johnny himself never gets bored, or at least is content to get bored with, the same sexual scene over and over as long as it safeguards his masculinity. Whilst the mechanical repetition of sex acts makes the numbers lose their identity, it helps Johnny and *City of Night*'s narrator consolidate theirs.

The case is very similar in DeLynn's novel. Sexual seriality there is a way of reducing sex to just another thing that people do, but this, actually, doesn't embody the loss of identity which Bersani claims is the keynote of serial impersonal sex. In *Don Juan* the narrator, a bit like Johnny Rio, counts the women she has loved and feels 'proud of this number' which confirms her sense that she is a 'real Don Juan' (DeLynn 1990: 8). The momentary twinge of sadness she feels as she notes how much of that love has not been reciprocal is replaced by the end of the section by pity for the women who have loved her that she has scorned: 'tears of pity for these possibly imaginary beings welled up in my eyes' (ibid.: 9). This early passage foreshadows the intense self-regard that the narrator demonstrates throughout and is the source of much humour in the novel. For example, one reason that she gives for repeatedly returning to the lesbian bars that are her regular haunts is, in her words, to 'remind me of myself' (ibid.: 4). Later, also considering the particularities of the bar, she marvels: 'And yet, in spite of the obvious superiority of all aspects of my being, in the bar I was treated just like an ordinary person' (ibid.: 73). At the end of the novel, the narrator comes out of a New York bar and is struck with a sense of futility as she observes the people around her and also the significance of her own being. 'This disturbed me, of course, but in the immense vanity of my self-love and self-hate it was just one more way in which I managed to prove to myself and whoever was listening that I was the most incredible human being in the entire world' (ibid.: 240). What comes through repeatedly is the narrator's narcissism and vanity. But, as the reference to both 'self-love' and 'self-hate' suggests, this is vanity not only as self-regard but also as futility or lack of purpose.[5] The kind of reduction in meaning and significance that the seriality of sex brings about is the result not only of a loss of self but also of an intense investment in self.

Rechy and DeLynn help us tune in to the fact that limitless extensibility and limited identity are *both forms of reduction*. In so far as forms of reduction or 'lessness' are what Bersani is interested in, there need not be a distinction between them. Whilst Johnny Rio's cruising is described in depersonalising ways, or in ways that make it clear that the process takes him out of an individual personality, this does not mean it does not involve or consolidate some form of 'identity'. Driving towards LA at the beginning of the novel, Johnny is described as being in a 'curious trance', 'sailing automatically' (Rechy 1967: 19). Later, in the midst of collecting numbers, Johnny counts 'automatically' (ibid.: 122). He moves 'like a somnambulist' (ibid.: 73), 'like one hypnotized, reacting to some awful demand beyond his consciousness' (ibid.). When he enters the cruising areas of Griffith Park he feels as if he has 'interrupted the walk of somnambulists' (ibid.: 144). He feels himself 'succumbing to the trance he's sensed in others' (ibid.: 182). This may be a surrendering of personality, and, clearly, Johnny is not interested in individual personalities, such as when he shows discomfort in any kind of conversation with potential sexual partners (ibid.: 103). But at the same time we cannot say that he is not interested in identity, albeit an identity that turns him only into a bearer of generic qualities. He is, as we have seen, 'butch' and 'very male' (ibd.: 16). Moreover, he constantly ensures his status as generic by looking in mirrors (ibid.: 17, 23, 92). He is himself an 'irresistible number' (ibid.: 92); like the other numbers he is anonymous, but not without identitarian qualities. Moreover, the accumulation of numbers helps define his identity as a successful sexhunter. He seeks assiduously to collect them: twenty-three ('Seven to go! he counts (ibid.: 197)), twenty-four ('Only six more!' (ibid.: 202)), twenty-five ('though he only attempted to jerk Johnny off' (ibid.: 203)), twenty-six (a 'tall, well-dressed man' who 'licks Johnny's balls' (ibid.: 205)), twenty-seven ('Three to go! Johnny counts' (ibid.: 207)), twenty-eight ('Two to go' (ibid.: 216)), twenty-nine ('Only one to go' (ibid.: 220)), and, finally, thirty ('The game is over. Johnny won' (ibid.: 224)). Johnny's victory, however, is only a consolidation of the generic sexcruiser that he is. His generic status is only confirmed by the fact that we never see inside Johnny, or get first-hand insight into his personality: the third-person narration in the novel ensures that he only ever appears fully generic.

Johnny's anxious guarding of masculinity is just one aspect of the highly limited gendering of the worlds Rechy presents. In *The Sexual Outlaw*, Jim recites mantra-like what he sees and feels surrounding him whilst out cruising: 'Male, male, male' (Rechy 1977: 106). En route to the Rushes, Endore passes through 'blocks and blocks populated by men [...] only by men, homosexual men': 'only men' (Rechy 1979: 16). For Chas, the cruisebar in *Rushes* is so exciting because it offers him the 'sense of communion with other like men' (ibid.: 25). Elsewhere, Rechy encourages gay men to call themselves 'Trojans' as a means of celebrating the heroism of their masculine promiscuity (Rechy 2004: 162). However, where critics have recognised Rechy's investment in masculinity it is to refuse its capacity to limit. Kevin Arnold, for example, recognises a tension between Rechy's investment in sexual and gendered subject positions which embody dominant values and his simultaneous rejection of dominant subject positions (like the position of 'gay writer') as limiting. Arnold (2011: 125) acknowledges Rechy's investment in 'so-called normative strictures of identification', such as normative masculinity. However, he concludes in favour of an 'impossibility' at the centre of Rechy's normative representations which means that they do not capture anything like a 'truth' of the sexual subject (ibid.: 119). The impossibility of this truth then makes these normative representations the occasion for the play of desire rather than the simple entrenchment of convention. In Arnold's words, redolent of the post-structuralist positions explored earlier, the 'limit therefore is not also a *limitation*' (ibid.: 129, original italics). The example he gives of a truth that is never realised in Rechy's fiction is the fantasy of the coincidence between masculinity and homosexuality. However, in a list of 'easy classification[s]' that features 'queen, score, hustler, [and] fairy' the narrator of *City of*

Night also includes the 'masculine homosexual' (Rechy 1963: 239). In *Rushes*, Chas imagines that '[o]nly homosexual men can be truly masculine' (Rechy 1979: 25). Arnold's impossibility that prevents the deployment of subject positions from becoming problematic limitations is not so impossible after all. That is, Rechy's representations are reductively normative: there is not necessarily grounds for imagining a salvific impossibility at their heart that prevents them from being reduced to themselves. Compelled as we may feel to side with Arnold when it is something as problematic as conventional masculinity at stake, positions like his ultimately tell us more about criticism's desire to line up against the sameness in limitation than about Rechy.

To lose individuality and personality in Rechy's fiction, then, is not necessarily to come to correspond with a mobility of forms, but also to take on the fixity of 'lifeless manikin people' (Rechy 1963: 256). This process, though, can be thrilling. Tim, the only hustler character in *Rushes*, is 'raided by excitement and fear' as he hustles: he is 'determined to abandon even the vestiges of his identity beyond the night, compressing its experiences into a pastless present' (Rechy 1979: 131). Tim is a hustler before he is an individual. Importantly, this is not an abandonment of identity, but rather a surrender to it: to the limited identity of the hustler, to an identity that has nothing in it from 'beyond the night'. In *City of Night*, the narrator finds himself in a hustling bar full of 'sallow-faced youngmen' with 'artificial manikin faces like masks' (Rechy 1963: 110). Like the über-macho men criticised in *Rushes* for looking '[i]ncreasingly alike', these 'youngmen' become a type, as much from a factory line as the shop mannequins to which they are frequently compared. Whether one anonymous 'youngman' or a collective of 'youngmen', they appear throughout Rechy's fiction (Rechy 1963: 16, 26, 40, 58, 62, 103, 168, 172, 232, 256, 363; Rechy 1967: 14, 29, 56, 81, 126, 247; Rechy 1977: 23, 77, 87, 115, 216, 248; Rechy 1979: 12). The sexworld requires them to be nothing other than types – 'youngmanoutofajob', 'dontgiveadamnyoungman', 'youngmanlostinthebigcity' (Rechy 1963: 36) – such that they get to be interchangeable: 'theres [*sic*] dozens just like you – all of you even get to look alike – pictures in a fuckedup album' one irate score says (ibid.: 31). In a bathhouse in San Francisco, the narrator of *City of Night* observes attendants 'selected as to type' (ibid.: 256). In Rechy's later novel *Bodies and Souls* (1983), we learn that there are only 'two main types of malehustlers' (Rechy 1983: 309). Rather than daring representations of non-identity, Rechy writes, in the words of Gary Indiana (1999: n.p.), 'types [that] lack the kind of interiority a fictional character needs for the reader to care about his or her fate'. Unlike Guillaume Dustan, whom Bersani addresses, and whose novel of interminable sex has the redeeming air of the avant-garde, Rechy's work, to quote Indiana again, 'resemble[s] the middle-to-lowbrow fictions of a Jackie Collins' (ibid.). Bersani has been celebrated by one recent reader for the way in which his insights into non-identity have been enabled by his career as a professor of French, by the 'dailiness of his engagement with specific kinds of French complexity — linguistic to be sure but, more consequentially, literary and theoretical' (Savoy 2011: 243). If we can understand Dustan to occupy a similar place of consequential French complexity in Bersani's work, then it is perhaps clear why he is not interested in a figure like Rechy, who in some ways seems to exemplify the same ideas as Dustan. Devoid of continental glamour and difficulty that belong as much to the French post-structuralist theory cited earlier as to Dustan, Rechy strays into the abjectly simple and limited terrain of types.[6]

This is not to say that Rechy has been without interest for those who have endorsed Bersani's terms for understanding sameness. Tim Dean, for example, has adopted a Bersanian position in relation to a number of phenomena, including Rechy's work. We have seen (in the Introduction) some of Dean's theoretical commitments in a special issue of the journal *Umbr(a)* on 'Sameness' (2002), where he suggests that the figure of the gay clone models access to a 'zone of undifferentiation' that thwarts 'identity' in the same way as Bersani's homo-ness (Dean 2002: 30). The clone figures a 'sameness irreducible to identity' and is an 'allegorical figure of what Bersani calls "inaccurate self-replication"', but Dean is keen that the clone not be seen as merely a 'model of stifling conformism' (ibid.: 31). Dean has also recently applied similar terms directly to Rechy's work, suggesting that Rechy's characters perform true forms of transgression, which for Dean is a concept that has been domesticated by its association with the contravention of external laws or norms. For example, according to Dean's account, lesbian and gay sexualities do not constitute transgression in the true sense, as they only flaunt external prohibitions on non-heterosexual behaviour. For Dean, true transgression, by contrast, involves the transcending of an internal limit, an internal coherence or identity that names like 'lesbian' and 'gay' designate. Therefore, in Dean's words, 'transgression concerns not the law but *the limit*' (Dean 2010: 70, original italics). According to Dean, this internal limit is what Rechy's writing is concerned with transcending. Rechy's hustlers 'repeatedly violate not only municipal laws and social norms but their own internal limits' and so Dean imagines them as 'walking embodiments of the eros of transgression' (ibid.: 72).[7]

By contrast, I would suggest that it is by virtue of their conformity, identity and limitation that Rechy's types are of interest. By investing in these forms of sameness, whilst also in some ways exemplifying Bersani's understanding of homo-ness, Rechy's fiction allows purchase on those forms of sameness that Bersani and those, like Dean, who have adopted his terms, still have to keep at arm's length. If we are really keen to think about sameness, then surely we have to think about why even those who claim to be interested in sameness feel the need to argue against an abject version of it too ('irreducible to identity'). That is, it is not always clear why sameness needs to be described as 'irreducible' to its abject forms, as if these abject forms of sameness stand alone as clear and inarguable problems. There is an abiding orientation against sameness even in work that has explicitly sought to address it. Certain forms of sameness – identity, conformism, limitation, reduction – seemingly cannot be rescued from themselves and therefore provide the means for even work that takes sameness as its object to align with a broader set of value-judgements against the sameness of the homo.

Rechy's work remains invested in the kinds of irredeemable sameness that Bersani and others have to reject in order to secure a form of rhetorical propriety. If Bersani seeks to dislodge identity, his approach ignores how the sameness associated with identity might also be seen to effect the kind of reduction of individuality that he celebrates. Whilst cruising may facilitate the self's loss of its expressive particularity, identity – surrendering oneself to nothing more than one's maleness, for example – might also perform the same work of self-dispossession. The identities established by Rechy's cruisers are not expressions of tyrannical individuality, but rather ways of making that individuality less than itself. As if they were mannequins, their 'irreducible complexity' is reduced to a blank particularity. The 'identity' of Rechy's characters may also be a form of 'reduced being' or a mode of being 'less than what we really are'. That is, it is not necessarily clear that the reductive forms of sameness Bersani decries above – for example, 'particular subjectivity', an 'untroubled optical identity', a 'specular image of the ego' – actually function as the enemy of his project to move away from models of relating based on the sovereignty of differentiation and individuality. It is not clear why these forms of reduction should bother him when in the context of his broader argument he has sought to embrace reduction and sameness. The convenient rhetorical leverage that opposing reduction provides, however, indicates that as long as there is a form of bad sameness that can be rejected in favour of good sameness – 'untroubled identity' in favour of 'limitless extensibility' – rhetorical and theoretical integrity is maintained. However, far from transcending limitation, breaking apart the fixity it designates, Rechy's fiction would seem to bring into question the queer theoretical idealism that holds that, for queers, limitations are there only to be transcended.

Rechy redux

Up to now I have identified an occasional discrepancy between Rechy the author (as in his interviews) and the fictions he creates. Lest this seem like a self-difference that prevents Rechy from being reducible to himself, I also want to note how the writer and his work are clearly integrated. With the reiteration in his autobiography, *About My Life and the Kept Woman* (2008), of much that has already been written into his fiction, it is as if the many repetitions already in his body of work are consolidated, as if his oeuvre is in some sense reduced to itself. As one reviewer notes, it is in the second half of Rechy's autobiography that he 'rehashes literary quarrels and repeats old gossip' (Swartley 2008: 72). On his arrival in New York, Rechy (2008: 210) meets a man at the YMCA who tells him that if he is interested in making money he should try hustling in Times Square. So does the narrator of *City of Night* (Rechy 1963: 26). In Times Square, Rechy (2008: 210) is greeted by a neon sign that flashes the word 'F★A★S★C★I★N★A★T★I★O★N'. So is the narrator of *City of Night* (Rechy 1963: 34). Rechy's first client as a hustler is a man he calls Mr Klein who propositions him with the words, 'I'll give you ten bucks, and I don't give a damn for you' (Rechy 2008: 211). The narrator of *City of Night* is propositioned by a Mr King with exactly the same words (Rechy 1963: 27). Rechy experiences the desire for lots of anonymous contacts that feels 'like a geometrical progression that keeps on multiplying', 'thirty in one week' (Rechy 2008: 317), 'twenty-seven sexual contacts in the park in one day' (ibid.: 323). He feels the compulsive need for 'More. More' (ibid.), just as we have seen Johnny Rio do in *Numbers*. Like many of his protagonists, Rechy (ibid.: 216) describes developing a 'rigid set of requirements' for sexual contact, the principal one of which is 'to be desired without reciprocation'. Rechy is arrested under false pretences after a vice cop claims to have seen another man performing oral sex on him from a vantage point that does not offer the necessary view (ibid.: 327). This is the event that precipitates the whole plot of *This Day's Death* (1969) in which Jim Girard must deal with the anxiety of keeping his arrest from his dying mother. It also features twice in *The Sexual Outlaw* (Rechy 1977: 101, 215–17).

It is no great discovery to note these overlaps between Rechy's fictions and his life. Charles Casillo (2002: 187) stresses that 'fiction mixe[s] easily with biography' in Rechy's work and goes on to prove the point by constructing his own biography out of large chunks of quotation from Rechy's writing (ibid.: 19, 24, 36, 39, 52, 55, 94, 96, 97). Rechy is keen to stress the philosophical significance of this blurring of lines. He writes, 'of the literary forms, autobiography is the most fraudulent' because it claims the status of truth when it is based on selected memory (Castillo and Rechy 1995: 123). Fiction, therefore, is the 'most honest of the literary forms' because it makes no claims to tell the truth (ibid.). This observation itself is something that Rechy often repeats. In a review of a biography of Jack Kerouac, for example, he writes that 'Fiction carries more truth than biography; the former does not pretend to tell "the" truth, the latter does and so dissembles' (Rechy 2004: 101). In his autobiography, wondering if he has betrayed the people he met whilst living the life of a hustler by writing about them in fiction, he asks, 'But wasn't greater honesty also possible in fiction' (Rechy 2008: 307). This is why, elsewhere, he conjures the idea of his own 'autobiography as novel' (Rechy 1977: 48). However, I am interested not in the epistemological status of autobiography, or even Rechy's own philosophy on it (which is not all that noteworthy), but, rather, what it means for Rechy's oeuvre to contain so much repetition, to be in a sense reducible to a series of repeated anecdotes and positions. The effect this creates is of a literary oeuvre constructed, not around the limitless extensibility of a transcendent creativity and imagination (the kind of creativity that we saw him describe at the beginning of this chapter as knowing 'no limit') but around repetition and reduction. The irreducibly complex agency of Rechy's creativity is compromised by his adherence to a limited autobiographical repertoire.

For example, Rechy repeatedly returns to the veiled representation of celebrities he has met. The exploitative director: named as George

Cukor in Rechy's autobiography (Rechy 2008: 252), but appearing also as a nameless 'famous director' in *The Sexual Outlaw* (Rechy 1977: 87) and as another nameless 'director' who is 'one of the kings' in *City of Night* (Rechy 1963: 172–3). Rechy (2008: 252) describes Cukor as dismissive and unfriendly with a 'handsome man' on hand to serve drinks. In *City of Night*, Skipper 'is briefly the favourite of a famous Hollywood director', but is soon usurped by a new man, 'the director's current "discovery"' (Rechy 1963: 172–3). In *The Sexual Outlaw*, the narrator meets a nameless 'famous director' who 'courts an army of drifting youngmen': 'All are sure they'll become big stars. Not one has, not one will' (Rechy 1977: 87). Then there is the celebrated writer and his younger lover: named as Christopher Isherwood and Don Bachardy in Rechy's autobiography (Rechy 2008: 290), but also appearing as Sebastian Michaels and Tony Lewis in *Numbers* (Rechy 1967: 160–2). Just as Isherwood makes a move on Rechy when Bachardy is supposedly away at art school and then sulks when Rechy (2008: 291–3) rejects him, so Sebastian Michaels attempts to seduce Johnny Rio, forcing him to hitchhike from Michaels's home in the Santa Monica Canyon in the middle of the night (Rechy 1967: 162). The famous entertainer is another figure to reappear: Liberace, who is the 'honored guest' at a dinner party to which Rechy (2008: 261) has been invited, but also appears as the 'famous star' who gropes the narrator at a dinner party in a similar scenario in *The Sexual Outlaw* (Rechy 1977: 87). Plus, it is perhaps this extra personal connection that prompts his defence of Liberace in a review of Darden Pyron's biography of the singer (Rechy 2004: 215–16).

Less glamorous, more everyday encounters also come up repeatedly. Rechy (2008: 295) meets a man called Bob – 'in his upper thirties, slender, tall, good-looking in an undramatic way ... like an engineer, which he was'. Rechy enters into a more sustained relationship with Bob, seeing him 'week after week, often daily' (ibid.: 296). Rechy states bluntly that much of what happened between him and Bob was 'veiled' in the chapter of *City of Night* called 'White Sheets' (ibid.: 306), although he changes Bob's name to Jeremy (Rechy 1963: 371). In *Numbers*, Bob is reincarnated as Tom, an 'architect then in his late 30's' (Rechy 1967: 31), a man with whom Johnny Rio has previously had a more enduring affair, but who has moved on in the three years that Johnny has been away. In Casillo's biography, Bob is given the name Bryce Mckoy, which we are told is a pseudonym. Bryce is an 'attractive architect in his 40s' with whom Rechy develops a 'cautious friendship' (Casillo 2002: 128). Casillo also discusses the other monikers under which Bob is identified throughout Rechy's oeuvre (ibid.: 190). Aside from Bob-Tom-Jeremy-Bryce, Rechy (2008: 255) describes sitting in the Carousel Bar in Venice Beach with a 'married man' he had met earlier, when there is a raid on the bar by the police. In *City of Night*, the narrator also meets a married man on the beach (Rechy 1963: 240), with whom he goes to the Carnival Bar, although the man first mistakenly calls it the Merry-Go-Round (ibid.: 246) (not quite but almost the Carousel). In another scenario, Rechy (2008: 52–7) reports being invited to a hotel room by his teacher – Miss Edwards – in order to show her his story, but then has a sexual encounter with her. Johnny Rio reports a similar encounter with a teacher in *Numbers* (Rechy 1967: 47) and Lyle Clemens also becomes erotically involved with his teacher Miss Stowe (Rechy 2003: 57). We might wonder why anyone who has reportedly had over seven thousand sexual contacts (Rechy 1977: 46) would feel the need to repeat in this way.

But particular sexual scenarios, as well as particular people, pop up repeatedly. Just as he is happy to flaunt brushes with fame, Rechy seems keen to share the highlights of his scandalous sex life. The autobiographical voice of *The Sexual Outlaw* reports the hosting of a 'mock slave auction' in a bathhouse in Los Angeles (Rechy 1977: 270). The auction is raided by the police and becomes an occasion for Rechy to protest against police interest in victimless crimes (ibid.: 281). The same thing happens to Chas in *Rushes* (Rechy 1979: 27). Moreover, in *Rushes*, Endore complains that gay men are 'mim[ing]' the violence that is often perpetrated against their own (ibid.: 94): '[p]antomined "slave auctions"', he thinks, have unfortunately become popular (ibid.). An entire section of *Bodies and Souls* is dedicated to a similar slave auction event (Rechy 1983: 133–60).

As well as often repeated biographical events, Rechy also often has recourse to a fairly fixed set of opinions and concerns. Predictably enough, perhaps, he repeatedly writes about bodybuilding and gay male cultures. In a review of Bob Paris's *Gorilla Suit*, Rechy (2004: 181) writes that bodybuilding is 'homoerotic at its core'. One of the reasons for this is the intimacy between men that some of the exercises encourage. As Rechy (2004: 139) writes in an essay titled 'Muscles and Mascara', 'exercises often seem to mime sexual acts'. 'Spotting', for example, which is nominally to add support to a partner lifting a heavy weight involves 'one man straddl[ing] the head of a prone lifter' (ibid.). Spotting appears again in Rechy's review of *Gorilla Suit*, alongside 'donkey raises', which are calf exercises in which in order to add weight a 'helper mounts the buttocks of a lifter, who is bent over' (ibid.: 183). At one point in *Numbers*, Johnny Rio finds himself amongst bodybuilders in Venice Beach and observes men doing 'donkey raises': 'When you first come on it, the spectacle is startling: Each couple – in brief trunks – appears to be performing a distinctly recognizable sex act' (Rechy 1967: 66). Bodybuilding, Rechy (2004: 137) tells us in 'Muscles and Mascara', 'fits squarely in the realm of gay theater'.

Similarly, often key to Rechy's repeated thoughts about gay S/M culture is his sense of its overstated and theatrical masculinity which contrasts with the apparently more authentic masculinity of the hustler. In *The Sexual Outlaw*, Jim notes that the hypermasculinity on display in an LA bar creates a sense of 'male drag' (Rechy 1977: 238). In *Rushes*, Endore recognises something 'as clearly homosexual as drag' (Rechy 1979: 19) in the postures and clothing of the men in the bar. Roxy, a drag queen who has forced her way into the male-only space, implicates Chas in this association between male posturing and theatrical display: 'You know why my drag makes you uncomfortable[?]' she asks him: 'Because yours is just as gay as mine' (ibid.: 153). Rechy reports having this exact same experience himself (Castillo and Rechy 1995: 122). Bodybuilding culture is similarly effeminate: in an essay Rechy (2004: 55) writes that 'iron-pumped muscles [...] are as exaggerated a form of decoration as high drag'. In the review of Bob Paris's *Gorilla Suit*, he writes that Paris's muscles are 'not unlike sequined drag' (Rechy 2004: 184).

This idea of gay drag is just one of Rechy's preoccupations that manifest in redux form in his more recent writing. In *The Coming of the Night* (1999), for example, one character, Clint, is the mouthpiece for Rechy's (1999: 68) sense of the theatrical masculinity of gay male culture, which is as 'identifiably gay as drag queens'. It is through the characters of Clint (who experiences a series of uneasy flashbacks to previous S/M situations (ibid.: 69, 93–4, 118, 181)) and Dave (a leather man who thinks of gay S/M as '*true* liberation' (ibid.: 43, original italics)) that Rechy negotiates his own ambivalence about S/M cultures that we have seen manifest in his criticism of its forms of overt display. (More repetition: the leather man character in *Bodies and Souls* combines these two names: his stage name is Clint Dave (Rechy 1983: 140).) Rechy

(1999: 88) even conjures another exploitative and closeted Hollywood director in the form of Dick Gellman whose 'bizarre "private entertainments"' are the subject of one of the narrative streams in the novel.

A longstanding preoccupation of Rechy's that also makes its way obliquely into the novel is Alfred Chester's 1963 review of *City of Night*. Chester (1963: 6) complains that the stories in *City of Night* 'do not bring anything new to literature': they are 'mostly about the same old queens doing the same old things'. This famous early review is one that irked Rechy to such an extent that, in its wake, as Casillo (2002: 155) tells us, he 'rarely gave an interview without mentioning [it]'. Not only does he mention it repeatedly in interviews (Castillo and Rechy 1995: 119; Isherwood 1996: 59) but he also maintains a section of his website detailing his protests at what he thinks are other unfair reviews, including a series of letters written to the *New York Review of Books* protesting against the inclusion of Chester's review in a published selection of their essays.[8] He even writes a sarcastic reference to Chester into *The Coming of the Night*: a porn actor storms off set with the assurance to the director who has just tried to fire him that he can go and work for 'Alfred Chester' (Rechy 1999: 219). Rechy's repeated protest about the unjustness of the Chester review, however, ignores its truth: Rechy's writing is concerned more with the 'same old' than with the different. His seemingly constant preoccupation with the review and reviewers only reinforces the sense of Rechy's attachment to the 'same old' issues.

Rechy has commented that he is 'surprised at times to write down a thought for including in a future book' only to find 'that same thought in an earlier book' (Castillo and Rechy 1995: 123). It is strange that this should be a surprise though, when this consolidation of interests seems to be a structural principle of his oeuvre. Following Bersani, we might imagine Rechy's repetitions of himself to form a series of 'inaccurate replications' that demonstrate his awareness of his writing's extensibility, its not being confined to one sovereign place. This would ignore the correlative fact that Rechy's repetitions also consolidate his writing, fix and limit its interests and preoccupations. However, this reduced oeuvre might also constitute a mode of self-dispossession in so far as it indexes not the free and easy creativity of a limitless individuality but the surrender of this individuality to a form, an idealised image, an identity that in some sense reduces it and its scope for harbouring difference. The effect is to encourage us to see Don Weise's sense of the width in the 'wide array' of issues in which Rechy is apparently interested – which we encountered in the first section of this chapter – as a case of perhaps protesting too much.

Queer limitation

Finally, then, is there an answer to Rechy's question about the effects of gay minoritarianism: 'Are we to be reduced to one collective mass?' (Pally 1986: 53). Aside from the fact that the question assumes no answer is required, I argue that Rechy's fiction asks an arguably more pertinent question in response: what exactly is so bad about reduction anyway? I have suggested that the terms Rechy uses in his question have a peculiar rhetorical capacity, not only as he deploys them but equally as they are employed in scholarship about him and in scholarship more broadly. If forms of reduction are very helpful for organising against, if they generate very persuasive energies, if they gather very effectively forms of agreement in disapprobation, then we perhaps must wonder where this capacity comes from. In the context of Rechy's critical reception, we have seen that what has seemed most reductive about him are emphatically gay phenomena. Coupled with the presentation in his fiction of gay male sexuality through modes of reduction, I have argued that Rechy's reception makes him an ideal staging ground for thinking through the relation between the effectiveness of reduction as a means to discredit or critique and the always implicitly undesirable sameness which is definitionally linked to homosexuality. In so far as this association is what lends reduction its power, the way in which reduction is evoked only to be condemned is of a piece with broad assumptions against sameness that queer scholarship frequently displays and that I have been charting throughout this book.

On one hand, the work of Leo Bersani helps us understand Rechy's representation of serial sex, as well as the broader fictional and non-fictional patterns in queer culture that this relates to. But, nevertheless, that culture has been reductive in ways that scholarship is less good at recognising. Whilst Rechy in many ways embodies the terms that Bersani makes available for understanding sameness and reduction in queer theory, he also offers the opportunity to consider the forms of sameness that remain abject even in Bersani's work. Whilst Bersani distinguishes between salutary and non-salutary forms of reduction, ultimately utilising recognisable rhetorical protocols that work through reliance on an implicit opposition to apparently bad forms of sameness,

Rechy's writing embodies the abject forms of reduction that Bersani rejects: most notably identity and limitation. If we therefore label Rechy or his work 'reductive', which it seems fair to do (many have done), we should feel free to do so only because his fiction immobilises the definitive censure the term carries with it. But more than just writing reductive fiction, or giving voice in another format to queer culture's preoccupation with serial sex, Rechy also gestures to the particular formal links between reductiveness as an idea and the sameness that has also defined homosexuality. We saw at the beginning, for example, how homosexuality, more than any other idea, seems to Rechy and a range of commentators to be more limiting and reductive than anything else. Rechy's writing and reception provide an opportunity to explore where the limited, the reductive and the homo converge. Rather than seeking constantly to push past Rechy's limits, then, rather than conceding, with Judith Butler, that 'we can – and must – push the limits', we might instead try interrogating what makes those limits seem so hopelessly, abjectly, reductive.

Notes

1 For example, describing this scenario, Iris Marion Young (1990: 165) writes that the 'ideal of a universal humanity without social group differences allows privileged groups to ignore their own group specificity'. More recently, drawing on the work of Alain Badiou, James Penney has critiqued queer theory by providing an example of the dynamic Young describes. For Penney (2014: 4), queer scholars focus too restrictively on sexual identity and are therefore faulted for failing to address their work to a 'humanity generically conceived'.
2 The foundational work I have in mind here is the text by Sedgwick cited in the first section of the Introduction. It is notable for the terms that I have begun to examine that Sedgwick (1990: 11n19) describes her formulation as possibly requiring a 'drastic reductiveness'.
3 This structure is also central in much of Butler's other work. In *Excitable Speech* (1997) hate speech is re-signified via intervention in the necessary repetition that gives language its authority so that a formerly offensive word or phrase is not 'reducible' to its previous usage (Butler 1997b: 40). In *Antigone's Claim: Kinship between Life and Death*, Butler (2000: 23) suggests that Antigone 'figures the limits of intelligibility' and so is the occasion for the interrogation of the limits of acceptable forms of kinship (ibid.). In *Precarious Life: The Powers of Mourning and Violence* (2004), the necessary dispossession

of the subject in sociality is both a limit and a 'fecundity' (Butler 2004b: 19): it prevents us from ever fully knowing what constitutes the human and keeps it 'in its frailty and at the limits of its capacity to make sense' open to the possibility of renewal (ibid.: 151). In *Giving an Account of Oneself* (2005), Butler (2005: 46, 45) writes that a generalised awareness of our dependence on a constitutive sociality (an awareness that we are 'constitutively limited') can be the occasion for a mode of ethics not 'reducible to acts of judgment'. That is, our necessary limitations protect us from a mode of ethics limited to judgement.

4 DeLynn explores similar ideas in her collection *Bad Sex Is Good: Fiction and Essays* (1998). The collection features a number of extracts from *Don Juan*.
5 The opening story in *Bad Sex Is Good* draws attention to this double meaning of vanity (DeLynn 1998: 1).
6 There is perhaps some indication of Dustan's own indebtedness to Rechy in a casual reference from *Dans ma chambre*. The narrator of the novel listens to Soft Cell's song 'Numbers', which seems obliquely to gesture to Rechy's novel of the same name (Dustan 1998: 19).
7 Notably, Dean (2010: 70) distances himself from a Freudian account of taboo by calling it 'reductive'. Moreover, he has reprised his interest in breaking through limits in his recent account of barebacking culture (Dean 2009).
8 www.johnrechy.com/so_protest.htm.

Coda
Same again

Does queer theory matter any more? Something like this has been asked frequently enough in recent times that even the question itself is starting to lose its interest. Does anybody care about the answer? As well as the charges of *political* irrelevance that we saw in Chapter 1, more recently scholars have addressed a sense that queer theory has become *temporally* irrelevant too. In a commentary on the state of the field, Michael Warner (2012: n.p) has written of the 'widespread impression' that queer theory is a 'thing of the past'. In their earlier introduction to 'After Sex? On Writing Since Queer Theory' (2007), a special issue of *South Atlantic Quarterly*, Janet Halley and Andrew Parker also suggest that part of their motivation for editing the issue is an increasing sense that queer theory is past its sell-by date. While all of these scholars ultimately dispute the suggestion that queer theory should be binned, they none the less respond to what is perhaps more prominently a casual or anecdotal sense that it has nothing left to live for: even if not quite dead, queer theory is fatigued, inert or in need of inspiration. In his distinctly more dismissive *After Queer Theory*, James Penney (2014: 1) tells us that 'queer discourse has run its course, its project made obsolete by the full elaboration of its own logic'. It is an 'exhausted project' (ibid.), an 'intellectually dead discourse[]' (ibid.: 3), one of whose principal genres is simply to 'repeat old mantras from the 1990s' (ibid.). Whether embracing or rejecting the idea that queer work is outliving any possible relevance, all of these positions testify to the potential of queer theory itself to seem to veer too much towards the 'same old' in contemporary thought.

But one of the things this book has been concerned with exploring is the rhetorical dimension of positions like Penney's. I have attended to the traction that can be established by associating any idea, person, body of work, political strategy, argumentative move or other phenomenon with sameness. In particular, I have accounted for this traction through recourse to one of queer theory's 'old mantras': the insistence that homo/hetero sexual definition influences structures of value that may not seem emphatically to have anything to do with sexuality. According to the way in which I have interpreted this mantra throughout the preceding pages, I would argue that what allows Penney to discredit queer theory through associating it with the obsolete, the repetitive and the old is the sameness that these ideas carry in them: evoking them relies on the widespread assumption that only what can be related to difference deserves legitimacy and attention. I have traced similar assumptions throughout queer theoretical writing. Via engagement with figures and works from queer literary history, I have charted how these works put pressure on central rhetorical strategies in queer scholarship that are effective in so far as they similarly evoke a maligned sameness. In the first chapter, I focused primarily on two Henry James novels which enable insight into the historical link between queer identity and uselessness (or, idiomatically, the failure to 'make a difference'). I argue that these novels help us to reassess the enduring commitment to usefulness even in queer scholarship on failure and negativity. The second chapter explored how lesbian feminist speculative fiction has imagined forms of reproduction as crucial to utopian worlds and then staged these fictions as a counterpoint to the assumption in queer theory that reproduction will only ever be linked to heteronormativity. In the third chapter, we saw that early twentieth-century lesbian middlebrow writing formally and thematically associates lesbianism with the kinds of normativity that queer theory has defined itself against. Focusing on John Rechy, the final chapter examined the reductiveness of the fiction and practice of queer sexual seriality. Whereas queer theory opposes reductionism and its link to a maligned 'logic of identity', these novels show how queer culture has in parts nevertheless been reductive in precisely this way. The idea that queer theory has nothing left to give simply because it is old, repetitive or boring seems to function in a similar way to some of these concepts: that is, through an implicit sense that what we should be motivated by is the new, the innovative and, above all, the different.

However, in an era of gay marriage and widespread gay visibility, when other minorities seem more urgently to need protection, it is perhaps easy to see why people might be inclined to bring the importance of queer theory into question. As the editors of 'After Sex?' note, the sense of queer theory's waning relevance has come in part from the fact that the 'activist energies that helped to fuel queer academic work in the United States have declined sharply since the early 1990s' (Halley and Parker 2007: 421). Indeed, a theoretical orientation that is often narrated as emerging from the context of the AIDS crisis or (specifically in the UK) the social engineering of section 28 will perhaps seem to many a lot less urgent in our current social and political climate in which queer people are often invited into the institutions of the state and the emergency of deadly disease seems to some to have been eased through medical advances and awareness-raising. Much of the queer theoretical work by which I have been influenced in this book, however, has tended to reject the idea of queers' steady progress away from political emergency and danger towards general acceptance. Moreover, this work has often sought to hold on to what can seem outdated or unhelpful in the context of apparent social progress. As we have seen, Heather Love looks at queer literary figures from the past whose approaches to their queerness may seem backward or unhelpful for contemporary political strategies. These figures, she argues, can alert us to structural similarities between current and past situations. For Love, we have not necessarily reached a stage of enlightenment in which feeling bad for queers can be consigned once and for all to the history book. Furthermore, I would add that the fact that something is from the past is not in itself grounds for moving beyond it. Indeed, to discredit something just because it seems like more of the same is a way of avoiding engaging with the issues raised by whatever is thus dismissed. As Jane Elliott (2006: 1701) has written, quoted earlier in the Introduction, the rejection of something simply on the basis of its routinisation is to ignore the fact that 'things may stay true longer than they stay interesting'. Moreover, as I will discuss in more detail below, the notion that queer theory should be relevant only as a political tool in the current moment ignores the many other motivations that may drive theoretical enquiry into queer culture and ways of being such as pleasure, interest or even the scholarly purpose that is taken for granted as the basis for non-politicised academic fields.

 Primarily it is the conviction that not all the social or political battles for queers have yet been won that has prevented me from arguing for abandoning social difference as an object of analysis, whether in the form of race, gender, sexuality, class, nationality, dis/ability or any other consequential social form. Even as many may no longer find this list of social forces interesting, I join others in the conviction that there is surely still truth in the effects they have on social life. Some scholars, like Alain Badiou, have invited us to move away from paying any attention at all to social categories like these, in order to elaborate a project that can enable a generic emancipation. James Penney, cited briefly above, has made a similar argument. By contrast, I have not wanted to make a statement to the effect that what a number of scholars named the 'politics of difference' has passed or become redundant, as if the categories that gave rise to those projects no longer engender forms of social abjection. Instead, one thing I have wanted to do is to pay attention to rhetorical strategy. Politics of difference approaches often justify themselves simply through their commitment to *difference*. At the same time, where scholars seek to discredit these approaches they are rendered as 'identity politics', which are styled as offering only limitation and restriction in the face of broader projects for change. I have meant to supplement the 'politics of difference' with the 'politics of sameness', or the framework I have established through these pages in which default oppositions to sameness can be interrogated. If anything, my ambition has been to refocus attention on how social forms manifest in culture and what kinds of tactics or moves or solutions are most amenable to them, which might, paradoxically, not always mean strategies that bear any relation to difference and its related ideas.

I would return, then, briefly, to what in the Introduction I suggested was an important influence on the project undertaken in this book. In *Object Lessons*, Robyn Wiegman (2012: 1) explores how what she calls 'identity knowledges' invest in particular objects of study or analytic moves as the guarantee of their own political usefulness. One example that I addressed in Chapter 3 is queer theory's attachment to anti-normativity, which in many ways defines the field and is frequently imagined to secure the fundamental queerness of phenomena and scholarly approaches. As Wiegman shows, though, a staunch commitment to anti-normativity by no means necessarily always works to queer positive ends. The explicit intent of *Object Lessons*, however, is not to move away from identity knowledges like queer theory, or even to suggest that they change wholesale the way they do business, but rather to get inside their motivations and ambitions. Wiegman's project is to 'show why identity knowledges are so compelling by attending to the

Coda: Same again 191

promises they make and the wishes and prohibitions that sustain them' (ibid.: 343). She is very sympathetic to the value of the promise of social transformation that they provide. Indeed, her project is to try to explore the ways in which investments in this promise can sometimes be too much for the objects that are often taken to be able to deliver on it. I have attempted something that I imagine to be similar in this book. In my case, I have also tried to account for what seems most compelling in queer theoretical writing, which has meant, counterintuitively, reading its frequent orientations against sameness in relation to a broader de-privileging of homosexuality. As with Wiegman's work, I think the project undertaken here could have modest practical effects in encouraging closer attention to the ways in which forms of sameness function as a convenient shorthand which can sometimes distract from a clearer focus on those social forces we might more emphatically want to oppose. I have wanted to make the suggestion that it can be helpful to separate social phenomena like exclusion, marginalisation and structural inequality from the forms of sameness with which they have often been given shape, or through which they are often imagined to be brought about, so as to focus greater attention on their specificity and how they actually function.

Of course, there may well be historical reasons that scholarship in identity knowledge fields like queer theory has tended to organise itself rhetorically around forms of difference. At various points throughout the preceding pages we have seen that a significant historical influence on queer scholarship has been post-structuralist theory, which provides perhaps the most academically prestigious and strongest account of the metaphysical and practical necessity of difference. For scholars like Judith Butler and Lee Edelman, the inevitability of self-difference is offered against the impossibility of sameness in the form of concepts like identity, Imaginary wholeness and the transcendental signified. Post-structuralist theoretical co-ordinates seem to necessitate the insistence that difference simply *is the case*, in the way that heterosexuality functions as what simply *is the case*, as the incontrovertible background to everyday life. I would argue, then, that the fact that many of the literary figures I have addressed here wrote before the widespread dissemination of post-structuralist ideas may be a reason that their works remain unconvinced of the values of difference that many post-structuralist-inflected contemporary theorists endorse. Detailed historical work has been done on how post-structuralist thought came to have such a powerful influence on the American intellectual field from which queer theory primarily emerged (Cusset 2008). Others have provided broader histories, locating the shift towards human worldviews based on singularity and difference, and away from worldviews based on resemblance, at the beginning of Western modernity in the sixteenth century (Silverman 2009). However, arguably more work remains to be done on the particular ways in which forms of difference have come to seem more important, valid and persuasive than forms of sameness. Indeed, such work may address the historical coincidence of, on the one hand, the rise of post-structuralism with its insistence on difference and, on the other, the increasing visibility of same-sex communities in the Euro-American academy and world from the middle of the twentieth century. Whilst some might imagine these two historical phenomena to work in tandem, with post-structuralism sometimes providing a philosophical or theoretical analogue for the new social movements that emerged from the middle of the twentieth century (like gay liberation movements) (Cusset 2008: 145–54), there might also be occasion to imagine the efforts of post-structuralist thinkers to strongly assert the non-negotiability of difference as a reactive effort in the face of increasingly visible attachments to sameness in the form of an increasing gay public presence. Such historical inquiry has been beyond the scope of this book, which has focused less on constructing a full genealogy of difference in queer theory than on exploring the way it has been privileged in contemporary theoretical formations. I none the less gesture to such a historical account here because it would seem to corroborate a sense encountered throughout the preceding pages that the influence of post-structuralist theory has been central for the way in which queer scholarship has kept difference, the hetero, at the heart of its endeavours.

Perhaps most significantly, the centrality of post-structuralism to queer theory is what has prevented the field from taking any real interest in any way in identity. In the context of post-structuralism, as we have seen, identity, self-sameness, is only ever a politically questionable fiction. Yet, of all the 'identity knowledge' fields which have been influenced by post-structuralism, it is queer theory which has most powerfully rejected the identities which have, in theory, been at the core of the knowledge it has established: that is, lesbian and gay identities. For example, the field-forming *Lesbian and Gay Studies Reader* (Abelove et al. 1993), which contained many of the canonical texts of what would become queer theory, never really served to found a field called 'lesbian

Coda: Same again

and gay studies'. Indeed, some commentators have become so hostile to lesbian and gay identities that these identities have been reimagined as the most pernicious vectors of modern state power (Puar 2007; Eng 2010). In the Introduction, we saw how some have been adamant that queer theory should provide more than a 'survey of gay male aesthetics' (Eng, Halberstam and Muñoz 2005: 12). While this may be true and laudable, surely the imperative to abandon identity should not make any interest in gay aesthetics seem intrinsically politically suspect. Nor is it clear immediately why it is queer theory in particular that is the most appropriate context in which to situate the move beyond what is emphatically attached to gay males. After all, where else are they going to go? Throughout this book, I have focused on aesthetic objects produced in the contexts of various lesbian and gay identities, from the late nineteenth century when, historians have claimed, such identities first became recognisable and available, to the present day. In resisting the vocabulary of difference that has largely been bequeathed to queer theory by post-structuralism, I have also done so via readings of works arguably tied in what is for some a politically or theoretically undesirable way to forms of lesbian and gay identity. One thing that a field called 'lesbian and gay studies' could do is to examine the culture produced by lesbians and gays in this way. This is in part what I have attempted here and the model this provides is a further upshot of the analysis I have offered in the preceding chapters. I have suggested through my readings that there is scope for a queer studies with a renewed willingness to dwell specifically on lesbian and gay phenomena. Can the cultural production produced by lesbians and gays sustain scholarly and critical attention? What do we learn from it that we can't from other things? Should we not be expected to honour the pleasure that many queer people have found in these identities and in this culture?

Against such suggestions, the impulse that mostly tends to drive scholarly and activist energies in gender and sexuality studies is to move on to whatever seems most politically and socially current. The constitution of the discipline as primarily a political field with its sights set on intervening in contemporary social relations, as well as the commitment to the malleability and flexibility of gender and sexual identities that is at the discipline's core, have left little choice for proponents but to focus on what's new, what's different and what's changing in the social sphere. In order to be itself, the field has had to position itself at the vanguard of the social experience of gender and sexual identity. We can see this in the various 'waves' of feminism, as well as in the positions outlined above which in different ways have suggested that queer theory is no longer needed because it is apparently politically superseded. As we have seen, moving on from fixed sexual identities was key to the philosophical project of queer theory. Writing in a less theoretical vein in the late 1990s in a book tellingly titled *Gay and After* (1998), Alan Sinfield (1998: 1) argues that 'we may be growing out of "gay"'. He suggests that new kinds of sexual formations show that 'gay and lesbian' may not be the last word on same-sex sexual identities any more and that further 'subcultural work' (ibid.: 5) is required to make forms of sexual dissidence appropriate for the new millennium. As the 'After' of his title and the reference to growing up suggest, Sinfield's suggestion is that 'gay' is a thing of the past. But it is an arguably curious demand that makes gayness seem past-it in this way. The implicit conclusion is that 'gay' is interesting or important as a category only in so far as it can be said to completely explain a lived social reality, or could summarise the collective lived social realities of sexual dissidence in 1998. Other objects of study do not need to bear this burden in order to be afforded validity as objects of study. Yet, objects within gender and sexuality studies are strongly subject to this expectation. Because of the field's constitution as a political tool, the only valid objects have been seen as those at the cutting edge of a social or political battle. The idea that we might study lesbian or gay phenomena and culture, or phenomena and culture pertaining to any other particular sexual formation, because they are interesting or revealing (or because it's fun to do so) does not seem to feature as a common assumption. But this book has been as much about readings in gay culture as anything else. The primary motive has been not to tune in to the most up-to-date knowledge of the landscape of sexual and gender expression but, to quote myself above, to pursue the 'pleasure, interest or even the scholarly purpose that is taken for granted as the basis for non-politicised academic fields'. I have implicitly argued to think of lesbian and gay phenomena as interesting and worthy of study aside from a perceived sense that to do this is to perform political work.

David Halperin has done something similar in his recent book *How to Be Gay* (2012). Whereas Sinfield looks forward (to what is 'after'), Halperin looks back to an apparently outmoded gay culture to consider what is distinctive about it. Halperin (2012: 63) argues that it is only the now institutionalised assumptions of queer theory that have prevented scholars from investigating the distinctive patterns and objects that have constituted gay culture, which has a singularity and a consistency that queer theory teaches us to see as fantasmatic or implicitly problematic. By contrast, Halperin sees what he calls 'traditional gay male culture' (ibid.: 50) as a specific 'way of being' (ibid.: 12) that can be parsed. For him, aspects of traditional gay culture (e.g., opera music, *Mildred Pierce*) capture something in their aesthetic forms which echo aspects of marginalised sexual life or social form: they testify more fully to what it means to be gay in a heterosexist world, or else they 'realize gay desire rather than denoting it' (ibid.: 112). This culture therefore offers a more expansive way of being gay and, like any culture, is something that has to be learned through structures for cultural reproduction: 'material support, organization, and a queer public sphere' (ibid.: 26). My book bears a number of similarities to Halperin's project. Firstly, I share his guiding assumption that there is such a thing as gay culture that can sustain scholarly attention, and the works I have examined are drawn from that culture. Secondly, I have also explored the 'relation between sexuality and social or aesthetic form' (ibid.: 35). As I discussed in the Introduction the boring repetitiveness of coming out stories (their aesthetic form) stems from the repetitiveness of marginalised existence (gay social form). Finally, with Halperin, I recognise that gay cultures, as learned ways of being, require structures for support and maintenance. In Chapter 2, I noted that logics and structures for reproduction are *most crucial* to minority cultures that do not enjoy these as standard.

However, Halperin ultimately ends up distancing his understanding of 'traditional gay male culture' from the cultural products produced by actual lesbian and gay people. For Halperin, 'traditional gay male culture' means the range of responses that gay men, principally before the liberation movements of the later twentieth century, have tended to entertain in relation to putatively mainstream cultural objects such as Joan Crawford or opera or Broadway musicals. According to the narrative that Halperin constructs, gay liberation brings with it an affirmative gay identity which replaces the older culture and looks on it as a backward and outmoded collection of stereotypes. Moreover, this new affirmative identity is a political identity based on ways of having sex rather than broader ways of being: the identity of gay liberation replaces the 'pleasure or feeling or *subjectivity*' of the earlier culture (ibid.: 70, original italics). Halperin singles out lesbian feminism and the gay 'clone' as icons of this new affirmative identity (ibid.: 48), apparently unable to see these as involved in any project of culture-making or way of being. Halperin is not the only one to feel this way. He describes teaching a course on 'gay male studies' (ibid.: 109) only to find that his students prefer to find queer meanings in 'non-gay representations' rather than in 'reading gay novels' (ibid.: 110). To evoke the coming out stories discussed in the Introduction once more, we have seen in that context how boredom can be the product of cultural objects that are too closely tied to gay identity. But surely there is also pleasure or feeling or even subjectivity to be found in clone culture or lesbian separatism or coming out stories. Why does their emphatic relation to gayness or lesbianism prevent them from also constituting ways of being or cultures?

Throughout this book, I have charted aesthetic objects that have not only been tied to gay and lesbian identities but that have also registered as disappointments in a similar way to the 'gay novels' that Halperin's students disdain. For example, Radclyffe Hall's writing has been considered middle-brow, Charlotte Perkins Gilman's texts are didactic tracts rather than literary creations and reviewers have baulked at the way John Rechy writes novels full of simplistic, unsophisticated types. Even when concerned with Henry James, a figure often imagined to have a high aesthetic pedigree, I have turned to novels that have been considered lesser works: Jonathan Freedman (1990: 145), for example, says that *Roderick Hudson* is not one of 'James's great imaginative achievements'. The judgements that have been made about these objects echo the judgements of Halperin and his students. What is too directly linked to gay or lesbian identity is liable to seem like an aesthetic disappointment. Rather than a new framework for investigating and attending to gay culture and the products it generates, Halperin's analysis, in the end, toes the line of queer theory's anti-identitarianism. If we really want to follow through on Halperin's ambition to chart the links between sexual and aesthetic forms within culture, then we have to question how what is tied emphatically to lesbian and gay identities seems so culturally and aesthetically disappointing, even to gay consumers, and think about the gay-aversiveness that would seem to underpin this.

One of the things that I would hope that this book enables, then, is for other scholars to see value, or at least interest, in the cultural production that is tied in literal and, perhaps, for some, unimaginative ways to lesbian and gay identities. This would by no means require the total scrapping of queer theory which, for example, James Penney has called for. Instead, it would follow in the footsteps of the thinkers addressed

Coda: Same again

at length in the Introduction who have sought to alter the terms on which queer theory does business such as Love, Freeman, Halberstam and Amin. On one hand, I have suggested that we supplement the 'politics of difference' with the 'politics of sameness'. This would mean continuing to assert the value of attending to the ways in which social forces like sexuality, race, gender and class enable forms of domination and abjection. But it would also mean questioning whether it is necessary to organise against forms of sameness in order to oppose or interrogate domination and social abjection. It is valuable to question the extent to which ideas like normativity, reductionism, reproduction and the status quo should really in themselves be targets of opposition, or if they evoke forms of sameness as convenient rhetorical shorthands to signal social ills, capitalising on the capacity of sameness to seem unjust, unpalatable, unwanted. On the other hand, my approach means not taking queer theory into some unchartered new future but rather returning to the opportunity that was latent but never fully realised in the original imagining of the field as a 'lesbian and gay studies'. Such a field would be more interested in the specificities of the objects and cultures created by lesbian and gay people than committed to the imperatives of a late twentieth- and early twenty-first-century theoretical formation. Rather than offering a fundamental change to current work, then, I could say that my intention in the preceding pages has been to encourage queer work to be even more like itself, in so far as its ambitions are to specifically address forms of marginalisation and social exclusion as experienced by non-heterosexual people, rather than necessarily to endorse theoretical positions privileging, often in abstract terms, difference over sameness.

The suggestion that queer theory should be forgotten because it is old, repetitive or obsolete does not have the desired effect of convincing me that it should be forgotten about. Yet, as I have tried to show, there's certainly scope for rethinking the field's relation to sameness, which means, relatedly, rethinking those cultural objects which seem hopelessly tied to specific sexual identities. Rather than heading off in some bold new direction for the field, then, we could have another go at what the field at one point promised to be, or else to put it differently, try trying the same old thing again.

References

Printed sources

Abelove, Henry, Michèle Aina Barale and David Halperin, eds. (1993) *The Lesbian and Gay Studies Reader*. London: Routledge.

Adams, Stephen. (1980) *The Homosexual as Hero in Contemporary Fiction*. London: Vision.

Ahmed, Sara. (2006) *Queer Phenomenology: Orientations, Objects, Others*. Durham, NC: Duke University Press.

Ahmed, Sara. (2012) *On Being Included: Racism and Diversity in Institutional Life*. Durham, NC: Duke University Press.

Ahmed, Sara. (2017) *Living a Feminist Life*. Durham, NC: Duke University Press.

Aldama, Frederick Luis. (2005) 'John Rechy's bending of brown and white canons', in *Brown on Brown: Chicano/a Representations of Gender, Sexuality, and Ethnicity*. Austin: University of Texas Press: 47–72

Allen, Judith A. (2009) *The Feminism of Charlotte Perkins Gilman: Sexualities, Histories, Progressivism*. Chicago: University of Chicago Press.

Allison, Dorothy. (1995) *Skin: Talking About Sex, Class and Literature*. London: Pandora.

Alvarez, Alma Rose. (2007) *Liberation Theology in Chicana/o Literature: Manifestations of Feminist and Gay Identities*. London: Routledge.

Amin, Kadji. (2017) *Disturbing Attachments: Genet, Modern Pederasty, and Queer History*. Durham, NC: Duke University Press.

Anderson, Amanda. (2006) *The Way We Argue Now: A Study in the Cultures of Theory*. Princeton: Princeton University Press.

Arnold, Kevin. (2011) '"Male and Male and Male": John Rechy and the scene of representation', *Arizona Quarterly* 67.1: 115–34

Badiou, Alain. (2001) *Ethics: An Essay on the Understanding of Evil*, trans. Peter Hallward. London: Verso.

References

Barber, Karen, and Sarah Holmes, eds. (1994) *Testimonies: Lesbian Coming-Out Stories*. Boston: Alyson Publications.

Bartel, Kim. (2005) 'Unmoored from "the shore of the real": Henry James, *Roderick Hudson*, and the advent of the modern in nineteenth-century painting', *Henry James Review* 26.2: 168–88

Bartkowski, Frances. (1989) *Feminist Utopias*. Lincoln: University of Nebraska Press.

Baudrillard, Jean. (2000) *The Vital Illusion*, ed. Julia Witwer. New York: Columbia University Press.

Bederman, Gail (1995) '"Not to *Sex* – But to *Race!*": Charlotte Perkins Gilman, civilized Anglo-Saxon womanhood, and the return of the primitive rapist', in *Manliness and Civilization: A Cultural History of Gender and Race in the United States, 1880–1917*. Chicago: University of Chicago Press: 121–69

Bell, Matt. (2011) 'When Harry met Harry', in Madhavi Menon, ed., *Shakesqueer: A Queer Companion to the Complete Works of Shakespeare*. Durham, NC: Duke University Press: 106–13

Berg, Allison. (2002) *Mothering the Race: Women's Narratives of Reproduction, 1890–1930*. Urbana and Chicago: University of Illinois Press.

Berlant, Lauren, and Michael Warner. (1995) 'What does queer theory teach us about *X*?' *PMLA* 110.3: 343–9

Berlant, Lauren, and Michael Warner. (2003) 'Sex in public', in Robert J. Corber and Stephen Valocchi, eds, *Queer Studies: An Interdisciplinary Reader*. Malden: Blackwell: 170–83

Bersani, Leo. (1990) *The Culture of Redemption*. Cambridge, MA: Harvard University Press.

Bersani, Leo. (1995) *Homos*. Cambridge, MA: Harvard University Press.

Bersani, Leo. (2010) *Is the Rectum a Grave? and Other Essays*. Chicago: Chicago University Press.

Bersani, Leo, and Ulysse Dutoit. (1993) *Arts of Impoverishment: Beckett, Rothko, Resnais*. Cambridge, MA: Harvard University Press.

Bersani, Leo, and Ulysse Dutoit. (2004) *Forms of Being: Cinema, Subjectivity, Aesthetics*. London: BFI.

Bersani, Leo, and Adam Phillips. (2008) *Intimacies*. Chicago: Chicago University Press.

Bloomer, Jeffrey. (2014) 'The "boyfriend twin" and our tendency to date people who look like us', *Slate*, 10 April. https://slate.com/human-interest/2014/04/boyfriend-twin-photos-do-gay-men-date-people-who-look-similar-to-them.html. Last accessed: 24 March 2019

Botshon, Lisa, and Meredith Goldsmith. (2003) 'Introduction', in Botshon and Goldsmith, eds, *Middlebrow Moderns: Popular American Women Writers of the 1920s*. Boston: Northeastern University Press: 3–21

Bristow, Joseph. (1995) *Effeminate England: Homoerotic Writing after 1885*. [n.p.]: Open University Press.

Broderick, Ryan. (2014) 'There's a new Tumblr that collects photos of boyfriends who look like each other', *Buzzfeed*, 8 April. www.buzzfeed.com/ryanhatesthis/the-new-boyfriend-twins-tumblr. Last accessed: 24 March 2019

Brown, Wendy. (1995) *States of Injury: Power and Freedom in Late Modernity*. Princeton: Princeton University Press.

Bruce-Novoa, Juan. (1992) 'Homosexuality and the Chicano novel', in Wayne R. Dynes and Stephen Donaldson, eds, *Homosexual Themes in Literary Studies*. New York: Garland: 33–41

Butler, Judith. (1997a) *The Psychic Life of Power: Theories in Subjection*. Stanford: Stanford University Press.

Butler, Judith. (1997b) *Excitable Speech: A Politics of the Performative*. London: Routledge.

Butler, Judith. (1999 [1990]) *Gender Trouble: Feminism and the Subversion of the Identity*. London: Routledge.

Butler, Judith. (2000) *Antigone's Claim: Kinship between Life and Death*. New York: Columbia University Press.

Butler, Judith. (2004a) *Undoing Gender*. London: Routledge.

Butler, Judith. (2004b) *Precarious Life: The Powers of Mourning and Violence*. London: Verso.

Butler, Judith. (2005) *Giving an Account of Oneself*. New York: Fordham University Press.

Butler, Judith. (2011 [1993]) *Bodies that Matter: On the Discursive Limits of 'Sex'*. London: Routledge.

Butler, Judith, Ernesto Laclau and Slavoj Žižek. (2000) *Contingency, Hegemony, Universality: Contemporary Dialogues on the Left*. London: Verso.

Carter, Julian. (2009) 'Gay marriage and pulp fiction: homonormativity, disidentification, and affect in Ann Bannon's lesbian novels', *GLQ: A Journal of Lesbian and Gay Studies* 15.4: 583–609

Casillo, Charles. (2002) *Outlaw: The Lives and Careers of John Rechy*. Los Angeles: Advocate Books.

Casillo, Charles. (2003) 'This time, Rechy takes on Tom Jones', *LA Times*, 7 November, http://articles.latimes.com/print/2003/nov/07/entertainment/et-casillo. Last accessed: 24 August 2012

Castillo, Debra, and John Rechy. (1995) 'Interview: John Rechy', *Diacritics* 25.1: 113–25

Charnas, Suzy McKee. (1981 [1978]) *Motherlines*. Sevenoaks: Coronet.

Chester, Alfred. (1963) 'Fruit salad', *New York Review of Books* 1.2: 6–7

Christian, Karen. (1997) *Show and Tell: Identity as Performance in U.S. Latina/o Fiction*. Albuquerque: University of New Mexico Press.

Cohen, Ed. (1993) *Talk on the Wilde Side: Towards a Genealogy of a Discourse on Male Sexualities*. London: Routledge.

Combahee River Collective. (1983 [1977]) 'A black feminist statement', in Cherríe Moraga and Gloria Anzaldúa, eds, *This Bridge Called My Back: Writings by Radical Women of Color*. New York: Kitchen Table: 210–18

Cornell, Drucilla. (1992) *The Philosophy of the Limit*. London: Routledge.

Cottom, Daniel. (2003) *Why Education Is Useless*. Philadelphia: University of Pennsylvania Press.

Crenshaw, Kimberle. (1989) 'Demarginalizing the intersection of race and sex: a black feminist critique of antidiscrimination doctrine, feminist theory, and antiracist politics', *University of Chicago Legal Forum* 140: 139–67

Crenshaw, Kimberle. (1991) 'Mapping the margins: intersectionality, identity politics, and violence against women of color', *Stanford Law Review* 43: 1241–99

Culler, Jonathan, and Kevin Lamb. (2003) 'Introduction: dressing up, dressing down', in Culler and Lamb, eds, *Just Being Difficult?: Academic Writing in the Public Arena*. Stanford: Stanford University Press: 1–12

Cusset, François. (2008) *French Theory: How Foucault, Derrida, Deleuze, & Co. Transformed the Intellectual Life of the United States*, trans. Jeff Fort. Minneapolis: University of Minnesota Press.

Dean, Tim. (2002) 'Sameness without identity', in Mikko Tuhkanen, ed., 'Sameness', special issue of *Umbr(a): A Journal of the Unconscious*: 25–41

Dean, Tim. (2009) *Unlimited Intimacy: Reflections on the Subculture of Barebacking*. Chicago: University of Chicago Press.

Dean, Tim. (2010) 'The erotics of transgression', in Hugh Stevens, ed., *The Cambridge Companion to Gay and Lesbian Writing*. Cambridge: Cambridge University Press: 65–80

Dellamora, Richard. (1990) *Masculine Desire: The Sexual Politics of Victorian Aestheticism*. Chapel Hill: University of North Carolina Press.

Dellamora, Richard. (2011) *Radclyffe Hall: A Life in the Writing*. Philadelphia: University of Pennsylvania Press.

DeLynn, Jane. (1991 [1990]) *Don Juan in the Village*. London: Serpent's Tail.

DeLynn, Jane. (1998) *Bad Sex Is Good: Fiction and Essays*. New York: Painted Leaf Press.

Denisoff, Dennis. (2006) 'Vernon Lee, decadent contamination and the productivist ethos', in Catherine Maxwell and Patricia Pulham, eds, *Vernon Lee: Decadence, Ethics, Aesthetics*. Basingstoke: Palgrave Macmillan: 75–90

Derrida, Jacques. (1978) 'Structure, sign and play in the discourse of the human sciences', in *Writing and Difference*, trans. Alan Bass. London: Routledge and Kegan Paul: 278–93

Derrida, Jacques. (1982) 'Différance', in *Margins of Philosophy*, trans. Alan Bass. Chicago: University of Chicago Press: 1–28

Derrida, Jacques. (2002) *Positions*, trans. Alan Bass. London: Continuum.

Dinshaw, Carolyn, Lee Edelman, Roderick Ferguson et al. (2007) 'Theorizing queer temporalities: a roundtable discussion', in Elizabeth Freeman, ed., 'Queer Temporalities', special issue of *GLQ: A Journal of Lesbian and Gay Studies* 13.2–3: 177–95

Ditum, Sarah. (2018) 'Never-ending nightmare: why feminist dystopias must stop torturing women', *Guardian*, 12 May. www.theguardian.com/books/2018/may/12/why-the-handmaids-tale-marks-a-new-chapter-in-feminist-dystopias. Last accessed: 13 April 2019

Doan, Laura. (2001) *Fashioning Sapphism: The Origins of a Modern Lesbian English Culture*. New York: Columbia University Press.

Doan, Laura, and Jay Prosser, eds. (2001) *Palatable Poison: Critical Perspectives on The Well of Loneliness*. New York: Columbia University Press.

Duggan, Lisa. (2002) 'The new homonormativity: the sexual politics of neoliberalism', in Russ Castronovo and Dana D. Nelson, eds, *Materializing Democracy: Toward a Revitalized Cultural Politics*. Durham, NC: Duke University Press: 175–94

Duquette, Elizabeth. (2002) '"Reflected Usefulness": exemplifying conduct in *Roderick Hudson*', *Henry James Review* 23.2: 157–75

Dustan, Guillaume. (1998) *In My Room*, trans. Brad Rumph. London: Serpent's Tail.

Edel, Leon. (1987) *Henry James: A Life*. London: Collins.

Edelman, Lee. (1994) *Homographesis: Essays in Gay Literary and Cultural Theory*. London: Routledge.

Edelman, Lee. (2004) *No Future: Queer Theory and the Death Drive*. Durham, NC: Duke University Press.

Edwards, Tim. (1998) 'Queer fears: against the cultural turn', *Sexualities* 1.3: 471–84

Elliott, Jane. (2006) 'The currency of feminist theory', *PMLA* 121.5: 1697–703

Ellmann, Richard. (1999) 'Henry James among the aesthetes', in John R. Bradley, ed., *Henry James and Homo-Erotic Desire*. Basingstoke: Macmillan: 25–44

Eng, David. (2010) *The Feeling of Kinship: Queer Liberalism and the Racialization of Intimacy*. Durham, NC: Duke University Press.

Eng, David, J. Halberstam and José Esteban Muñoz. (2005) 'Introduction', in Eng, Halberstam and Muñoz, eds, 'What's Queer about Queer Studies Now?', special issue of *Social Text* 23.3–4: 1–17

English, Elizabeth. (2015) *Lesbian Modernism: Censorship, Sexuality and Genre Fiction*. Edinburgh: Edinburgh University Press.

Epps, Brad. (2001) 'The fetish of fluidity', in Tim Dean and Christopher Lane, eds, *Homosexuality and Psychoanalysis*. Chicago: Chicago University Press: 412–31

Epstein, Steven. (1996) 'A queer encounter: sociology and the study of sexuality', in Steven Seidman, ed., *Queer Theory/Sociology*. Oxford: Blackwell: 145–67

Evans, Lynne. (2014) '"You See, Children Were the – the Raison d'être": the reproductive futurism of Charlotte Perkins Gilman's Herland', *Canadian Review of American Studies / Revue Canadienne d'Etudes Americaines* 44.2: 302–19

Federici, Silvia. (2012) *Revolution at Point Zero: Housework, Reproduction and Feminist Struggle*. Oakland: PM Press.

Ferguson, Roderick A. (2004) *Aberrations in Black: Towards a Queer of Color Critique*. Minneapolis: University of Minnesota Press.

Ferguson, Roderick A. (2012) *The Re-Order of Things: The University and Its Pedagogies of Minority Difference*. Minneapolis: University of Minnesota Press.

Firestone, Shulamith. (1972) *The Dialectic of Sex*. London: Paladin.

Fitting, Peter. (1985) '"So We All Became Mothers": new roles for men in recent utopian fiction', *Science Fiction Studies* 12.2: 156–83

Fitting, Peter. (1990) 'The turn from utopia in recent feminist fiction', in Libby Falk Jones and Sarah Webster Goodwin, eds, *Feminism, Utopia, and Narrative*. Knoxville: University of Tennessee Press: 141–58

Flatley, Jonathan. (2010a) 'Like: collecting and collectivity', *October* 132.1: 71–98

Flatley, Jonathan. (2010b) 'Unlike Eve Sedgwick', *Criticism* 52.2: 225–34

Flatley, Jonathan (2017) *Like Andy Warhol*. Chicago: Chicago University Press.

Floyd, Kevin. (2009) *The Reification of Desire: Toward a Queer Marxism*. Minneapolis: University of Minnesota Press.

Foster, David William. (2006) *El Ambiente Nuestro: Chicano/Latino Homoerotic Writing*. Tempe: Bilingual Press / Editorial Bilingüe.

Foucault, Michel. (1998 [1978]) *The History of Sexuality, Volume 1: The Will to Knowledge*, trans. Robert Hurley. London: Penguin.

Foucault, Michel. (2003) *Abnormal: Lectures at the Collège de France, 1974–75*, trans. Graham Burchell, eds Valerio Marchetti and Antonella Salomoni. New York: Picador.

Fraiman, Susan. (2003) *Cool Men and the Second Sex*. New York: Columbia University Press.

Franklin, Sarah. (2007) *Dolly Mixtures*. Durham, NC: Duke University Press.

Freedman, Jonathan. (1990) *Professions of Taste: Henry James, British Aestheticism, and Commodity Culture*. Stanford: Stanford University Press.

Freeman, Elizabeth. (2007) 'Still after', in Janet Halley and Andrew Parker, eds, 'After Sex? On Writing Since Queer Theory', special issue of *South Atlantic Quarterly* 106.3: 495–500

Freeman, Elizabeth. (2010) *Time Binds: Queer Temporalities, Queer Histories*. Durham, NC: Duke University Press.

Freibert, Lucy M. (1983) 'World views in utopian novels by women', in Marleen Barr and Nicholas D. Smith, eds, *Women and Utopia: Critical Interpretations*. London: University Press of America, 1983: 67–84

Fusco, Katherine. (2009) 'Systems, not men: producing people in Charlotte Perkins Gilman's *Herland*', *Studies in the Novel* 41.4: 418–34

Fuss, Diana. (1989) *Essentially Speaking: Feminism, Nature, and Difference*. New York: Routledge.

Galana, Laurel. (1975) 'Radical reproduction: X without Y', in Gina Covina and Laurel Galana, eds, *The Lesbian Reader: An Amazon Quarterly Anthology*. Oakland: Amazon Press: 122–37

Gamson, Joshua. (1996) 'Must identity movements self-destruct?: a queer dilemma', in Steven Seidman, ed., *Queer Theory/Sociology*. Oxford: Blackwell: 395–420

Ganobcsik-Williams, Lisa. (1999) 'The intellectualism of Charlotte Perkins Gilman: evolutionary perspectives on race, ethnicity, and class', in Jill Rudd and Val Gough, eds, *Charlotte Perkins Gilman: Optimist Reformer*. Iowa City: University of Iowa Press: 16–44

Gard, Roger, ed. (1968) *Henry James: The Critical Heritage*. London: Routledge and Kegan Paul.

Gardner, Burdett. (1987) *The Lesbian Imagination (Victorian Style): A Psychological and Critical Study of 'Vernon Lee'*. London: Garland.

Gearhart, Sally Miller. (1984 [1979]) *The Wanderground: Stories of the Hill Women*. Boston: Alyson Publications.

Gilbert, Sophie. (2018) 'The remarkable rise of the feminist dystopia', *The Atlantic*, 4 October. www.theatlantic.com/entertainment/archive/2018/10/feminist-speculative-fiction-2018/571822/. Last accessed: 13 April 2019

Gilman, Charlotte Perkins. (1991 [1908]) 'A suggestion on the negro problem', in Larry Ceplair, ed., *Charlotte Perkins Gilman: A Non-Fiction Reader*. New York: Columbia University Press: 176–83

Gilman, Charlotte Perkins. (1998 [1898]) *Women and Economics: A Study of the Economic Relation between Men and Women as a Factor in Social Evolution*. Mineola: Dover Editions.

Gilman, Charlotte Perkins. (1999a [1915]) *Herland*, in Minna Doskow, ed., *Charlotte Perkins Gilman's Utopian Novels*. London: Associated University Presses: 150–269

Gilman, Charlotte Perkins. (1999b [1916]) *With Her in Ourland*, in Minna Doskow, ed., *Charlotte Perkins Gilman's Utopian Novels*. London: Associated University Presses: 270–387

Gilman, Charlotte Perkins. (1999c [1911]) *Moving the Mountain* (1911), in Minna Doskow, ed., *Charlotte Perkins Gilman's Utopian Novels*. London: Associated University Presses: 37–149

Gilman, Charlotte Perkins. (2011 [1935]) *The Living of Charlotte Perkins Gilman: An Autobiography*. [n.p.]: Read Books.

Gough, Val. (1995) 'Lesbians and virgins: the motherhood in Herland', in David Seed, ed., *Anticipations: Essays on Early Science Fiction and Its Precursors*. Liverpool: Liverpool University Press: 195–215

Gove, Ben. (2000) *Cruising Culture: Promiscuity, Desire and American Gay Literature*. Edinburgh: Edinburgh University Press.

Graham, Wendy. (1999) *Henry James's Thwarted Love*. Stanford: Stanford University Press.

Green, Adam Isaiah. (2002) 'Gay but not queer: toward a post-queer study of sexuality', *Theory and Society* 31.4: 521–45

Green, Adam Isaiah. (2007) 'Queer theory and sociology: locating the subject and the self in sexuality studies', *Sociological Theory* 25.1: 26–45

Griffith, Nicola. (1993) *Ammonite*. London: Grafton.

Halberstam, J. (2001) '"A writer of misfits": "John" Radclyffe Hall and the discourse of inversion', in Laura Doan and Jay Prosser, eds, *Palatable Poison: Critical Perspectives on* The Well of Loneliness. New York: Columbia University Press: 145–61

Halberstam, J. (2005) *In a Queer Time and Place: Transgender Bodies, Subcultural Lives*. New York: New York University Press.

Halberstam, J. (2011) *The Queer Art of Failure*. Durham, NC: Duke University Press.

Hall, Radclyffe. (1981 [1924]) *The Unlit Lamp*. London: Virago.

Hall, Radclyffe. (1994 [1928]) *The Well of Loneliness*. London: Virago.

Halley, Janet, and Andrew Parker. (2007) 'Introduction', in Halley and Parker, eds, 'After Sex? On Writing Since Queer Theory', special issue of *South Atlantic Quarterly* 106.3: 421–32

Halperin, David. (2012) *How to Be Gay*. Cambridge, MA: Harvard University Press.

Haralson, Eric. (2003) *Henry James and Queer Modernity*. Cambridge: Cambridge University Press.

Harker, Jaime. (2007) *America the Middlebrow: Women's Novels, Progressivism, and Middlebrow Authorship between the Wars*. Boston: University of Massachusetts Press.

Hausman, Bernice L. (1998) 'Sex before gender: Charlotte Perkins Gilman and the evolutionary paradigm of utopia', *Feminist Studies* 24: 489–510

Hayes, Kevin J., ed. (1996) *Henry James: The Contemporary Reviews*. Cambridge: Cambridge University Press.

Heise, Thomas. (2011) 'Wasted dreams: John Rechy, Thomas Pynchon, and the underworlds of Los Angeles, 1960s', in *Urban Underworlds: A Geography of Twentieth Century American Literature and Culture*. New Brunswick: Rutgers University Press: 169–212

Hemmings, Clare. (2001) '"All my life I've been waiting for something …": theorizing femme narrative in *The Well of Loneliness*', in Laura Doan and Jay Prosser, eds, *Palatable Poison: Critical Perspectives on* The Well of Loneliness. New York: Columbia University Press: 179–96

Hennessy, Rosemary. (2000) *Profit and Pleasure: Sexual Identities in Late Capitalism*. London: Routledge.

Herring, Scott. (2010) *Another Country: Queer Anti-Urbanism*. New York: New York University Press.

Hinds, Hilary. (2009) 'Ordinary disappointments: femininity, domesticity, and British middlebrow fiction, 1920–1944', *Modern Fiction Studies* 55.2: 293–320

Hoagland, Sarah Lucia. (1988) 'Introduction'. in Sarah Lucia Hoagland and Julia Penelope, eds, *For Lesbians Only: A Separatist Anthology*. London: Onlywomen Press: 1–14

Hocquenghem, Guy. (1993 [1978]) *Homosexual Desire*, trans. Daniella Dangoor. Durham, NC: Duke University Press.

Holleran, Andrew. (1982) 'The Petrification of Clonestyle', *Christopher Street*, October: 14–17

Holmes, Sarah, ed. (1988) *Testimonies: A Collection of Lesbian Coming Out Stories*. Boston: Alyson Publications.

Holmes, Sarah, and Jenn Tust, eds. (2002) *Testimonies: Lesbian and Bisexual Coming-Out Stories*. Los Angeles: Alyson Publications.

hooks, bell. (1992) *Black Looks: Race and Representation*. Boston: South End Press.

Humble, Nicola. (2001) *The Feminine Middlebrow Novel, 1920s to 1950s: Class, Domesticity, and Bohemianism*. Oxford: Oxford University Press.

Indiana, Gary. (1999) 'Midnight's Child', *LA Times*, 29 August. http://articles.latimes.com/1999/aug/29/books/bk-4731. Last accessed: 20 February 2014

Isherwood, Charles. (1996) 'Beyond the Night', *The Advocate*, 15 October.

Jagose, Annamarie. (2015) 'The trouble with antinormativity', in Robyn Wiegman and Elizabeth A. Wilson, eds, 'Queer Theory Without Antinormativity', special issue of *differences* 26.1: 26–47

Jakobsen, Janet R. (1998) *Working Alliances and the Politics of Difference: Diversity and Feminist Ethics*. Bloomington: Indiana University Press.

James, Henry. (1980 [1875]) *Roderick Hudson*, ed. Tony Tanner. Oxford: Oxford University Press.

James, Henry. (1962) *The Art of the Novel: Critical Prefaces* (1907–9), intro. R.P. Blackmur. London: Charles Scribner's Sons.

James, Henry. (1995 [1890]) *The Tragic Muse*, ed. Philip Horne. Harmondsworth: Penguin.

Johnson, Barbara. (1980) *The Critical Difference: Essays in the Contemporary Rhetoric of Reading*. Baltimore: Johns Hopkins University Press.

Johnson, Barbara. (1987) *A World of Difference*. Baltimore: Johns Hopkins University Press.

Johnson, David E. (1998) 'Intolerance, the body, community', *American Literary History* 10.3: 446–70

Jones, Richard H. (2000) *Reductionism: Analysis and the Fullness of Reality*. Lewisburg: Bucknell University Press.

Kaplan, Caren. (1994) 'The politics of location as transnational feminist practice', in Inderpal Grewal and Caren Kaplan, eds, *Scattered Hegemonies: Postmodernity and Transnational Feminist Practices*. Minneapolis: University of Minnesota Press: 137–52

Key, Ellen. (1909) *The Century of the Child*. New York: Putnam.
Koestenbaum, Wayne. (1990) 'Wilde's hard labor and the birth of gay reading', in Michael Cadden and Joseph A. Boone, eds, *Engendering Men: The Question of Male Feminist Criticism*. New York: Routledge: 176–90
Kolossa, Alexandra. (2004) *Keith Haring: 1958–1990: A Life for Art*, trans. Michael Scuffil. London: Taschen.
Lane, Ann J. (1990) *To 'Herland' and Beyond: The Life and Work of Charlotte Perkins Gilman*. New York: Pantheon.
Lane, Christopher. (1996) 'The impossibility of seduction in Henry James's *Roderick Hudson* and *The Tragic Muse*', *American Literature* 68.4: 739–64
Lanser, Susan S. (1989) 'Feminist criticism, "The Yellow Wallpaper," and the politics of color in America', *Feminist Studies* 15: 415–41
Libretti, Tim. (2004) 'Sexual outlaws and class struggle: rethinking history and class consciousness from a queer perspective', *College English* 67.2: 154–71
Lilla, Mark. (2017) *The Once and Future Liberal: After Identity Politics*. New York: HarperCollins.
Lochrie, Karma. (2005) *Heterosyncrasies: Female Sexuality When Normal Wasn't*. Minneapolis: University of Minnesota Press.
Lorde, Audre. (1984) *Sister Outsider: Essays and Speeches*. Freedom: The Crossing Press.
Love, Heather. (2007) *Feeling Backward: Loss and the Politics of Queer History*. Cambridge, MA: Harvard University Press.
Love, Heather. (2015) 'Doing being deviant: deviance studies, description, and the queer ordinary', in Robyn Wiegman and Elizabeth Wilson, eds, 'Queer Theory Without Antinormativity', special issue of *differences* 26.1: 74–95
Mamo, Laura. (2007) *Queering Reproduction: Achieving Pregnancy in the Age of Technoscience*. Durham, NC: Duke University Press.
Marcus, Sharon. (2007) *Between Women: Friendship, Desire, and Marriage in Victorian England*. Princeton: Princeton University Press.
Martin, Biddy. (1997) 'Extraordinary homosexuals and the fear of being ordinary', in Elizabeth Weed and Naomi Schor, eds, *Feminism Meets Queer Theory*. Bloomington: Indiana University Press: 109–35
Martin, Robert K. (1978) 'The "high felicity" of comradeship: a new reading of *Roderick Hudson*', *American Literary Realism* 11: 100–8
Matheson, Neil. (1999) 'Talking horrors: Henry James, euphemism, and the specter of Wilde' *American Literature* 71.4: 709–50
Mendelssohn, Michèle. (2003) 'Homosociality and the aesthetic in Henry James's *Roderick Hudson*', *Nineteenth-Century Literature* 57.4: 512–41
Mendelssohn, Michèle. (2007) *Henry James, Oscar Wilde and Aesthetic Culture*. Edinburgh: Edinburgh University Press.
Menon, Madhavi. (2008) *Unhistorical Shakespeare: Queer Theory in Shakespearean Literature and Film*. Basingstoke: Palgrave Macmillan.

Menon, Madhavi. (2015) *Indifference to Difference: On Queer Universalism*. Minneapolis: University of Minnesota Press.

Milman, Lena. (1895) 'A few notes upon Mr. James', *The Yellow Book* 7, October: 71–83

Mohanty, Chandra Talpade. (2003) *Feminism without Borders: Decolonizing Theory, Practicing Solidarity*. Durham, NC: Duke University Press.

Moon, Jennifer. (2006) 'Cruising John Rechy's *City of Night*: queer subjectivity, intimacy, and counterpublicity', *disClosure* 15: 42–59

Moraga, Cherríe, and Gloria Anzaldúa. (1983) 'Introduction', in Moraga and Anzaldúa, eds, *This Bridge Called My Back: Writings by Radical Women of Color*. New York: Kitchen Table.

Morton, Donald. (1996) 'Changing the terms: (virtual) desire and (actual) reality', in Donald Morton, ed., *The Material Queer: A LesBiGay Cultural Studies Reader*. Boulder: Westview: 1–33

Muñoz, Josè Esteban. (1999) *Disidentifications: Queers of Color and the Performance of Politics*. Minneapolis: University of Minnesota Press.

Muñoz, Josè Esteban. (2009) *Cruising Utopia: The Then and There of Queer Futurity*. New York: New York University Press.

Murtaugh, Daniel J. (1996) 'An emotional reflection: sexual realization in Henry James's revisions to *Roderick Hudson*', *Henry James Review* 17.2: 182–203

Nadkarni, Asha. (2014) *Eugenic Feminism: Reproductive Nationalism in the United States and India*. Minneapolis: University of Minnesota Press.

Newman, Louise. (1999) *White Women's Rights: The Racial Origins of Feminism in the United States*. Oxford: Oxford University Press.

Nichols, Ben. (2019) 'Reproduction lines: feminism, management, and Charlotte Perkins Gilman', in James Dorson and Jasper Velinden, eds, *Fictions of Management: Efficiency and Control in American Literature and Culture*. Heidelberg: Winter.

Nichols, James. (2014) '"Boyfriend twins" Tumblr documents lookalike gay boyfriends', *Huffington Post*, 9 April. www.huffingtonpost.co.uk/2014/04/09/boyfriend-twins_n_5118091.html?guccounter=1. Last accessed: 24 March 2019

Nissen, Axel. (2009) *Manly Love: Romantic Friendship in American Fiction*. Chicago: Chicago University Press.

O'Brien, Mary. (1981) *The Politics of Reproduction*. Boston: Routledge and Kegan Paul.

O'Connell, Rachel. (2015) 'Reparative Pater: retreat, ecstasy, and reparation in the writings of Walter Pater', *ELH* 82: 969–86

Ohi, Kevin. (2005) '"The Author of 'Beltraffio'": the exquisite boy and Henry James's equivocal aestheticism', *ELH* 72.3: 747–67

Ohi, Kevin. (2015) *Dead Letters Sent: Queer Literary Transmission*. Minneapolis: University of Minnesota Press.

Ortiz, Ricardo. (1993) 'Sexuality degree zero: pleasure and power in the novels of John Rechy, Arturo Islas, and Michael Nava', *Journal of Homosexuality* 26.2–3: 111–26

Ortiz, Ricardo. (1995) 'John Rechy and the grammar of ostentation', in Philip Brett, Sue-Ellen Case and Susan Leigh Foster, eds, *Cruising the Performative: Interventions into the Representation of Ethnicity, Nationality, and Sexuality*. Bloomington: Indiana University Press: 59–70

Pally, Marcia. (1986) 'A visit with author John Rechy: caught between worlds in the American wasteland', *The Advocate*, 23 December.

Parvulescu, Anca. (2017) 'Reproduction and queer theory: between Lee Edelman's *No Future* and J M Coetzee's *Slow Man*', *PMLA* 132.1: 86–100

Pater, Walter. (1986 [1873]) *The Renaissance: Studies in Art and Poetry*, ed. Adam Phillips. Oxford: World's Classics.

Penney, James. (2014) *After Queer Theory: The Limits of Sexual Politics*. London: Pluto.

Pérez-Torres, Rafael. (1994) 'The ambiguous outlaw: John Rechy and complicitous homotextuality', in Peter F. Murphy, ed., *Fictions of Masculinity: Crossing Cultures, Crossing Sexualities*. New York: New York University Press: 204–25

Prosser, Jay. (2001) '"Some primitive thing conceived in a turbulent age of transition": the transsexual emerging from *The Well*', in Laura Doan and Jay Prosser, eds, *Palatable Poison: Critical Perspectives on* The Well of Loneliness. New York: Columbia University Press: 129–44

Puar, Jasbir. (2007) *Terrorist Assemblages: Homonationalism in Queer Times*. Durham, NC: Duke University Press.

Puar, Jasbir. (2012a) '"I would rather be a cyborg than a goddess": becoming-intersectional in assemblage theory', *philoSOPHIA* 2.1: 49–66

Puar, Jasbir. (2012b) 'Coda: the cost of getting better: suicide, sensation, switchpoints', *GLQ: A Journal of Lesbian and Gay Studies* 18.1: 149–58

Puar, Jasbir. (2013) 'Rethinking homonationalism', *International Journal of Middle East Studies* 45.2: 336–9

Rechy, John. (1963) *City of Night*. New York: Grove.

Rechy, John. (1967) *Numbers*. New York: Grove.

Rechy, John. (1970 [1969]) *This Day's Death*. London: MacGibbon & Kee.

Rechy, John. (1972) *The Fourth Angel*. London: W.H. Allen.

Rechy, John. (1977) *The Sexual Outlaw: A Documentary*. New York: Grove.

Rechy, John. (1979) *Rushes*. New York: Grove Press.

Rechy, John. (1999) *The Coming of the Night*. New York: Grove Press.

Rechy, John. (2001 [1983]) *Bodies and Souls*. New York: Grove.

Rechy, John. (2003) *The Life and Adventures of Lyle Clemens*. New York: Grove.

Rechy, John. (2004) *Beneath the Skin: The Collected Essays of John Rechy*. New York: Carroll & Graf.

Rechy, John. (2008) *About My Life and the Kept Woman*. New York: Grove Press.

Renault, Mary. (2005 [1944]) *The Friendly Young Ladies*. London: Virago.
Rensenbrink, Greta. (2010) 'Parthenogenesis and lesbian separatism: regenerating women's community through virgin birth in the United States in the 1970s and 1980s', *Journal of the History of Sexuality* 19.2: 288–316
Rich, Adrienne. (1976) *Of Woman Born: Motherhood as Experience and Institution*. New York: Norton.
Robinson, Paul. (2005) *Queer Wars: The New Gay Right and Its Critics*. Chicago: University of Chicago Press.
Rohy, Valerie. (2012) 'On homosexual reproduction', *differences: A Journal of Feminist Cultural Studies* 25.1: 101–30
Rohy, Valerie. (2015) *Lost Causes: Narrative, Etiology, and Queer Theory*. Oxford: Oxford University Press.
Roof, Judith. (1996) *Come as You Are: Sexuality and Narrative*. New York: Columbia University Press.
Rowe, John Carlos. (1998) *The Other Henry James*. Durham, NC: Duke University Press.
Ruehl, Sonja. (1982) 'Inverts and experts: Radclyffe Hall and the lesbian identity', in Rosalind Brunt and Caroline Rowan, eds, *Feminism, Culture and Politics*. London: Lawrence and Wishart.
Russ, Joanna. (2010 [1975]) *The Female Man*. London: Gollancz.
Salamensky, Shelley. (1999) 'Henry James, Oscar Wilde and "fin-de-siecle talk": a brief reading', *Henry James Review* 20.3: 275–81
Salamensky, Shelley. (2011) '"The man of the hour": Oscar Wilde, performance, and proto-modernity in Henry James's *The Tragic Muse*', *Henry James Review* 32.1: 60–74
Saldívar, José David. (1997) *Border Matters: Remapping American Cultural Studies*. Berkeley: University of California Press.
Savage, Dan, and Terry Miller. (2012) *It Gets Better: Coming Out, Overcoming Bullying, and Creating a Life Worth Living*. London: Plume.
Savoy, Eric. (2011) '*Casse-toi!* – or the calling of Leo Bersani', *Henry James Review* 32.3: 242–8
Saxey, Esther. (2008) *Homoplot: The Coming-Out Story and Gay, Lesbian and Bisexual Identity*. New York: Peter Lang.
Schulman, Sarah. (1995) *My American History: Lesbian and Gay Life during the Reagan/Bush Years*. London: Cassell.
Schulman, Sarah. (2012) *The Gentrification of the Mind: Witness to a Lost Imagination*. Berkeley: University of California Press.
Sedgwick, Eve Kosofsky. (1990) *Epistemology of the Closet*. Berkeley: University of California Press.
Sedgwick, Eve Kosofsky. (1993) *Tendencies*. Durham, NC: Duke University Press.
Seidman, Steven. (1993) 'Identity and politics in a "postmodern" gay culture: some historical and conceptual notes', in Michael Warner, ed., *Fear of a Queer*

Planet: Queer Politics and Social Theory. Minneapolis: University of Minnesota Press: 105–42

Seidman, Steven, ed. (1996) *Queer Theory/Sociology*. Oxford: Blackwell.

Seitler, Dana. (2008) *Atavistic Tendencies: The Culture of Science in American Modernity*. Minneapolis: University of Minnesota Press.

Shugar, Dana. (1995) *Separatism and Women's Community*. Lincoln: University of Nebraska Press.

Silverman, Kaja. (2009) *Flesh of My Flesh*. Stanford: Stanford University Press.

Sinfield, Alan. (1994) *The Wilde Century: Effeminacy, Oscar Wilde and the Queer Moment*. London: Cassell.

Sinfield, Alan. (1998) *Gay and After*. London: Serpent's Tail.

Sofer, Naomi Z. (1999) 'Why "different vibrations … walk hand in hand": homosocial bonds in *Roderick Hudson*', *Henry James Review* 20.2: 185–205

Souhami, Diana. (1998) *The Trials of Radclyffe Hall*. London: Weidenfeld and Nicolson.

Spivak, Gayatri Chakravorty, and Sneja Gunew. (1993) 'Questions of multiculturalism', in Simon During, ed. *The Cultural Studies Reader*. London: Routledge: 193–202

Spring, Justin. (2010) *Secret Historian: The Life and Times of Samuel Steward, Professor, Tattoo Artist, and Sexual Renegade*. New York: Farrar, Strauss and Giroux.

Stanley, Julia Penelope, and Susan J. Wolfe, eds. (1980) *The Coming Out Stories*. Watertown: Persephone Press.

Stein, Arlene, and Ken Plummer. (1996) '"I can't even think straight": "queer" theory and the missing sexual revolution in sociology', in Steven Seidman, ed., *Queer Theory/Sociology*. Oxford: Blackwell: 129–44

Stevens, Hugh. (1998) *Henry James and Sexuality*. Cambridge: Cambridge University Press.

Stevens, Hugh. (2010) 'Normality and queerness in gay fiction', in Stevens, ed. *The Cambridge Companion to Gay and Lesbian Writing*. Cambridge: Cambridge University Press: 81–96

Stryker, Susan, and Aren Z. Aizura. (2013) 'Introduction: transgender studies 2.0', in Stryker and Aizura, eds, *The Transgender Studies Reader 2*. London: Routledge: 1–12

Swartley, Ariel. (2008) 'No Country for Young Men: John Rechy's Tragic, Picaresque Memoir', *Los Angeles*, February: 68–72

Tuhkanen, Mikko. (2002a) 'Becoming same: Deleuze and Bersani', in Tuhkanen, ed., 'Sameness', special issue of *Umbr(a): A Journal of the Unconscious*: 131–45

Tuhkanen, Mikko. (2002b) 'Clones and breeders: an introduction to queer sameness', in Tuhkanen, ed., 'Sameness', special issue of *Umbr(a): A Journal of the Unconscious*: 4–7

Turner, William B. (2000) *A Genealogy of Queer Theory*. Philadelphia: Temple University Press.

Valverde, Mariana. (1992) '"When the mother of the race is free": race, reproduction, and sexuality in first wave feminism', in Franca Iacovetta and Mariana Valverde, eds, *Gender Conflicts: New Essays in Women's History*. Toronto: University of Toronto Press: 3–26

Vázquez, David J. (2011) *Triangulations: Narrative Strategies for Navigating Latino Identity*. Minneapolis: University of Minnesota Press.

Vicinus, Martha. (2004) '"A legion of ghosts":Vernon Lee (1856–1935) and the art of nostalgia', *GLQ: A Journal of Lesbian and Gay Studies* 10.4: 599–616

Warner, Michael. (1990) 'Homo-narcissism; or, heterosexuality', in Joseph A. Boone and Michael Cadden, eds, *Engendering Men: The Question of Male Feminist Criticism*. London: Routledge: 190–206

Warner, Michael. (1993) 'Introduction', in Warner, ed., *Fear of a Queer Planet: Queer Politics and Social Theory*. Minneapolis: University of Minnesota Press: vii–xxxi.

Warner, Michael. (1999) *The Trouble with Normal: Sex, Politics, and the Ethics of Queer Life*. Cambridge, MA: Harvard University Press.

Warner, Michael. (2012) 'Queer and then?', *Chronicle of Higher Education*. 1 January. http://chronicle.com/article/QueerThen-/130161/. Last accessed: 29 September 2014

Warrick, Pamela. (1996) 'Righting a wrong from long ago', *LA Times*, 15 September. http://articles.latimes.com/1996-09-15/news/ls-44044_1_long-ago. Last accessed: 24 August 2012

Weeks, Jeffrey. (1977) *Coming Out: Homosexual Politics in Britain from the Nineteenth Century to the Present*. London: Quartet Books.

Weeks, Jeffrey. (1989) *Sex, Politics and Society: The Regulation of Sexuality since 1800*. Harlow: Longman.

Weinbaum, Alys Eve. (2004) *Wayward Reproductions: Genealogies of Race and Nation in Transatlantic Modern Thought*. Durham, NC: Duke University Press.

Weinbaum, Alys Eve. (2019) *The Afterlife of Reproductive Slavery: Biocapitalism and Black Feminism's Philosophy of History*. Durham, NC: Duke University Press.

West, Cornel. (1990) 'The new cultural politics of difference', in Russell Ferguson, Martha Gever, Trinh T. Minh-ha and Cornel West, eds. *Out There: Marginalization in Contemporary Cultures*. London: MIT Press: 19–36

Whitlock, Gillian. (1987) 'Everything is out of place: Radclyffe Hall and the lesbian literary tradition', *Feminist Studies* 13.3: 554–82

Wiegman, Robyn. (2012) *Object Lessons*. Durham, NC: Duke University Press.

Wiegman, Robyn. (2015) 'Eve's triangles, or queer studies beside itself', in Robyn Wiegman and Elizabeth A. Wilson, eds, 'Queer Theory Without Antinormativity', special issue of *differences* 26.1: 48–73

Wiegman, Robyn, and Elizabeth A. Wilson. (2015) 'Introduction: antinormativity's queer conventions', in Robyn Wiegman and Elizabeth A. Wilson, eds,

'Queer Theory Without Antinormativity', special issue of *differences* 26.1: 1–25

Wilde, Oscar. (1973) 'The soul of man under socialism', in *Complete Works of Oscar Wilde*, intro. Vyvyan Holland. London: Collins: 1079–104

Wilde, Oscar. (1994 [1891]) *The Picture of Dorian Gray*. Harmondsworth: Penguin.

Wilson, Michael. (1993) 'Lessons of the master: the artist and sexual identity in Henry James', *Henry James Review* 14.3: 257–63

Winning, Joanne. (2001) 'Writing by the light of *The Well*: Radclyffe Hall and the lesbian modernists', in Laura Doan and Jay Prosser, eds, *Palatable Poison: Critical Perspectives on* The Well of Loneliness. New York: Columbia University Press: 372–93

Woods, Gregory. (1999) 'The art of friendship in *Roderick Hudson*', in John R. Bradley, ed., *Henry James and Homo-Erotic Desire*. Basingstoke: Macmillan: 69–77

Woolf, Virginia. (1942) 'Middlebrow. to the editor of the "New Statesman"', in *The Death of the Moth and Other Essays*. London: Hogarth Press: 113–19

Young, Iris Marion. (1990) *Justice and the Politics of Difference*. Princeton: Princeton University Press.

Zacharias, Greg W. (1990) 'James's morality in *Roderick Hudson*', *Henry James Review* 11.2: 115–32

Internet resources

Boyfriend Twin blog. https://boyfriendtwin.tumblr.com/. Last accessed: 2 January 2020

Rechy, John. 'A Writer Protests'. www.johnrechy.com/so_protest.htm. Last accessed: 29 September 2014

Index

Page references for chapter notes are given in the form 186 n.7

abjection 89–90, 115–16, 130
abnormality 129–33
action 58–60, 62–3, 64–6, 68
Adams, Stephen 151
aestheticism 6, 8, 34–5, 39–40, 42–4, 68
   Pater, Walter 39, 43–4, 53–4, 60–1
   and uselessness 53–4, 60–1, 71–2
   Wilde, Oscar 2, 18, 39, 43
Ahmed, Sara 2, 90
Aizura, Aren 122
Allison, Dorothy 27
ambivalence 62–3, 65–6
Amin, Kadji 5, 23–4, 25–6, 197
Anderson, Amanda 162
anti-identitarianism 18–26, 46, 121, 151–2, 165–70, 192–3, 196
anti-normativity 115–19, 125–6
anti-redemption 5, 23–4, 116–17, 155–6, 163–5
Anzaldúa, Gloria 20–1
apoliticalness 49–51
appearance, similarity of 1, 10–11, 22–3, 170, 176–7
Arnold, Kevin 174–5
art
   and procreation 58
   and uselessness 53–61, 73 n.5
   see also aestheticism; culture; literature

artists 54–6
assemblage 19, 20, 162
   see also intersectionality
assimilation 106–7, 116, 119–20, 124–5, 128–35
Atwood, Margaret
   The Handmaid's Tale 79
   The Testaments 79
autobiography 26–34, 156, 178–9

Bachardy, Don 180
Badiou, Alain 14–15, 16, 190
Barber, Karen 31
Baudrillard, Jean 50
Bederman, Gail 106
Berlant, Lauren 124
Bersani, Leo 6–7, 11
   and anti-identitarianism 121, 177–8
   and anti-redemption 23
   homo-ness 12–13, 36, 163–6, 176
   and ontological breakdown 12–14, 16, 17
   and reductionism 36–7, 155–6, 163–6, 184–5
   and sex 169–70
bodybuilding 181–2
books 31–2
boredom 27–8, 33–4, 92, 136–7
Boyfriend Twin (blog) 1

Bussy, Dorothy, *Olivia* 114
Butler, Judith 11–12, 21, 117, 125–6, 158–60, 185 n.3

Camus, Renaud, *Tricks* 153, 169
capitalism 19, 47–8, 161
Carter, Julian 117
Casillo, Charles 152, 179, 180–1
catalogues 8, 36–7, 153
   see also Rechy, John
change 15
   aversion to 82–3, 137–9, 170
   lack of 10, 12, 175, 178
   making 6, 8, 42–3, 45, 52, 59, 70–1
   redundancy of 92–3
   social 45–6, 79, 154
Charnas, Suzy McKee, *Motherlines* 77, 78–9, 81, 97–8, 99, 100, 102
Chester, Alfred 183
Child, the (Edelman) 76–7, 83
children 93–4, 99
chrononormativity 121
class, social 92, 96–7
clones (gay men) 10–11, 22–3, 170, 176–7
clones (genetic) 50, 92, 98–9
clothing 10–11, 182
Combahee River Collective 20
coming out stories 26–34, 114
commonality 15–16
community 93–5, 130–2, 148
   women-only 77–9, 81, 97–104
complexity 8, 27, 76, 118, 152, 154, 159–60
conformity 10–11, 117–18, 123
connectedness 163–4, 166
conservatism 122–3, 129–30
continuity 78–9, 82–3, 88
convention 120, 135–40
copying/copies 18, 35, 56
   clones (gay men) 10–11, 22–3, 170, 176–7
   clones (genetic) 50, 92, 98–9
Cornell, Drucilla 159–60
Cottom, Daniel 43–4, 45, 53, 70, 72–3
cruising 163–4, 165–6, 167–8
Cukor, George 179–80

culture
   gay 38 n.3, 181–2, 194–6
   literary 32–3
   middle-brow 142–3
   reproduction of 80
   S/M 182–3

Daughter Visions (newsletter) 100, 101–2
Dean, Tim 11, 12, 17, 176–7, 186 n.7
death drive 50, 76–7
deconstruction 13–14, 160
   see also post-structuralism
de-differentiation 11, 12–14
Delany, Samuel, *Times Square Red/Times Square Blue* 153, 169
Deleuze, Gilles 20
DeLynn, Jane, *Don Juan in the Village* 153, 169–70, 172–3
Derrida, Jacques 11, 13, 20, 159–60
desire 14, 169–70
différance (Derrida) 11, 159–60
difference
   and abjection 4–5, 87–8
   commodification of 19–20, 21
   complexity 8, 27, 76, 118, 152, 154, 159–60
   de-differentiation 11, 12–14
   diversity 19–20, 162
   inconsistency 66–7
   making a 6, 8, 42–3, 45, 52, 59, 70–1
   necessity of 86–7
   non-negotiable 84–5
   pluralism 19–20, 162
   politics of 2–3, 9–10, 20–1, 160–1, 190
   privileging of 17, 24, 70–1, 162, 197
   and repetition 12
   as sameness 15
   sameness of 19–20
   sex 93, 95, 107–8, 142–3
   social 9–10, 14, 15–16, 18–19, 162, 189–90
   universality of 13–15
   see also change; individuality
discourse, reverse 4–5
diversity 19–20, 162

Doan, Laura 114, 142
doing 58–60, 62–3, 64–6, 68
Donisthorpe, G. Sheila, *Loveliest of Friends!* 114
drag 80, 182
Duquette, Elizabeth 63–4
Dustan, Guillaume 176, 186 n.6
dystopian fiction 79, 98

Edelman, Lee 5, 14, 80–1, 82, 116
   and homosexuality 49–50
   and reproductive futurism 35, 50, 52, 76–7, 83–8, 142
   and uselessness 40, 41
education 103–4, 106–7
Elliott, Jane 33, 189
Eng, David 18–19, 21–2, 48, 53, 161
English, Elizabeth 117, 141, 143
Epstein, Steven 46, 48, 162
essentialism 17, 76, 162
eugenics 105, 109–10
exclusion 4–5, 115–16, 128–9, 149

family 78, 91–2
   motherhood 93–5, 99, 136–7
Fear of a Queer Planet (anthology) 45–6
Federici, Silvia 80, 90, 109
femininity 107, 120–1, 141–2, 146, 147
feminism 20–1, 28
   and normativity 126
   and racism 104–11
   and reproduction 75–6, 90
   separatist 81
   see also middle-brow fiction; speculative fiction
fiction
   dystopian 79, 98
   genre 143
   see also lesbian fiction; middle-brow fiction; Rechy, John; speculative fiction; utopian fiction
fin-de-siècle period 6, 8, 39
fixity 10, 12, 175, 178
Flatley, Jonathan 17, 148, 149
Foster, David William 157
Foucault, Michel 4–5, 124–5
Fraiman, Susan 117, 121, 141–2
Freedman, Jonathan 60–1

Freeman, Elizabeth 5, 40, 41, 51–2, 105, 121, 140, 197
Fusco, Katherine 95
Fuss, Diana 17, 162
futurism, reproductive 50, 52, 76–7, 83–8, 142

Ganobcsik-Williams, Lisa 107
gay-aversiveness, in queer theory 6–7, 22–3
gay culture 38 n.3, 181–2, 194–6
gay identity 26, 151–2, 157–8, 193–6
gay men 10–11, 22–3, 153, 165–72, 176–7
gay pride 115–16, 119–20
gay sex 153, 165–70, 171–2
Gearhart, Sally Miller, *The Wanderground* 77, 79, 97–8, 100, 103–4
gender
   difference 107–8, 142–3
   femininity 107, 120–1, 141–2, 146, 147
   masculinity 49–50, 63, 146, 171–2, 174–5, 181–3
   norms 125, 158–9
   performativity 11–12
   and race 107
   transitivity 126–7
Genet, Jean 23–4
genre fiction 143
Gilman, Charlotte Perkins 8–9, 75, 77–8, 90–1, 96, 112 n.4
   and racism 105–10
   Herland 37, 77, 78, 81–2, 91–7, 100, 102, 106–7
   Moving the Mountain 96, 106–7
   With Her in Ourland 92
   Women and Economics 78, 93, 95, 107–8
   "The Yellow Wall-paper" 110
Gough, Val 97
Graham, Wendy 63
Griffith, Nicola, *Ammonite* 77, 79, 97–9, 101, 102, 103, 112 n.5

Halberstam, Jack (Judith) 5, 18–19, 40, 41, 48, 51, 52, 53, 197

Index

Hall, Radclyffe 119–20, 128, 141
  The Unlit Lamp 36, 120, 135–40
  The Well of Loneliness 7–8, 35–6, 37, 114–16, 119–20, 128–35, 146–8
Halley, Janet 187, 189
Halperin, David 38 n.3, 39, 121, 194–6
Handmaid's Tale, The (TV programme) 79
Haring, Keith 10–11
Herring, Scott 121–2, 123–4
heterogeneity *see* difference
heteronormativity 78, 111–12, 122–3
  and reproduction 35, 82–3, 88–9
heterosexuality 17, 58–9, 94–6, 117–18, 133–4
  erasure of 142–3
  and reproduction 76–7, 96–7
Hinds, Hilary 146
historical materialism, and queer theory 47–9
Hoagland, Sarah Lucia 105
Hocquenghem, Guy 6, 39–40, 169
Holmes, Sarah (ed), *Testimonies* 31–2
homoeroticism 181–2
homogeneity *see* sameness
homonationalism 19, 21–2
homo-ness (Bersani) 12–13, 36, 163–6, 176
homonormativity 121–2
homophobia 6–7, 18, 22–3, 24, 79–80, 88–9, 121
homosexuality 1–3, 12–13
  culture of 38 n.3, 181–2, 194–6
  reproduction of 80, 88–9
  and sameness 2–3, 7, 14–15, 86–7, 142–3
  *sinthom*osexual (Edelman) 87
  and uselessness 39–40
  see also sexual definition

identity 11–12, 14, 18–26, 159–60, 185 n.1
  gay 26, 151–2, 157–8, 193–6
  lesbian 26, 35–6, 119, 120–1, 193–6
  queer 42–3, 119, 120–1
  and reductionism 159–60, 177–8
  refusal of 11, 192–3, 196
  see also anti-identitarianism

identity knowledges 190–1
identity politics 9–10, 15–16, 18–19, 46, 190
Imaginary (Lacan) 84–5
imitation 44, 56–7, 63
inconsistency 66–7
Indiana, Gary 176
indifference 14
individuality 56–7, 95–6
  loss of 166–7, 170–8
instrumentalism 95–6
intersectionality 18–21, 48, 105, 154, 161–2
  assemblage 19, 20, 162
intimacy 167
irreducibility 159–60
Isherwood, Christopher 180
'It Gets Better' project 29–30

Jagose, Annamarie 125–6
Jakobsen, Janet 20, 162
James, Henry 40–5, 53–73
  The Ambassadors 61
  Roderick Hudson 34, 40–5, 53–4, 55–8, 60–1, 62–4, 69–71
  The Tragic Muse 34, 40–5, 54–7, 58–61, 64–9, 70–1
Johnson, Barbara 13–14

Key, Ellen 75
Koestenbaum, Wayne 18, 22–3

Lacan, Jacques 11, 83–5
language use 59–60, 67–71, 74 n.6
Lanser, Susan 110
Lehmann, Rosamond, *Dusty Answer* 114
lesbian fiction 6
  middle-brow 8, 27, 35–6, 114–16, 120–1, 141–7
  speculative 77–9, 97–104
  see also Charnas, Suzy McKee; Gearhart, Sally Miller; Gilman, Charlotte Perkins; Griffith, Nicola; Hall, Radclyffe; Renault, Mary; Russ, Joanna
lesbian identity 26, 35–6, 120–1, 193–6

lesbians 28–9, 31–2, 102–3, 112 n.4, 119–20
lesbian separatism 81, 99–100
Liberace 180
liberalism 19, 21–2, 154, 161
libraries 32
likeness *see* similarity
Lilla, Mark 16
limits 159–60, 171, 176–7, 185
  lack of 167–8, 170
lists 8, 36–7, 153
  see also Rechy, John
literature 6, 7–8, 96
  autobiography 26–34, 156, 178–9
  coming out stories 26–34, 114
  and culture 32–3
  repetition in 178–81, 183–4
  see also fiction
Lochrie, Karma 117
Loddon, D.L., *Do They Remember?* 114
Lorde, Audre 20–1
Love, Heather 5, 8, 40, 41, 47, 189, 197
  and abjection 24, 130, 132, 134–5
  and anti-redemption 23
  and normativity 115–16, 121, 128, 142, 143, 149
  and uselessness 50–1

Marcus, Sharon 117, 141, 143
marginalisation 4–5, 115–16, 128–9, 149
marriage 58–9, 78, 95, 119–20, 123
Martin, Biddy 117, 121, 124, 126, 142
masculinity 49–50, 63, 146, 171–2, 174–5, 181–3
maternalism 9, 106, 110
McCalla, Deidre 29
McKee Charnas, Suzy *see* Charnas, Suzy McKee
memory 32–3, 103–4
men, gay 10–11, 22–3, 153, 165–72, 176–7
Menon, Madhavi 14, 17, 162
metaphor, and reproduction 89–90
metronormativity 121–2, 123–4, 150 n.3

middle-brow fiction 6, 8, 35–6, 114–21, 141–7
  see also Hall, Radclyffe; Renault, Mary
Miller Gearhart, Sally *see* Gearhart, Sally Miller
mimicry 56–7
monotony 27–8, 33–4, 92, 136–7
Moraga, Cherríe 20–1
Morton, Donald 47, 48–9
motherhood 93–5, 99, 136–7
  maternalism 9, 106, 110
multiculturalism 162
Muñoz, José Esteban 18–19, 48, 53, 162

Nadkarni, Asha 109–10
narcissism 1, 2, 49–50
National Gay and Lesbian Survey (UK), *What a Lesbian Looks Like* 28
nationalism 19, 21–2
negativity 23–4, 40–1, 83, 89, 115–16
neoliberalism 19, 161
Newman, Louise 107
non-redemptiveness 5, 23–4, 116–17, 155–6, 163–5
  see also redemption
normalisation 116–17, 118, 123–5, 132–5, 140, 149–50
normativity 6, 8, 35–6, 114–50
  and abnormality 129–33
  anti-normativity 115–19, 125–6
  assimilation 106–7, 116, 119–20, 124–5, 128–35
  chrononormativity 121
  conformity 10–11, 117–18, 123
  conventional 120, 135–40
  and feminism 126
  homonormativity 121–2
  metronormativity 121–2, 123–4, 150 n.3
  ordinariness 6, 8, 117, 140–9
  and similarity 147–50
  transgender 122
  see also heteronormativity
norms 121–8, 158–9

Index

O'Brien, Mary 75
ontological breakdown 11, 12–14, 17
ordinariness 6, 8, 117, 120–1, 140–9
originality, lack of 63, 66–7
Ortiz, Ricardo 151

paradox 66–7, 86–8
Parker, Andrew 187, 189
parthenogenesis 91–2, 100
Parvulescu, Anca 80, 82, 89
passivity 49–50
Pater, Walter 39, 43–4, 53–4, 60–1
Penney, James 15–16, 185 n.1, 187–8, 190, 196
perfection 67–8, 78, 92–3, 105, 108
performativity 11–12, 20
Perkins Gilman, Charlotte *see* Gilman, Charlotte Perkins
Pickles, *Queens* 153, 169
pluralism 19–20, 162
politics 58–60, 64–5
  activism 49–50
  affirmative 115–16
  conservatism 122–3, 129–30
  of difference 2–3, 9–10, 20–1, 160–1, 190
  homonationalism 19, 21–2
  identity 9–10, 15–16, 18–21, 46, 190
  liberalism 19, 21–2, 154, 161
  queer 4–5, 25–6, 45–53, 117–19
  and race 105–8
  and reproduction 80, 83–4
  and uselessness 40–2, 45–53, 72
  see also feminism
Portillo, Tina 31
post-structuralism 17–18, 20–1, 83–4, 191–2
  and difference 13–14
  and irreducibility 159–61
  and political intervention 45–6
  and reductionism 154, 162
practicality 43–5, 46–7, 53–4, 62, 73 n.5
pride 115–16, 119–20
privilege 53
  of difference 17, 24, 70–1, 162, 197
procreation 44, 58

Puar, Jasbir 19, 20, 21–2, 162
Purnell, Brontez, *The Cruising Diaries* 153, 169

queerness 42–3, 119, 120–1
  and futurism 86–8
  and signification 84–5, 86–7
  and uselessness 71–3
queer studies 42, 48
queer theory 2–5, 10–18
  and abjection 115–16
  anti-identitarianism 18–26, 46, 121, 151–2, 165–70, 192–3, 196
  anti-redemption 5, 23–4, 116–17, 155–6, 163–5
  assemblage 19, 20, 162
  and capitalism 47–8
  as cultural critique 47
  gay aversiveness 6–7, 22–3
  and historical materialism 47–9
  and identity 18–26
  intersectionality 18–21, 48, 105, 154, 161–2
  and normativity 115–19, 121–8
  and reductionism 155–6, 158–65
  rejection of theory in 48–9
  and reproduction 79–81, 82, 83–90
  and sociology 46–7, 48
  and uselessness 45–53

race 20–1
racialisation 108–9
racism 9, 81–2, 104–11
rape 100
reading 31–2, 110
Real (Lacan) 11
Rechy, John 36–7, 151–8, 165–86
  as 'gay writer' 151–2, 157–8
  About My Life and the Kept Woman 178–84
  Bodies and Souls 157, 175–6, 181, 182–3
  'The City of Lost Angels' 171
  City of Night 151–3, 156, 165, 172, 175, 178, 180–1, 183
  The Coming of the Night 153, 182, 183
  The Fourth Angel 156

Numbers 151–3, 165–9, 172, 173–4, 178, 180–1
Rushes 152, 156, 166–7, 169, 170, 175, 180–1
The Sexual Outlaw 152, 153, 156, 165–7, 169, 170, 179, 180–1
This Day's Death 156, 179
redemption
  lack of 40, 57, 60–1
  opposition to 5, 23–4, 116–17, 155–6, 163–5
reductionism 6, 8, 36–7, 151–86
  and anti-identitarianism 165–70
  and identity 159–60, 177–8
  in language 171
  and loss of individuality 166–7, 170–8
  opposition to 154–5
  opposition to/rejection of 158–65
  and post-structuralism 154, 162
  and repetition 178–84
  relating 12–13, 153, 155, 163, 166–7
Renault, Mary, *The Friendly Young Ladies* 36, 114, 120, 143–7, 148–9
Rensenbrink, Greta 100, 101–2
repetition 30–1
  in artistic practice 56
  and difference 12
  literary 178–81, 183–4
  and reductionism 178–84
  and sex 167–8, 172
repetitiveness 27, 28–9, 31, 33–4
replication 18, 35, 56
  clones (gay men) 10–11, 22–3, 170, 176–7
  clones (genetic) 50, 92, 98–9
reproduction 6, 8–9, 75–113
  asexual 91–2, 98–102
  clones (genetic) 50, 92, 98–9
  copying 18, 22–3, 35
  cultural 80
  and eugenics 105, 109–10
  and feminism 75–6, 90
  futurism of 50, 52, 76–7, 83–8, 142
  of good things 90, 104
  gynogenesis 102
  heteronormativity of 35, 82–3, 104
  and heterosexuality 76–7, 96–7
  of homosexuals 80, 88–9
  labour of 80–1
  lack of 39–40
  maternalism 9, 106, 110
  through memory 32–3, 103–4
  metaphorical 89–90
  and motherhood 93–5, 99, 136–7
  non-biological 79–81, 82–3, 88–90, 103–4
  parthenogenesis 91–2, 100
  procreation 44, 58
  and racialisation 108–9
  rationalisation of 90–1, 93–4, 104
  rejection of 35
  in scholarship 108–11
  and sexual activity 93, 102–3
  social 80, 89–90, 93–4, 98, 99, 103–4
  in speculative fiction 77–9, 90–104
  and technology 75, 78–9, 97–8
resemblance *see* similarity
reverse discourse 4–5, 33–4
Rich, Adrienne 75
Robinson, Paul 123
Rohy, Valerie 80, 82, 88–9
Roof, Judith 27–8
Roseanne (TV show) 27–8
Rowe, John Carlos 53
Ruehl, Sonja 114
Russ, Joanna, *The Female Man* 77, 78, 97–8, 99

sameness
  benefits of 8, 90, 104
  boredom 27–8, 33–4, 92, 136–7
  conformity 10–11, 117–18, 123
  continuity 78–9, 82–3, 88
  fixity 10, 12, 175, 178
  homo-ness (Bersani) 12–13, 36, 163–6, 176
  and homosexuality 2–3, 7, 14–15, 86–7, 142–3
  imitation 44, 56–7, 63
  and middle-brow culture 142–3
  mimicry 56–7
  narcissism 1, 2, 49–50
  ordinariness 6, 8, 117, 120–1, 140–9
  standardisation 78, 81–2, 95

Index

stereotypes 156, 157–8, 175–6
tradition 119, 136, 141, 147, 195
see also difference; normativity; reductionism; repetition; reproduction; similarity; uselessness
Savage, Dan 29
Saxey, Esther 28
Schulman, Sarah 27, 32–3
Sedgwick, Eve Kosofsky 2, 3–4
Seidman, Steven 45–6, 48, 162
self 11–12, 159–60, 163, 172–3
see also subjectivity
self-centredness 63–4
self-identity 159–60
sensuality 43–4, 53–4
separatism 81, 99–100
sex 93, 122–3, 157
  cruising 163–4, 165–6, 167–8
  desire 14, 169–70
  gay 153, 165–70, 171–2
  lesbian 102–3
  and repetition 167–8, 172
  serial 6, 8, 36–7, 166, 167–8, 172–3, 178
  and subjectivity 172–3
sex difference 93, 95, 107–8, 142–3
sexual definition 1–2, 3–4, 6, 8, 17
sexual identity
  gay 151–2, 157–8, 193–6
  lesbian 26, 35–6, 119, 120–1, 193–6
  queer 42–3, 119, 120–1
  see also anti-identitarianism
Shenton, David 11
Shugar, Dana 100
signification 13–14, 83–7
Silverman, Kaja 38 n.4
similarity 17, 38 n.4, 92, 147–50
  of appearance 1, 10–11, 22–3, 170, 176–7
Sinfield, Alan 114, 194
*sinthom*osexual (Edelman) 87
sociability 163–4
social change 45–6, 79, 154
social class 92, 96–7
social difference 9–10, 14, 15–16, 18–19, 162, 189–90
sociology 21, 46–7, 48

speculative fiction 8, 35, 37, 77–9, 91–104
  see also Charnas, Suzy McKee; Gearhart, Sally Miller; Gilman, Charlotte Perkins; Griffith, Nicola; Russ, Joanna
standardisation 78, 81–2, 95
Stanley, Julia Penelope (ed), *The Coming Out Stories* 29, 31–2, 114
stereotypes 156, 157–8, 175–6
Stevens, Hugh 117
Steward, Samuel 153
Stryker, Susan 122
stud files 8, 36–7, 153
  see also Rechy, John
subjectivity
  continuous 13
  extensible 163, 165, 168–9
  and sex 172–3
  and signification 14
  see also self
subversion 125–6
Symbolic (Lacan) 83, 84–5

talk 59–60, 67–71, 74 n.6
theory
  critique of 69–72
  uselessness of 40–2, 43–5, 51, 61, 66–7
  see also feminism; post-structuralism; queer theory
tradition 119, 136, 141, 147, 195
Tuhkanen, Mikko 17, 162
Tust, Jen (ed), *Testimonies* 31–2

universalism 14, 159
unoriginality 63, 66–7
urbanism 121–2, 123–4
usefulness 6, 8, 37, 95–6
  refusal of 61–71
  of uselessness 41, 72
uselessness 34–5, 37, 39–74
  and aestheticism 53–4, 60–1, 71–2
  and art 53–61, 73 n.5
  and failure 40–1
  and homosexuality 39–40
  political effects of 49–51
  and politics 40–2, 45–53, 72

and queerness 71–3
of queer theory 40–2
of sex 50
of theory 40–2, 43–5, 61, 66–7
usefulness of 41, 72
utility *see* usefulness
utopian fiction 77–9, 91–104
  see also Charnas, Suzy McKee;
  Gearhart, Sally Miller; Gilman,
  Charlotte Perkins; Griffith,
  Nicola; Russ, Joanna

Warhol, Andy 17, 148
Warner, Michael 2, 35, 117–18, 122–4, 187
Weeks, Jeffrey 114
Weinbaum, Alys Eve 106, 107, 108–9
Weise, Don 152, 183–4
West, Cornel 21, 161
wholeness 84–5, 86

Wiegman, Robyn 25–6, 117–19, 124–5, 126–7, 140, 190–1
Wilde, Oscar 2, 18, 39, 43
Wilson, Elizabeth A. 124–5, 127
Wolfe, Susan J. (ed), *The Coming Out Stories* 29, 31–2, 114
women
  lesbians 28–9, 31–2, 102–3, 112 n.4, 119–20
  motherhood 93–5, 99, 136–7
  and reproduction 142
  reproductive labour of 80–1
women-only communities 77–9, 81, 97–104
Woolf, Virginia 141, 142–3

Yellow Book, The (journal) 44
Young, Iris Marion 161, 185 n.1

Zacharias, Greg 63

EU authorised representative for GPSR:
Easy Access System Europe, Mustamäe tee 50,
10621 Tallinn, Estonia
gpsr.requests@easproject.com

www.ingramcontent.com/pod-product-compliance
Lightning Source LLC
Chambersburg PA
CBHW070238240426
43673CB00044B/1836